VISUAL QUICKSTART GUIDE

ADOBE
ENCORE DVD 1.5

FOR WINDOWS

Steve Tomich

Peachpit Press

Visual QuickStart Guide
Adobe Encore DVD 1.5 for Windows
Steve Tomich

Peachpit Press

1249 Eighth Street
Berkeley, CA 94710
510/524-2178
800/283-9444
510/524-2221 (fax)

Find us on the World Wide Web at: www.peachpit.com
To report errors, please send a note to errata@peachpit.com

Peachpit Press is a division of Pearson Education

Editor: Suzie Lowey
Production Coordinator: Andrei Pasternak
Copy Editor: Tracy Brown Collins
Compositor: Kelli Kamel
Indexer: FireCrystal Communications
Cover Design: The Visual Group
Cover Production: George Mattingly / GMD

ISBN 0-321-29392-4

9 8 7 6 5 4 3 2 1

Printed and bound in the United States of America

Acknowledgments

I'd like to thank all the people who contributed to this book.

From Adobe, Daniel Brown and Joe Bowden deserve thanks for some well-timed emails which helped a lot. Daniel also gets credit for the cocktail napkin quote.

Thanks to the folks at Snader and Associates, especially Joe Pettit for the generous loan of the camera. Tony Arata's timely assistance was a huge help, as well.

Thanks to everyone at Peachpit who had a hand in this book:

Suzie Lowey, for editing it.

Tracy Collins, for copyediting.

Andrei Pasternak for overseeing the production.

Marjorie Baer, for inviting me back for round two.

Special thanks to my family:

My wife Jo, and my boys Chris and Nick, for their patience and grace, even during deadlines.

TABLE OF CONTENTS

TABLE OF CONTENTS

TABLE OF CONTENTS

INTRODUCTION

Just as with recorded music, where the CD format overtook vinyl in a very short time, DVDs have replaced videotape as the medium of choice for distribution, from Hollywood movies to high-school video yearbooks. The high quality of both picture and sound, along with the additional features of DVD—interactive menus, alternate content, multiple languages—open up huge opportunities for creativity.

What this means for you is that you can do a *whole lot* with a DVD; you just need the right tools.

Which is where Adobe Encore DVD for Windows comes in.

What is Encore DVD?

Encore DVD is a DVD-authoring software application developed by Adobe Systems.

If you've been out shopping at all, you already know that a wide spectrum of DVD-authoring tools are available, from very expensive hardware-based systems to very inexpensive desktop software designed for the casual user.

Encore DVD fits in the middle of this spectrum. It is designed for professional users who want to combine DVD-authoring capabilities with design tools to control the creative process right down to the "burn disc" command.

A sophisticated tool in its own right, Encore DVD is also fully integrated with other world-class Adobe applications—Photoshop, After Effects, and Premiere. If you're familiar with the Adobe "look and feel," you'll be right at home in Encore DVD.

Who should use this book?

This book is designed for professionals who want to create high-quality DVDs with familiar, efficient Adobe tools. If you're an old hand at DVD titles, you'll be pleased with Encore DVD's ease of use and flexibility as you progress through the book. Even if you're new to the DVD-creation process, you'll be up and running quickly using the basic overview provided here.

What's in this book?

This is a *task-based* reference book. It contains simple, step-by-step instructions on the use of Encore DVD—setting up your system, understanding the Encore interface, importing assets, creating menus and links, and efficiently combining video, audio, graphic, and text elements into a finished product.

The focus of the book is on *using* Encore DVD. The technical aspects of the DVD world can get very complicated very quickly, so rather than bog you down in arcana, I discuss just the relevant technical aspects as concisely as possible.

The first part of this book gives you a bit of background on the technology and technique of DVD authoring, with suggestions on how to plan your project for maximum impact and minimum fuss. Chapter by chapter, you'll go through the steps of creating a DVD and outputting to disc.

Encore DVD is becoming a powerful tool for design and DVD creation in its own right, so the entire first part of this book emphasizes what you can do *just* with the features available in Encore DVD.

The second part of the book gives you an idea of what you can do when you combine the other members of the Adobe suite—Photoshop, After Effects, and Premiere—with Encore DVD. You'll also learn how to incorporate subtitling and multiple languages into your DVD in this section.

A Note on Windows Commands

As a user of Windows, you are no doubt aware that there are often several different ways to accomplish a task. Menu options, right-click contextual menus, keyboard shortcuts, and modifier keys all come into play—supposedly to make your high-tech life easier and as efficient as possible, if you could only remember which ones to use.

In order to make this book manageable, I mention or illustrate one or two useful methods to accomplish a task, rather than list every conceivable Windows alternative. In general, you can substitute your favorite Windows methodology for the procedures described in the book.

There *are* occasions in Windows and in Encore DVD where there are alternate ways of doing something—creating a timeline, for instance—that yield different results. In these situations, I cover each method and give you some suggestions about which one to use and when to use it.

System requirements

Encore DVD is remarkably unfussy in terms of setup. If you have a reasonably new and fast computer and are serious about investing in the right monitor(s), drives, and DVD burner, getting up and running is a breeze. For the latest specs, refer to www.adobe.com.

The following are the minimum system requirements:

◆ Intel Pentium III 800 MHz or faster processor (Pentium 4 and dual processor recommended)

◆ Microsoft Windows XP Professional or Home Edition, with latest Service Pack

◆ 256 MB RAM (512 or more recommended)

◆ 1 GB available hard disk space for application installation

◆ 5 GB of additional hard disk space recommended for extra content

◆ 10 GB or larger hard disc or disc array for ongoing work

◆ 1280 x 1024 32-bit color video display adapter and monitor with 16 MB VRAM or more (dual monitors recommended)

◆ Stereo sound card

◆ DVD-ROM drive

◆ Supported DVD burner (see www.adobe.com)

◆ QuickTime 6.5 software recommended

Part I:
The Basics

WELCOME TO ENCORE DVD

The world of DVD creation can be a very technical place. If you've spent any time in this world at all, you may have waded through *GOPs* and *BUPs* and *VOBUs* and *I-frames* and *bit budgets*. The great thing about Adobe Encore DVD is that its considerable engineering sophistication is "under the hood" and out of your way, so you can concentrate on designing a DVD that's interesting to watch.

In this chapter, I'll outline the Big Picture of the DVD-creation process and introduce a few basic technical concepts. Most of the chapter is, however, devoted to getting you familiar with the Encore DVD interface. Once you're comfortable with the interface and begin working with it on your own projects, you'll find out just how flexible Encore DVD is. There are usually several different ways to accomplish a task. I'll cover as many as I can in the space of this book, but you'll also discover many others on your own.

Creating a DVD

Whether the DVD you plan to create needs only the most basic design or something quite elaborate, Encore DVD has a powerful toolset to meet your needs. **Figure 1.1** shows an example of a final product from Encore DVD with all the elements you're familiar with from your experience watching movies on a home DVD player. While it's a little hard to appreciate the interactive aspects in this screenshot—the buttons, the layers, the links—they're all there. The process of creating a DVD can be broken down into three main phases:

◆ **Creating your source material**

Creating the source material happens "upstream" of Encore DVD. How it is gathered and prepared, however, affects how you will use Encore DVD to create your DVD. More on how to prepare source material in Chapter 2.

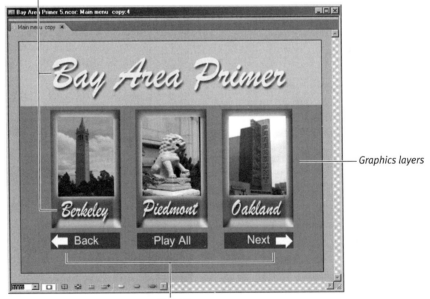

Text layers

Graphics layers

Buttons

Figure 1.1 A very basic example of a DVD design, created with Encore DVD.

CREATING A DVD

◆ **Authoring**

Because the actual authoring process—creating a disc's menus and linking structures and verifying navigation—forms the bulk of this book, it deserves a little explication now. Here are the basic steps, in a typical order:

Import your edited video, audio, and graphics files into an Encore DVD project (see Chapter 2 for more information).

Create one or more timelines. Each timeline will have tracks for video, audio, and, optionally, subtitle information (see Chapter 3 for more information).

Create one or more menus to enable viewers to navigate through the content of your DVD (see Chapter 4 for more information on the basics, and Part II of the book for advanced techniques).

Add buttons to your menus to allow users to interact with, and navigate within, your DVD (see Chapter 4 for more information).

Link the tracks on your DVD to your menu buttons and to functions on a DVD player's remote control (see Chapters 5 and 6 for more information).

Preview and test your DVD as you design it (see Chapters 5 and 6).

◆ **Producing final output**

The final phase is outputting your project, which entails the following:

Using Encore DVD's disc-management tools to determine the final quality and type of MPEG-2 transcoding (see Chapter 6).

Burning your DVD project to disc. For small runs, your output can go straight to a desktop DVD burner. For larger distribution or very large projects, you'll create a disc image, disc file, or output your project to a DLT (digital linear tape). These outputs can be taken to a replication service for the final disc production. All of this is in Chapter 6.

CREATING A DVD

DVD Basics

Briefly, DVD refers to a type of optical-disc storage technology similar to CD, but with far greater capacity. A typical DVD can hold 4.7 GB—roughly seven times the data that can be housed on a computer CD—and its capacity and flexibility has lifted it out of the strictly technical world of data storage and into all kinds of home entertainment and interactive media.

Which is why you're here.

A discussion of DVD can quickly become bogged down in such things as the details of *physical formats* (a vowels-optional world of DVD-R, DVD-RW, etc.) and *application formats* (such as DVD-ROM and DVD-Video). To keep up the momentum, I'll discuss only pertinent technical issues, and only as the book progresses.

But right now, the main concern is how to use Encore DVD to author DVDs—specifically, DVDs using the standards for DVD-Video that can play on a set-top player attached to your TV or on a computer with a DVD drive and DVD player. (In fact, you can assume that when I talk about "DVD" in this book, I'm specifically talking about DVD-Video.)

The DVD-Video specification

The DVD-Video specification is complex, but there are certain aspects of it that will play a big part in determining the DVDs you create and how you use Encore DVD to create them. The DVD-Video specification supports

- One track of MPEG-2 constant bit rate (CBR) or variable bit rate (VBR) compressed digital video

- Both NTSC and PAL formats

- Interlaced frame rates, in frames per second, of 29.97 (NTSC) and 25 (PAL)

Additional DVD Resources

If you're interested in more technical detail, lots of resources are available. Here are some I've found valuable:

- *DVD Authoring and Production,* Ralph Labarge, CMP Books, ©2001

- *Desktop DVD Authoring,* Douglas Dixon, New Riders, ©2002

- DVD Demystified FAQs: www.dvddemystified.com/dvdfaq.html.

- Adobe Evangelists, which is a good site for information and tips on a variety of Adobe products: www.adobeevangelists.com.

- Progressive frame rates of 23.976, 23.98, and 24 frames per second

- Frame sizes of 720×480 pixels (NTSC) or 720×576 pixels (PAL)

- Both 4:3 standard and 16:9 widescreen aspect ratios

- A maximum video data rate of 9.8 Mbps

- Up to 32 subtitle tracks

- Up to eight selectable audio tracks, in mono, stereo, and/or multichannel surround sound (playback of one track at a time)

- Three major audio formats, including PCM, MPEG-1 Layer 2, and Dolby Digital (also known as AC-3)

MPEG and Compression

MPEG stands for *Motion Picture Experts Group,* an international standards committee. At its core, the MPEG format is a compression scheme that takes large chunks of data (such as video and audio files) and compresses—or encodes—them into much smaller files. This is what makes the DVD-Video format possible. Compressed, a feature film can fit easily on a single DVD disc and maintain high picture and sound quality. Without compression, that same film would have to be spread across as many as 36 DVDs.

MPEG encoding is *lossy,* however, which means that the information in the original source is not copied exactly. An MPEG encoder samples dense information, such as color, and a minimal number of samples are retained. When the transcoded file is played back, the software in the DVD player is able to "fill in the blanks". It re-creates the original color accurately by extrapolating from the small set of stored color samples in the MPEG file.

The real power of MPEG, however, is this: In MPEG, an incoming stream of frames is broken down into groups of pictures, or *GOPs.* The MPEG encoder analyzes a GOP, takes note of the differences and similarities of frames in the entire group of pictures, eliminates redundancies, and stores the minimum amount of information necessary to re-create the pictures when the file is played back and displayed on a computer or TV screen.

There are several types of MPEG, but the current format for DVD-Video is MPEG-2. Encore DVD has a built-in MPEG-2 encoder, so the final output to DVD will always be MPEG-2. (In Encore-speak, MPEG-2 encoding is usually referred to as "transcoding," so I use that term from here on out.)

Determining how much compression to apply is always a balancing act between the demands of quality and the limitations of disc space and bandwidth. As you'll see in Chapter 6, Encore DVD offers several transcoding solutions to help you achieve the balance you want.

DVD BASICS

The Encore DVD Interface

The tasks you'll be asking Encore DVD to perform are grouped within very sleek, logically arranged windows, some of which have tabs and panes to further organize the tools inside them (**Figure 1.2**). If you're familiar with other Adobe products, you'll feel right at home with Encore DVD. The main windows are accessed via the main toolbar's Window menu (**Figure 1.3**). I'll be covering the windows in depth in the course of the book. For starters, the following sections are a brief overview of what they are and what they do.

THE ENCORE DVD INTERFACE

Toolbox   Project window   Properties palette

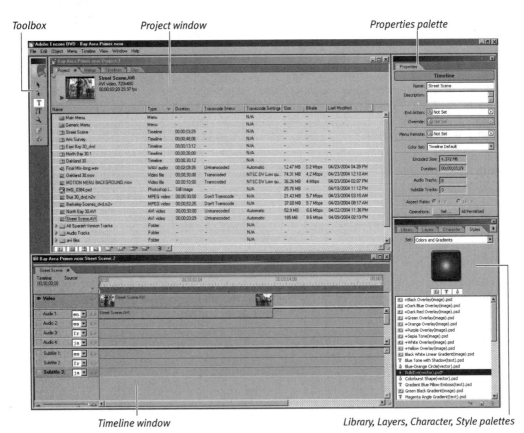

Timeline window   Library, Layers, Character, Style palettes

Figure 1.2 Encore DVD's interface as you begin a project. Note the main windows—you'll be spending lots of time with each of them.

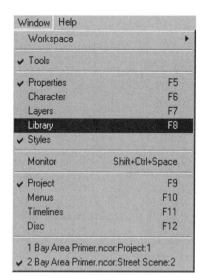

Figure 1.3 The various Encore DVD windows can be opened and closed via the Window menu.

About the Project Window

When you create a new project or open an existing one, the Project window appears. This window has four tabs—Project, Menus, Timelines, and Disc—and provides an overview of your project and its elements and helps you manage your assets.

◆ **Project tab**

Select the Project tab in the Project window and you can see the audio, video, and still-image assets you are using in your project, along with the timelines and menus you create for that project (**Figure 1.4**). You can create folders here to group any of these items, to organize your project, and to save screen space.

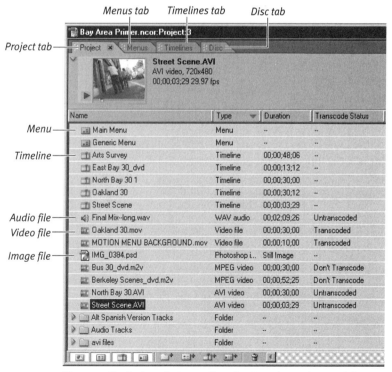

Figure 1.4 The Project window and its tabs. Note that each type of element in the project has its own distinctive icon.

As with Adobe Premiere Pro, when you select an asset, a thumbnail preview appears in the upper-left corner of the Project tab, along with information about that asset (**Figure 1.5**). If the asset contains video and/or audio, a play controller appears below the thumbnail, allowing you to view and hear the asset at play speed. Hide the thumbnail preview by clicking the x in its tab.

Along the bottom of the Project tab is a series of buttons (**Figure 1.6**). The four on the left are display toggle buttons, which can help you organize your project by alternately showing or hiding items in the tab. Click once to display an item, such as timelines or menus, and click again to hide those items. The four buttons on the right are shortcuts to create or delete items in the Project tab.

◆ **Menus tab**

Similar in appearance to the Project tab, the Menus tab lists the information associated with menus in your project (**Figure 1.7**). A column naming your menus, followed by other columns—End Action, Override, Aspect Ratio, Description, Color Set, etc.—can be displayed in the top pane of the tab.

The bottom pane is available when there are buttons associated with your menus. Pertinent data about their relationships with the menus are displayed. (See Chapter 4 for more details.)

◆ **Timelines tab**

The Timelines tab gives you a global view of the timelines in your project (**Figure 1.8**). Like the Menus tab, it has two panes. The top pane lists your timelines, with sortable columns to keep track of the elements in your timelines, along with actions such as End Action and Override that you program in later.

Figure 1.5 Project tab thumbnail preview.

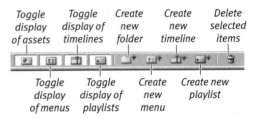

Figure 1.6 Project tab buttons.

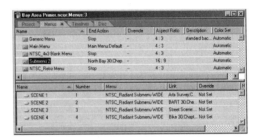

Figure 1.7 The Menus tab.

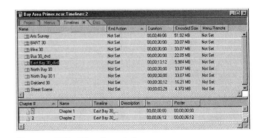

Figure 1.8 The Timelines tab.

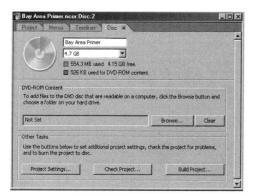

Figure 1.9 The Disc tab.

✔ Tips

■ You can make any of the tabs in the interface into its own window by dragging it to the Encore DVD desktop. Drag the window back and it becomes a tab again.

■ You'll find that your computer monitor quickly fills up with tabs, windows, palettes, etc. Encore DVD lets you manage your screen space with *workspaces*. More on that feature later on in this chapter.

■ When you select a timeline in the top pane of the Timlines tab, the bottom pane lists the chapter points you have marked in that timeline, along with their name and position information. Chapter points link specific points on timelines to buttons, menus, and other timelines (all explored in detail in Chapters 3 and 5).

◆ **Disc tab**

The Disc tab controls how your project will be output—either to a disc burner attached to your system or to a file or image that can be burned or replicated later (**Figure 1.9**). The tab has three sections. The top section is where the name of the DVD volume is selected. It also has a pop-up menu that allows you to choose the size of the volume you are going to create. This also displays the currently allocated space and enables Encore to update its "bit budget" as the project progresses. See Chapter 2 for more details.

The *DVD-ROM Content* section allows you to either archive or add supplemental content, such as related text files or applications, to a DVD. These files are generally outside the links-and-menu structure you've established in the project—they're accessible only through Windows Explorer and won't play on a set-top player. (See Chapter 6 for more information.)

The *Other Tasks* section contains the group of controls that make up the "final stop" of your project before it actually becomes a DVD. The Project Settings button enables the adjustment of output settings, the Check Project button allows you to analyze your project for navigational or throughput problems before burning, and the Build Project button manages the options for the final "write" of the project to disc or file.

ABOUT THE PROJECT WINDOW

About the Timeline Window

The Project window and its associated tabs allow you to gather and organize your material and manage a lot of the Encore DVD workflow, but the Timeline window is where the action is in terms of video, sound, and subtitle tracks (**Figure 1.10**).

The Timeline window will be familiar territory to Adobe Premiere users. Divided into three vertical panes, it allows you to sync up a video track, up to 8 audio tracks, and up to 32 subtitle tracks. For navigation, a zoom control and a scrollbar can be found at the bottom of the window. Chapter points are placed in the Timeline window to build links to buttons and menus, and Language Code pop-up menus are used to allow the DVD player to select among multiple languages you may employ in the audio tracks and subtitle tracks of your DVD.

✔ Tips

- You can create as many as 99 timelines in each project. They are displayed as tabs in the Timeline window, where they can be opened, closed, and rearranged at will.

- Although a timeline might look like something you'd see in an editing application such as Premiere Pro, you cannot edit together or combine multiple audio or motion video clips on a track. Still images, however, can be arranged as separate clips on a video track to create a slideshow. See Chapter 3 for more information.

- Track length can be adjusted by trimming (in a very Premiere Pro-like manner), but if you need to edit video or audio assets together, you must do it outside of Encore DVD and then import the results as a contiguous file into the project.

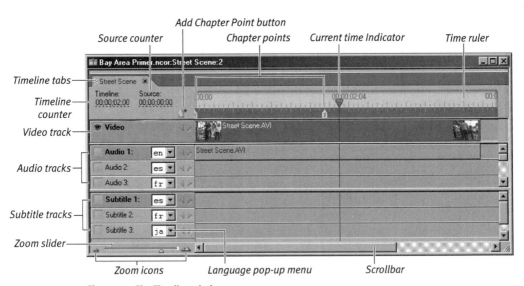

Figure 1.10 The Timeline window.

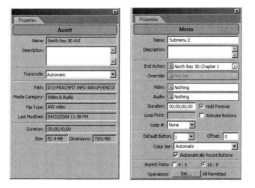

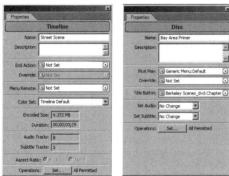

Figure 1.11 The Properties palette in four different views. (Its content and tools change depending on the element being described.)

About the Properties Palette

The Properties palette is a very powerful tool that displays and adjusts the properties of menus, timelines, buttons, and the like. It is context sensitive. As you can see in this example, the Properties palette has different controls for each selected item (**Figure 1.11**).

✔ Tip

- If you'd like to save some screen space, the Properties palette can be made into a tab by dragging into any window that contains the Library, Style, Character, or Layers tabs.

ABOUT THE PROPERTIES PALETTE

About the "Palette Window"

This is a bit of a misnomer, really. There is no such thing as a "Palette Window" in Encore-speak. However, when you create your first project, you'll see the next four important palettes grouped together as tabs in a single window (they can, of course, be separated and repositioned, if you like). They are used extensively in designing and modifying menus.

◆ **Layers palette**

Reminiscent of Photoshop, this palette gives you control over all the layers involved in buttons and menus (**Figure 1.12**). You can select and modify the layers independently.

◆ **Character palette**

This compact but powerful text tool has all the attributes you'd expect from the folks who brought you Illustrator (**Figure 1.13**). Font selection, kerning, sizing, color, and so on are all available here. It also supports Asian text.

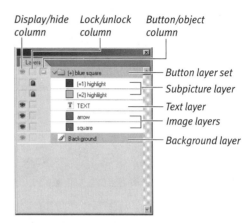

Display/hide column *Lock/unlock column* *Button/object column*

Button layer set
Subpicture layer
Text layer
Image layers
Background layer

Figure 1.12 The Layers tab.

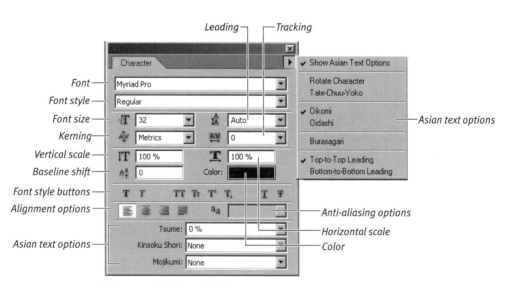

Leading *Tracking*

Font — Myriad Pro
Font style — Regular
Font size —
Kerning —
Vertical scale —
Baseline shift —
Font style buttons —
Alignment options —
Asian text options —

Show Asian Text Options
Rotate Character
Tate-Chuu-Yoko
Oikomi
Oidashi
Burasagari
Top-to-Top Leading
Bottom-to-Bottom Leading

Asian text options
Anti-aliasing options
Horizontal scale
Color

Figure 1.13 The Character tab.

◆ **Library palette**

This palette contains prebuilt templates, backgrounds, buttons, and vector-based shapes that can be used for designing menus in Encore DVD (**Figure 1.14**). You can build your entire DVD by incorporating and modifying these elements, and you can also add your own custom templates or raw graphic elements.

The Library groups its contents in default sets labeled General, Sports, Corporate, and the like, which are accessible through a pop-up menu. It displays an alphabetical list of the available items and a thumbnail picture of a selected item. Toggle buttons in the center of the palette are used to select the type of item displayed, such as menus, backgrounds, text, shapes, and so on.

At the bottom of the tab, there are several buttons. These are used to precisely place graphic elements and backgrounds into menus, to create a new menu, and to either add or delete items from the Library.

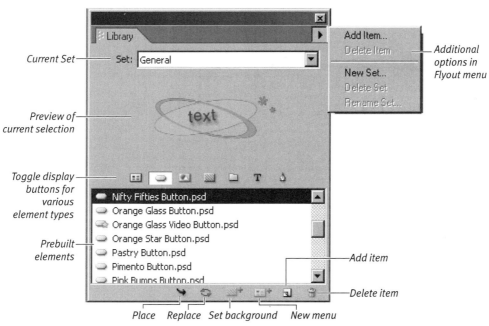

Figure 1.14 The Library tab.

ABOUT THE "PALETTE WINDOW"

◆ **Styles palette**

This palette contains a set of predefined styles to enable you to modify the appearance of an object in a menu (**Figure 1.15**). Like the Library palette, there are toggles to display the style types—Image, Text, or Shape. You can access the various styles with a pop-up menu and, as with the Library tab, the styles are grouped into sets. You can drag and drop styles onto objects in a menu or use the button at the bottom of the palette to apply the styles. You can also add your own styles to the palette and delete styles as well.

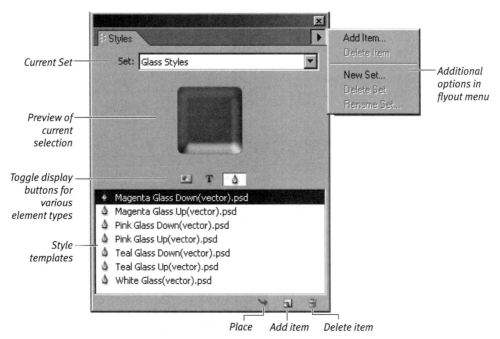

Figure 1.15 The Styles palette.

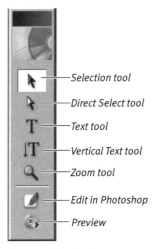

Selection tool

Direct Select tool

Text tool

Vertical Text tool

Zoom tool

Edit in Photoshop

Preview

Figure 1.16 The Toolbox.

About the Toolbox

Compared with the other windows in the interface, the Toolbox seems small and unassuming (**Figure 1.16**). But combined with the Menu Editor and the Monitor Window, it gives you a lot of power to design and modify text and buttons in menus and text in subtitles.

As with the rest of the Encore DVD interface, the functions of the tools are readily apparent. At the top, the black arrow icon represents the Selection tool, which allows you to select an *entire* layer set (such as a button and its related elements) together so the set can be manipulated as a unit.

The white arrow icon represents the Direct Select tool, which allows you to move individual layers *within* layered sets. The Text ("T" icon) and Vertical Text ("T" icon with the downward-pointing arrow) tools come next. They interact with the controls in the Character tab to create and modify text. The Zoom tool (the magnifying glass icon) has the function of allowing you to zoom into and out of the Menu Editor and the Timeline Window. The next two buttons are shortcuts. The Edit in Photoshop button opens the current menu in Photoshop for modification, and the last button, Preview, opens the Preview window and allows you to watch your project from the beginning.

About the Menu Editor

Three windows remain—the Menu Editor, Monitor, and Preview windows—and it's important that you get acquainted with them. These are the windows you'll use to actually build and view your menus, watch and listen to your timelines, and preview the project before you commit to burning a disc.

The Menu Editor (**Figure 1.17**) opens each time you create, open, or import a menu. It's a tabbed window, so you can open up several menus, work on them simultaneously, and copy and paste elements between them easily. The Menu Editor works closely with the various palettes, the Project window, and the Toolbox to allow you to enable and modify all the elements that make up a menu.

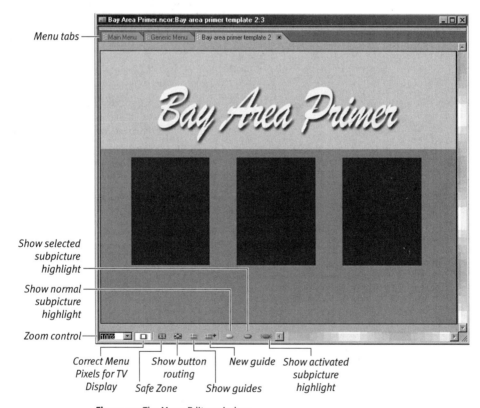

Figure 1.17 The Menu Editor window.

At the bottom of the Menu Editor are controls that let you change the view of the current menu. Using the Zoom control, you can zoom in or out as you work in the Editor. Using the "Correct Menu Pixels for TV Display" toggle, you can adjust the display of menus created with either square or nonsquare pixels. The Safe Zone button shows the outer area of the screen likely to be cropped off when viewed on a video monitor, while the New Guide and Show Guides buttons allow you to create and display any guidelines you might need to align elements in the menu. The Show Button Routing control allows you to program the way a DVD remote control navigates through the menu's buttons. The last three toggles allow you to display the Normal, Selected, and Activated highlight states of any buttons in the menu.

✔ Tip

- The Menu Editor can display in-screen aspect ratios of 4:3 or 16:9. If it opens up in the "wrong" aspect ratio for the material you're working on, check the aspect-ratio selectors at the bottom of the Properties palette and/or check the default menu listed in the Library palette (more information on this in Chapter 4).

About the Monitor Window

The Monitor window allows you to view and hear the content of a timeline (**Figure 1.18**). It has basic transport controls to play a timeline and zoom controls to size the picture within its window. The Monitor also has controls that will let you add chapter points (even during playback) and jump between chapter points. Another set of tools allows you to add, trim, and jump between subtitles. Depending on the aspect ratio of the video on your timeline, you can set the monitor's aspect ratio to either 4:3 or 16:9.

✔ Tip

■ The Monitor window is tied to timelines, so it will only display if there is a timeline active.

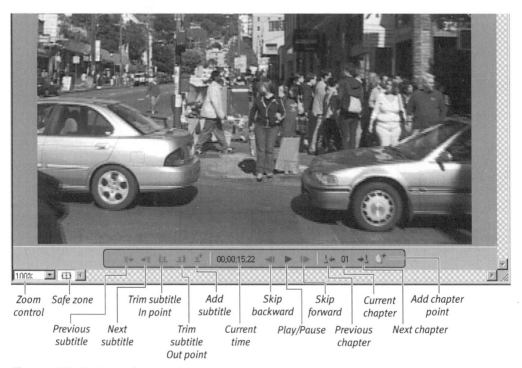

Figure 1.18 The Monitor window controls.

About the Preview Window

The Preview window (**Figure 1.19**) is similar in appearance to the Monitor window, but its function is more complex. When the Preview window is opened, Encore DVD can play back your entire project or selected segments of it, giving you an idea of how it will work on a DVD player.

The controls at the bottom of the window include a Zoom control, a "Render current motion menu" button, track selectors and information about the current content, and control areas that mimic the remote controls on a DVD player.

✔ Tip

■ Use the Preview shortcut on the Toolbox or choose File>Preview to open the Preview window and play your project from the beginning. A great timesaver is to right-click on a menu or timeline in the Project window, a chapter point in the Timeline window, or a button in the Menu Editor. Select Preview from Here from the contextual menu. The Preview window opens and playback begins from the selected point.

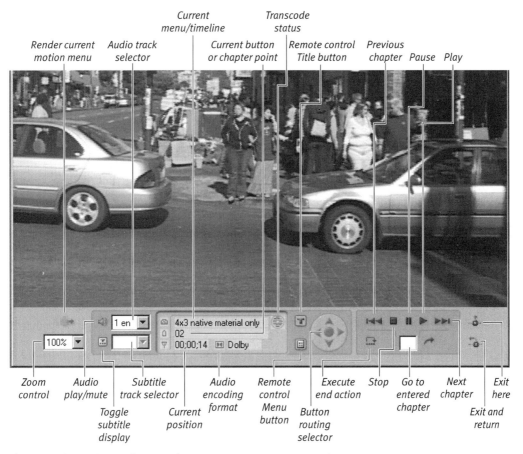

Figure 1.19 The Preview window controls.

About Workspaces

The placement of the various windows in the Encore DVD interface is called a *workspace*. Encore DVD provides workspace templates in the Window menu (**Figure 1.20**).

You can switch between the various workspace templates as you perform different tasks in Encore DVD. You are also free to arrange the windows in any way that suits you and save the arrangement as a custom workspace. When you create a new project, your saved custom workspaces will be available to you.

To create a custom workspace:

1. Click and drag on a window to change its size and position to taste.

   If a desired window or palette is not open, it can be accessed via the Window menu or keyboard shortcut (**Figure 1.21**).

2. Choose Windows>Workspace>Save Workspace.

   The Save Workspace dialog appears (**Figure 1.22**). Name the workspace and click Save.

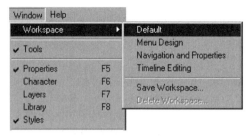

Figure 1.20 Encore DVD comes with some prebuilt workspaces to get you started.

Figure 1.21 You can open any tool or tab and add it to a workspace.

Figure 1.22 Name and save any customized workspace for later use.

ABOUT WORKSPACES

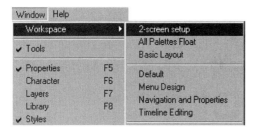

Figure 1.23 Custom workspaces are added to the top of the list.

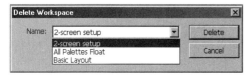

Figure 1.24 Custom workspaces can be deleted easily.

To open a custom workspace:

1. Choose Windows > Workspace. Any custom workspaces appear at the top of the list (**Figure 1.23**).

2. Select the desired custom workspace.

Encore DVD displays the selected workspace.

To delete a custom workspace:

◆ Choose Windows > Workspace > Delete Workspace.

The Delete Workspace dialog appears (**Figure 1.24**). Select the workspace from the pop-up menu and click Delete.

The workspace is deleted.

✔ Tips

■ Only custom workspaces can be deleted. Encore DVD's workspace templates are not available in the Delete dialog.

■ Most of the windows in Encore DVD can be resized; however, some, such as the Properties palette, Toolbox, and the Character palette, have fixed sizes.

ABOUT WORKSPACES

23

2

GETTING STARTED

The previous chapter offered a general look at the technology behind the DVD-creation process and showed you how the Encore DVD interface works.

This chapter will help you lay the foundation for your own DVD project. It covers the planning phase, where there are many choices to be made—both technical and nontechnical. For instance, determining who the audience is will have a big impact on how you create the final disc. If the audience is small and informal, you can plan on burning a short run of DVDs on your desktop, without worrying about copy protection or replication issues. The video standard (PAL or NTSC) that's in effect where you will distribute your final product, the original formats of your video, audio, and graphics sources—all these things (and more) come into play before you even launch Encore DVD.

After you've gathered up your various video, still images, and audio elements—called assets in Encore DVD—the next step is to start a project and begin importing both assets and menus into Encore DVD.

In this chapter, you'll learn the various methods for creating and managing projects, preparing and importing material, and using the Project, Menu, and Timelines windows to keep it all organized.

Making a Plan

One of the best comments about modern technology I've heard was that the most important invention was not the assembly line nor the transistor nor the memory chip; it was the cocktail napkin (**Figure 2.1**). Without it, many great ideas—roughly sketched among the rings and spills of exotic beverages—would be lost to time.

I'm not encouraging you to do your design work in bars—the lighting is usually not very good and it's easy to get distracted. What I'd like to emphasize is the importance of starting with a plan. Whether it's a crude drawing or a fancy flowchart (**Figure 2.2**), making a plan will help keep you organized and focused. A plan helps you decide what your final product will be, what sources you'll draw from, and how you want to pull it all together into a successful DVD.

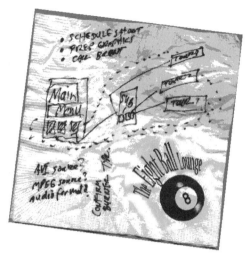

Figure 2.1 The planning process, happy hour, Tuesday evening. Three mai tais.

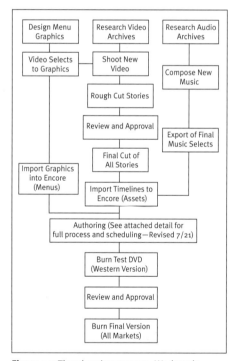

Figure 2.2 The planning process, Wednesday morning meeting. Two aspirin. Coffee, black.

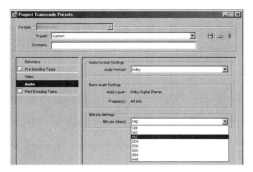

Figure 2.3 You have several transcoding options in dealing with your audio assets.

Table 2.1

Audio Formats for Import		
FORMATS	BIT DEPTH	SAMPLE RATE
WAV, MPG, M2P, MOV, MP3, WMA, AIFF, AIF, AC3	16 bits	48 kHz

Preparing Source Audio

You'll be concerned with three categories of source material as you work through the plan for your DVD: video, audio, and graphics. Because of video's relative complexity, I'll save that for last.

Audio files come in lots of flavors, and Encore DVD can handle most of them transparently. They can be mono, stereo, or, in the case of AC-3 (Dolby Digital) and MPEG, encoded in a surround-sound format. The basic spec for audio file import is shown in **Table 2.1**.

When you are ready to output to disc, there are three DVD-compliant formats to choose from: MPEG, PCM, and Dolby Digital. Your source audio will generally need to be transcoded to one of them (Dolby Digital being by far the most popular). You have several transcode settings to choose from, some of which are shown in **Figure 2.3**. I'll deal with these settings more extensively in Chapter 6.

✔ Tips

- You might have to deal with a mixture of audio formats and sample rates. For instance, any audio you source from audio CDs or MP3 downloads will have a native sample rate of 44.1 kHz. Encore DVD will always transcode audio to the standard DVD rate of 48 kHz.

- AIFF-C is an Apple-specific format and is not supported.

Preparing Source Graphics

Encore DVD has useful built-in graphics templates and tools, but you can also use Photoshop, After Effects, and other applications to create image files. If you do, here are some things to keep in mind:

◆ Format and export your graphics in the file types that Encore DVD will support: BMP, TGA, PICT, TIFF, GIF, JPEG, PNG, and PSD.

◆ Create your menus or backgrounds at their finished size to match the TV standard and aspect ratio you choose for your Encore DVD project (**Figure 2.4**). Encore DVD can accommodate graphics created in either square or nonsquare pixel formats. If you use the square-pixel templates available in Photoshop, Encore DVD will correctly interpret the menu size in Encore DVD. Photoshop CS has the additional option of nonsquare-pixel templates. See the sidebar "Covering All the Aspects" later in the chapter for more information.

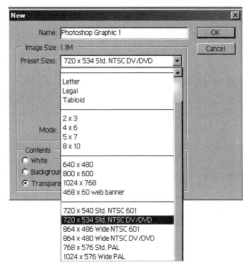

Figure 2.4 When you're creating graphics (in this case, in Photoshop), be conscious of the TV standard, pixel aspect ratio, and screen aspect ratio of your Encore DVD project.

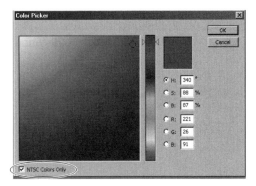

Figure 2.5 Note the NTSC Colors Only check box in Encore DVD's color picker. This will keep a selected color within the limits of what can be reproduced in a standard video signal.

◆ Use RGB colors when creating graphics, and use video-safe color palettes (**Figure 2.5**).

◆ Use vector shapes whenever possible to allow for resizing of graphics without quality loss.

◆ Create bitmapped buttons and other graphic elements (such as logos) at the largest size needed for the DVD. In terms of picture quality, it's always better to scale an object down, rather than up.

◆ As a rule, keep the number of buttons to a maximum of 36 in a standard aspect ratio (4:3) menu and a maximum of 18 in a widescreen (16:9) menu.

◆ Buttons should be created at a size of 70x60 pixels or greater for visibility.

◆ Use a font size of 20 points or greater, to ensure that text can be read easily on a TV screen.

◆ Set line thickness at 3 pixels or greater. Horizontal lines thinner than 3 pixels flicker when displayed on a TV screen. (You can also set lines to 2 pixels and add a blur.)

PREPARING SOURCE GRAPHICS

Preparing Source Video

At the beginning of a project, Encore DVD prompts you to choose a television standard—NTSC or PAL—for the DVD you will create. (NTSC is the standard for video in North America and Japan, whereas PAL is the standard for Europe.)

Table 2.2 shows the differences between these standards, in very general terms. The two standards are incompatible—you cannot use PAL sources in NTSC projects, and vice versa.

Encore DVD will import digital video files in three formats: QuickTime, AVI, and MPEG-2 (see the sidebar "Working with AVI, QuickTime, and MPEG-2" later in this chapter). **Table 2.3** lists the specifications that Encore DVD will accept in a video file.

Note that although Encore DVD will import only three kinds of digital video files, and outputs to disc in one TV standard (per project), Encore DVD can accommodate a lot of variation in frame rates, aspect ratios, and frame sizes—even in a single project.

This brings me to a key point: Encore DVD can accommodate these things, but you must manage them. While you can mix these video variants together, for best results, be consistent, plan ahead, and exert as much control over your source material as possible. See the sidebar for more information.

Table 2.2

NTSC and PAL TV Standards for DVD-Video

NTSC	PAL
Interlaced fields	Interlaced fields
59.94 fields/sec	50 fields/sec
29.97 frames/sec	25 frames/sec
720x480 pixels	720x576 pixels
525 scan lines/frame	625 scan lines/frame

Table 2.3

Accepted Video Formats for Import

VIDEO FORMAT	FRAME SIZE	ASPECT RATIO	FRAME RATE
AVI (NTSC)	720x480, 720x486, 704x480	4:3 or 16:9	23.976fps, 29.98 fps 24fps, 29.97fps, 30fps
AVI (PAL)	720x576, 704x576	4:3 or 16:9	25fps
MPEG-2 (NTSC)	720x480, 720x486, 704x480	4:3 or 16:9	23.976fps, 29.98 fps 24fps, 29.97fps, 30fps
MPEG-2 (PAL)	720x576, 704x576	4:3 or 16:9	25fps
QuickTime (NTSC)	720x480, 720x486, 704x480	4:3 or 16:9	23.976fps, 29.98 fps 24fps, 29.97fps, 30fps
QuickTime (PAL)	720x576, 704x576	4:3 or 16:9	25fps

Covering All the Aspects

You have a number of choices to make regarding how your content will be created, imported, previewed, and, finally, displayed to the viewer. It all starts at the pixel level and goes up from there. Here's how it works:

Pixel Aspect Ratio: Pixels come in two shapes—square and nonsquare—and Encore DVD has tools to help you cope with both of them. Square pixels occur in computer-generated graphics and visuals. Square pixels have a pixel aspect ratio (PAR) of 1.0.

In recent years, graphics programs (including, of course, Photoshop CS and After Effects) have included the option to work in either square or nonsquare pixels.

Nonsquare pixels are found in material shot with a digital video camera—they are part of both the NTSC and PAL television standards. When you view your DVD on a video monitor, what you're seeing is a screenful of nonsquare pixels.

Screen Aspect Ratio: Nonsquare pixels also come in two varieties: standard (4:3 screen aspect ratio), and widescreen (16:9 screen aspect ratio). As you know, with many digital video cameras you select a screen aspect ratio (SAR) before you begin shooting, depending on the type of video monitor you'll be using to display your footage.

To keep all this straight, here's a quick list of the different combinations (you'll need this information to understand how Encore DVD deals with importing your assets and to know how to make sure the assets are matched correctly to avoid any problems on the finished DVD):

- **Computer graphics:** square pixels, 1.0 PAR

- **NTSC standard (4:3):** nonsquare, .9 PAR

- **NTSC widescreen (16:9):** nonsquare, 1.22 PAR

- **PAL standard (4:3):** nonsquare, 1.066 PAR

- **PAL widescreen (16:9):** nonsquare, 1.422 PAR

In an easy and perfect world, your output needs and your source material all line up nicely in terms of pixel and aspect ratios. Here are some considerations in using Encore DVD in those situations where you have to mix and match:

Interpreting assets on import: When a video asset is imported, Encore DVD interprets the native pixel aspect ratio of that asset and imports it accordingly. Then, Encore DVD refers to the project's Preview Preferences and displays the video asset in the project's selected screen aspect ratio—either 4:3, 16:9, or letterbox (a 16:9 video asset within a 4:3 frame, with black bars at the top and bottom).

continues on next page

PREPARING SOURCE VIDEO

Covering All the Aspects *(continued)*

As you create and play timelines, Encore DVD is able to make sure that your video assets are neither "squeezed" nor "stretched" by being played back in the wrong aspect ratio. What you see is what you get, so if your video does not look right, you can re-import the asset using the Interpret Footage function to select the appropriate pixel aspect ratio to fit the desired screen aspect ratio.

The same idea applies to the maintaining the correct screen aspect ratio of a menu in Encore DVD. If it doesn't look right, check the aspect ratio setting in its Properties window.

Matching aspects: You can mix and match timelines and menus of different aspect ratios in a project. Try to make sure that 16:9 widescreen material is accessed via a 16:9 widescreen menu, and the same for 4:3. Shifting from a widescreen menu to a standard-size video playback and vice versa can be jarring to the viewer.

You cannot mix aspect ratios in the same imported asset. Encore DVD assigns one pixel aspect ratio setting upon import, so if you have a video asset with both 16:9 and 4:3 material in it, some of the material will always display incorrectly, both in Encore DVD and on the final DVD. To cope with this sort of problem, you can use Premiere Pro to reformat the video to one aspect ratio and then import it into Encore.

What will I see on my TV? Obviously, when you play standard 4:3 video on a DVD player and view it on a standard 4:3 video monitor, it will display correctly. The same goes for 16:9 video displayed on a widescreen monitor. (If you experience trouble here, check the settings of the player and monitor.) Here's what happens when you mix aspect ratios on playback:

◆ **16:9 video on a 4:3 monitor:** Encore DVD always retains the video's original 16:9 aspect ratio on the DVD, but it will always display 16:9 material in a letterboxed format on a 4:3 monitor. The letterboxing is embedded when Encore DVD creates the DVD, so it will override any other settings in the DVD player.

◆ **4:3 video on a 16:9 monitor:** The DVD player will perform what is sometimes described as "pillarboxing," presenting the 4:3 material in the center of the screen, with black bars at each side to fill the additional screen width. You may adjust the monitor to zoom in on the picture, but picture quality will deteriorate.

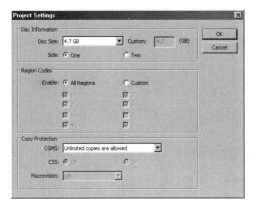

Figure 2.6 The Project Settings dialog.

Determining Disc Capacity

Along with all the technical choices you'll be making as you plan your DVD project, you face another challenge: matching the amount of source material you want to use to a disc size that makes sense, using a compression scheme that balances quality with space considerations. Whew!

This is important because, although DVDs do currently come in sizes up to 18 GB, if your project extends beyond the 4.7 GB capacity of a standard single-sided, single-layer disc, three things happen: burning discs on your desktop is no longer an option, the planning and expense of disc replication goes up substantially, and the end user's life can be complicated by the need to manage multiple discs to view your program.

Balancing out all these considerations requires a bit budget (see the sidebar later in this chapter).

Bit budgeting can get quite complicated. (See the Appendix for more details.) The good news is that Encore DVD can help keep track of the bit budget for your project as you work on it. First, however, you'll need to set the size of the destination disc.

To set the disc size:

1. In the Project window, click the Disc tab.

2. Click the Project Settings button.
   The Project Settings dialog opens
   (**Figure 2.6**).

continues on next page

3. Choose a size from the Disc Size menu.

To enter a custom disc size, choose Custom and then type a size in the text box or choose from the options shown (**Figure 2.7**). Now that Encore DVD knows the capacity of your destination disc, it will keep a running estimate of how much material in the project it will need to transcode and how much space that will take up on disc.

For an example of how that works, take a look at **Figure 2.8**. In this case, out of 4.7 GB total disc capacity, Encore DVD is estimating that about 270 MB is already "spoken for" by the assets in the project, leaving about 4.43 GB free. Every time a timeline is created or deleted, Encore DVD updates this number.

Now that you have gone through this process to determine disc size, another question arises: Which disc format (DVD-R, DVD-RW, and so on) is best for your project? Good news again: Encore DVD supports all of them. (See Chapter 6.)

✔ Tips

- The standard computer definition of a gigabyte is 1,024 megabytes, whereas the DVD standard defines a gigabyte as 1 billion bytes. Using the DVD standard, a typical DVD disc can hold 4.7 GB of data. Using the traditional computer standard, that 4.7 GB would be considered 4.37 GB, but because Encore DVD's calculations are based on the DVD standard, that's what I'll use in this book.

- You are not required to set the disc size at the beginning of a project, but it does allow you to keep track of available disc space as your project progresses.

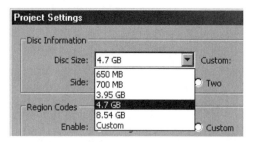

Figure 2.7 Setting the disc size. Note that you can set a custom size if you want (within the physical capacity of the disc).

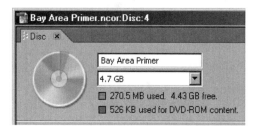

Figure 2.8 A close-up view of Encore DVD's internal bit budget feature.

- The numbers in the Disc Size area of the Disc tab are estimates, based on several variables, such as the number of timelines in the project and the method you choose for determining asset transcode settings—letting Encore DVD do it automatically, using a custom setting, or using a combination of the two. More detail on this can be found in Chapter 6.

Disc Capacity Considerations

Here are the basic things to keep in mind regarding disc capacity:

◆ The maximum data rate for a DVD is just over 10 megabits per second (Mbps).

◆ Of that, a maximum of 9.8 Mbps can be devoted to video data. The reality is, both these numbers are maximum rates. There is no absolute agreement on the "sweet spot" of data rates, as it is so dependent on the complexity of your source video. But you'll want to stay on the conservative side to ensure reliable playback on a wide variety of players. The highest bit rate available in for transcoding in Encore DVD is 9 Mbps. If you want to use a data rate near the maximum, burn some test discs and try them on different DVD players first.

◆ Video takes up by far the most space on your disc; you'll need to add up the total amount of video source footage you want to use.

◆ The other assets you'll use, such as audio and motion menus (menus that utilize moving video), take up less space on the disc but still must be accounted for.

◆ The different disc sizes give you some flexibility, but the only type you can burn on the desktop are single-sided discs with a maximum capacity of 4.7 GB.

As you consider all this, you'll need to leave a little "headroom" for the disc—you don't want to use up every single kilobyte of its capacity. An allowance of 5 percent extra for headroom is considered about right.

DETERMINING DISC CAPACITY

Starting a Project

Now that you've got a handle on what kind of sources you have and what kind of DVD you are going to create, it's time to start a project and get to work. First, an explanation of just what an Encore DVD project is.

Each time you create and save a new project, Encore DVD creates a project file and a project folder on the same directory level (**Figure 2.9**). As you import assets and menus and begin transcoding files, Encore DVD builds a hierarchy of folders to hold this data and updates them as you make changes (**Figure 2.10**).

The project file, with the suffix .ncor, is the nucleus of your project. Inside the project folder there are three items:

◆ **Preferences.** As you make changes to the interface—customizing the column view in a window, for instance—they are recorded here.

◆ **Cache folder.** This contains image files that Encore DVD will use for thumbnails.

◆ **Sources folder.** This is where Encore saves and manages several different kinds of data:

Figure 2.9 Encore DVD creates both a project file and a folder to store files associated with the project.

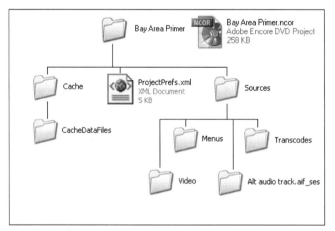

Figure 2.10 Encore DVD creates and manages files for your project.

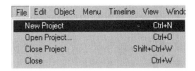

Figure 2.11 Creating a new project.

Figure 2.12 Setting the TV standard for the project. This step can be bypassed by checking the "Don't prompt for setting..." check box.

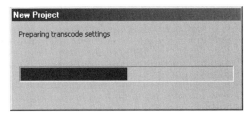

Figure 2.13 Encore is checking its list of transcode settings. These settings will play a big part when the project is ready for output.

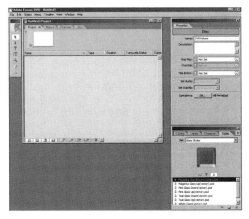

Figure 2.14 The project is up and ready to go.

▲ For video and audio material that has not been transcoded, Encore DVD stores a small pointer file, leading to the original source. The source itself is still wherever you stored it on your hard drive, and is not altered in any way.

▲ When a menu is created or imported, Encore DVD stores the entire menu file in its Menus folder, not just a pointer.

▲ When a motion menu is rendered (moving video and/or audio is stored as an MPEG-2 file), the entire file is stored. (More on motion menus in Chapter 9.)

▲ For MPEG-2 files that have been imported but not transcoded, Encore DVD creates a folder with the source file name and stores pointer information inside it, but it does not alter the original source.

▲ For files that it has transcoded, Encore DVD creates a Transcoded folder. This contains the actual transcoded files, which are stored inside subfolders.

These files are "under the hood"—they generally need no attention from the user.

To create a new project:

1. Choose File > New Project (**Figure 2.11**). Encore displays a New Project Settings dialog (**Figure 2.12**).

2. Select the video standard you will work in (NTSC or PAL) and click OK.

   (If you want to bypass this step, choose Edit > Preferences > General and check the "Don't prompt for setting..." box.)

   The program prepares transcode settings (**Figure 2.13**).

   Encore DVD's interface is displayed, in its Default workspace (**Figure 2.14**).

STARTING A PROJECT

To open an existing project:

1. Choose File > Open Project (**Figure 2.15**).

2. Navigate to the folder containing the project and select it.

Or

◆ Select a recent project from the list at the bottom of the File menu (**Figure 2.16**). The four most recent projects are listed in the order in which they were saved. Encore opens the selected project.

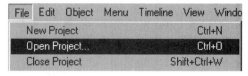

Figure 2.15 Opening an existing project from the File menu.

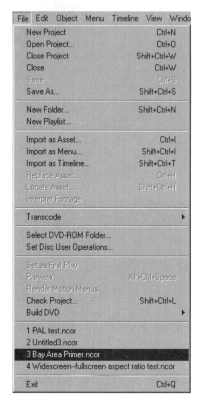

Figure 2.16 Encore DVD keeps a list of the last four projects, ready to reopen.

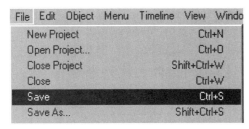

Figure 2.17 The File > Save menu.

Figure 2.18 When you save a project, make sure you give it a meaningful name and save it where you can find it again.

To save a project:

◆ Choose File > Save (**Figure 2.17**).

Or

◆ Choose File > Save As.

Encore DVD navigates to the most recently opened folder and allows you to name and save the project (**Figure 2.18**). Note that the project will be named Untitled unless you give it a specific name.

✔ Tips

■ Since Encore DVD's save process defaults to the last folder opened, pay attention— be sure that's where you want to save the file, and be consistent as to where you are saving your projects.

■ Encore allows you to save projects wherever you like, so it is prudent to create a specific folder in a specific place first and then save your work consistently to that folder.

■ It's wise to keep your project's assets—the source video, sound, and graphics files— organized in folders at the same directory level as the project file. Keeping the project and the assets together makes copying and backing up your work much easier.

■ As Encore DVD saves complex menus and MPEG-2 transcoded files in its Sources folder, make sure you have enough space on your hard drive(s) to accommodate all the necessary files.

■ Most processes can be reversed through the Undo (Edit > Undo) function and the History (Edit > History) feature. In addition, if you make a mistake in transcoding, you can right-click on the transcoded file in the Project tab and choose Revert to Original from the contextual menu to relink to your original file.

STARTING A PROJECT

39

Importing Assets

Assets are major building blocks of your project: video, audio, and still images. If you have prepared your source elements as outlined earlier in this chapter, you will be able to import them successfully as assets.

You can bring assets into a project either by importing them or by dragging and dropping them.

To import a file as an asset:

1. Select File > Import as Asset (**Figure 2.19**). The Import as Asset dialog opens (**Figure 2.20**).

2. Navigate to the folder that contains the file(s) you wish to import.

3. Select the desired file(s) and click Open.

Or

1. Select the Project tab in the Project window.

2. Navigate to the folder containing the files to import.

3. Select the desired file(s). Drag and drop them onto the Project tab.

✔ Tips

■ Other options in the menu allow you to locate or replace assets (**Figure 2.21**). If Encore DVD cannot find an asset, its name is displayed in italics in the Project window. You can browse for the asset's original file in Windows Explorer and then use Locate Asset to redirect the link from Encore DVD to the same file. Replace Asset can be used to change Encore DVD's link to a different file.

■ You can also import an asset or menu by double-clicking any blank area within the Project tab and making your selection from the contextual menu.

Figure 2.19 The first step in importing an asset.

Figure 2.20 Using the Import function to navigate and select a file. Note the list of formats that Encore DVD finds acceptable for import.

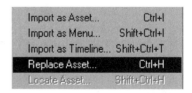

Figure 2.21 More asset management options in the File menu.

Figure 2.22 When it comes to importing a file as a menu, Encore DVD is interested in Photoshop files only.

Figure 2.23 The first step in importing a file as a menu.

Figure 2.24 The Menu Editor with several menus stacked in it and tabbed for use.

Importing Menus

While you use the same basic procedure to import menus that you do to import assets, menus differ from assets in one important aspect: They are, specifically, Photoshop files (**Figure 2.22**). The advantage to importing menus as Photoshop files is that it preserves the layers and layer sets associated with the files. Even when you create a menu within Encore DVD, it is saved in a Photoshop (PSD) format. (Chapter 4 deals with creating menus and Chapter 7 deals with Photoshop.)

To import a PSD file as a menu:

1. With the Project window active, choose File > Import as Menu (**Figure 2.23**) or double-click any empty area in the Project tab.

2. Navigate to the PSD file you want to import and select it. (You can select multiple files if you wish.)

3. Click Open.

   When the menu has been imported, it will be listed both in the Project and Menu tabs of the Project window. In addition, the Menu Editor window automatically opens.

   If you imported several menus simultaneously, they will all be displayed within the Menu Editor window as tabs (**Figure 2.24**).

✔ Tip

■ Here's another way to import a PSD file as a menu: Hold down the Alt key as you drag the file from Windows Explorer to the Project tab.

Organizing Your Content

You'll need to keep all the elements of your project organized, and Encore DVD gives you several different means for doing so. Three of the tabs in the Project window lead to extensive databases that help manage the various elements that will make up your final DVD (**Figure 2.25**).

There are too many columns in each tab to go through them all here. (See Chapter 1 for more details.) The Project tab has the most extensive set of controls, but the Timelines and Menus tabs also behave much like the Project tab in terms of accessing and customizing your column views. The Timelines and Menus tabs have upper and lower panes, as well, to accommodate lists of chapter points and buttons.

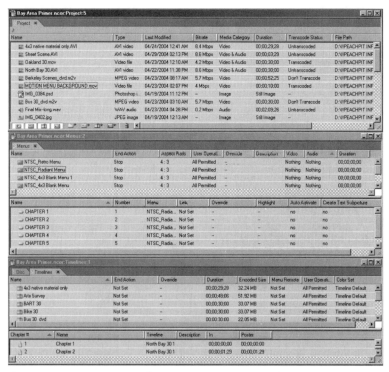

Figure 2.25 The three main tabs (Project, Menus, and Timelines) with just some of their data columns displayed.

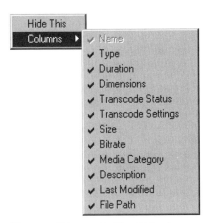

Figure 2.26 You can decide which columns are most useful, and select them with a checkmark.

Figure 2.27 You can also hide the columns that are not useful to you.

To show or hide information in Project window tabs:

◆ Right-click anywhere in a column name and choose the column you want to hide or show from the contextual menu (**Figure 2.26**).

A check next to the column name indicates that the column is shown.

Or

◆ To hide a column, right-click its column name and choose Hide This from the contextual menu (**Figure 2.27**).

To resize columns:

◆ Position the cursor over the right edge of the column you want to resize and, when the cursor becomes a resize cursor, drag the edge to the desired size.

Or

◆ Double-click the right edge of the column you want to resize. The panel resizes to the length of the longest line of text in that column.

To rearrange columns:

1. Drag the column name to a different location along the column header and release the mouse button.

2. Repeat for other columns.

✔ Tip

■ Each column can be sorted or reverse-sorted in standard Windows fashion. Clicking a column name will display an up arrow, and the column will be sorted in standard alphabetical or numerical order. Click again and a down arrow is displayed, indicating a reverse sort. You can only sort one column at a time.

ORGANIZING YOUR CONTENT

To view asset, menu, timeline, or playlist information in the Project tab:

1. Click on one of the toggle buttons on the bottom left of the tab: Assets, Menus, Timelines, Playlists (**Figure 2.28**).

   The default setting for all four buttons is the show state, which is indicated by a white outline. If the element type was previously shown, it is now hidden.

2. To restore the element type to view, click on the appropriate toggle button again.

✔ Tips

- This toggle function can be a great help when searching for specific elements in a large project because it allows you to filter out the types of elements you don't want to include in the search.

- Also at the bottom of the Project tab are four other buttons (**Figure 2.29**), which are essentially shortcuts for adding new folders, menus, and timelines to the Project tab (more on these in Chapters 3 and 4). The button with the trashcan icon deletes items from the Project tab.

To name or rename elements of the project:

Do one of the following:

- Select an item in any tab. Choose Edit > Rename and type a new name.

- Right-click on an item in any tab. Choose Rename from the contextual menu, and type a new name.

- With the Properties palette open, select an item in any tab. Type a new name in the Name box.

Toggle display of assets   *Toggle display of timelines*

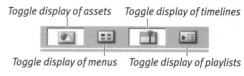

Toggle display of menus   *Toggle display of playlists*

Figure 2.28 Project tab display toggles.

Create new folder   *Create new timeline*   *Delete selected items*

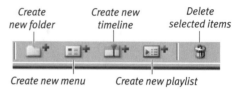

Create new menu   *Create new playlist*

Figure 2.29 More shortcuts and controls in the Project tab.

Working with AVI, QuickTime, and MPEG-2

AVI (Audio Video Interleave), QuickTime, and MGEG-2 are three of the most common computer video formats. Microsoft developed AVI QuickTime was developed by Apple Computer, and MPEG-2, as you learned in Chapter 1, was developed by a committee and adopted as an industry standard. Since Encore DVD can work with any of these three formats, you have a lot of latitude in choosing your source material and mixing sources in a project.

In terms of Encore DVD, the distinction between working with AVI, QuickTime and MPEG-2 files is their different temporal compression schemes. AVI and QuickTime are source video formats, and they contain every frame of the original video. MPEG-2 files, as mentioned in Chapter 1, break the video content into GOPs (Groups Of Pictures), usually about 15 frames long. Each GOP is analyzed, redundant information is "thrown away," and the video stream is created from the remaining information. The result is very good video quality in a much smaller file.

Your final DVD, of course, will store its video as an MPEG-2 stream. Here's how Encore DVD deals with the three main computer video formats:

◆ AVI files can be transcoded to MPEG-2 at any time in the Encore DVD project—either while you're working on the project or when it is being output to disc.

◆ QuickTime files must be transcoded on import. Encore DVD will display a message to that effect and allow you to choose from a list of transcoding presets.

◆ MPEG-2 files need not be transcoded in Encore DVD. In fact, transcoding an existing MPEG-2 file should be avoided, because picture quality will be affected. (If your project is too big to fit on a disc, this may be necessary, but only as a last resort.)

Many experienced DVD authors prefer to transcode all their source video into the MPEG-2 format before working in Encore DVD. This gives them a great deal of control over the picture quality and data rate, saves on storage space, and also saves time in Encore DVD, because the transcoding is performed "upstream" of the DVD authoring process. Both Premiere Pro and After Effects 6.5 have MPEG-2 in their list of output options. (See Chapters 8 and 9 for more information about transcoding to MPEG-2 and importing the video file into Encore DVD.)

However, Encore DVD's built-in transcoder gives you the option of working with a variety of assets, having some choice as to when to transcode them—in the background as you work on your project, or just before outputting to disc. This may be a better fit for your workflow, and allows you to get great results without having to be an experienced MPEG-2 compressionist.

ORGANIZING YOUR CONTENT

WORKING WITH TIMELINES

In this chapter, you'll learn all the basics of timelines: what they're made of, how to make them, and how to modify them. You'll learn how to get assets onto tracks and what to do with them once they're there. You'll find out how to use the controls in the Timeline window and how to use the Monitor window to view your work. You'll also learn about chapter points—how to make, move, and manage them—in preparation for building the navigational links in your project.

Most of this chapter is devoted to building timelines from video and audio assets. However, you can also create slideshows by assembling still images on a video track and laying in audio tracks if you wish. Because a timeline's video track works a bit differently when populated with a series of stills, I'll cover that at the end of the chapter.

Creating Timelines

As with most everything in Encore DVD, there are several different ways to create a timeline. You can

◆ Use the Import as Timeline option in the File menu to import video, audio, or still images into your project *and* create a timeline out of them, all in one step.

◆ Create timelines out of existing assets in the Project tab by selecting them and clicking the Create a new Timeline button at the bottom of the Project tab.

◆ Create empty timelines, and drag assets onto them from the Project tab.

The first two methods allow you to use your video and audio elements as the starting point and then transform them into timelines, retaining their original names. With the third method, you create an empty, untitled timeline, and then drag assets onto it. Of course, you can name and rename your timelines whenever you wish.

These methods all work just fine, and you may find yourself using any or all of them in your workflow. Regardless of the method you choose, your project's original assets remain unchanged. When an asset—actually, a copy of the asset—is attached to a timeline, the resulting file is called a *clip*.

About Assets, Clips, and Timelines

Assets—video, audio, and still images—are the raw materials you use to build timelines. Assets are stored in the Project tab and, as you'll recall from the last chapter, they are just *references* to the original source files—they are not the source files themselves.

Think of a timeline as a container. When an asset is associated with a timeline, a copy of the asset—a new pointer file—is created within the timeline, and that copy is called a *clip*. This scheme allows you to use the same asset many times in a project. Each clip is unique, however, and is related both to the original source file and to the timeline that contains the clip.

These relationships are reflected in the Properties palette (**Figures 3.1** and **3.2**).

The number and types of tracks you can place in a timeline depends on your project settings. Each timeline always has a single video track—even if that track has nothing on it. The video track cannot be deleted. However, audio tracks (and subtitle tracks, as you'll find out later in the book) can be added and deleted as needed.

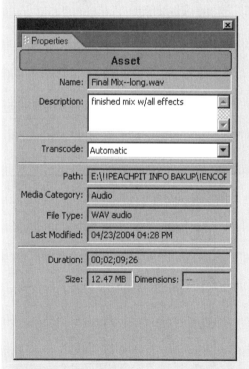

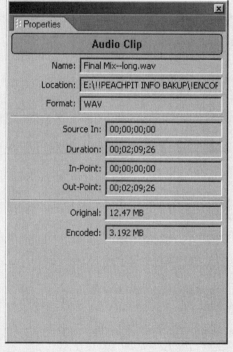

Figure 3.1 A sound file in the Project tab is an asset...

Figure 3.2 ...but when added to a timeline, it becomes a clip.

To import an asset as a timeline:

1. Choose File > Import as Timeline (**Figure 3.3**).

   Or

◆ Double-click in the Timelines tab.

   The Import as Timeline dialog opens (**Figure 3.4**).

2. Select a file to import and click Open.

   A new timeline is created, with the Timeline window and Monitor window displayed automatically (**Figure 3.5**). The timeline will have the same name as the file from which it was created.

   The new timeline and the imported asset are stored in the Project tab.

✔ Tips

■ The general rule is: If you select multiple video/image files or multiple audio files, Encore DVD will import them as separate timelines. However, there are some variations:

■ If you select one video or image file and one audio file to import, Encore DVD assumes that you want to combine them on the new timeline. If the video file has audio already embedded in it, Encore DVD still allows you to select one "extra" audio file. Encore DVD then takes both audio tracks, along with the video, and creates a new timeline. (This can be a useful shortcut, if, for instance, you have a sync-sound movie and a foreign language track that you want to import simultaneously.)

■ If you select one video or image file *and more than one* audio file to import, Encore DVD will import them all as separate timelines.

Figure 3.3 Importing an asset as a timeline.

Figure 3.4 You can use the Import as Timeline dialog to select the source files to import.

Figure 3.5 From source files to a timeline in one step.

CREATING TIMELINES

Figure 3.6 The Create a New Timeline button.

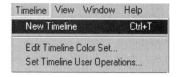

Figure 3.7 Creating a new timeline from the Timeline menu.

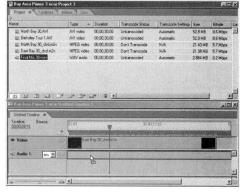

Figure 3.8 A little hard to see here, but this is an asset making the journey to the timeline.

To create a timeline from the Project tab:

1. Select an asset from the Project tab.

2. Click the Create a New Timeline button (**Figure 3.6**).

   Or

◆ Right-click and select New Timeline from the contextual menu.

A new timeline is created, with the Timeline window and Monitor window displayed automatically. The timeline will be named for the asset from which it was created.

✔ Tip

■ You can select multiple assets in the Project tab. Encore DVD will follow the same rules as above, in terms of combining video and audio elements onto timelines.

To create a timeline from the Timeline menu:

1. Choose Timeline > New Timeline (**Figure 3.7**).

A new, untitled timeline is created and placed in both the Project and Timelines tabs of the Project window. The Timeline window and Monitor window also open (if they weren't open already), with *Untitled* displayed in each of them.

2. Drag individual video and audio assets out of the Project tab and place them on the timeline (**Figure 3.8**).

For further information on placing multiple assets on timeline tracks, see the section "Placing Assets on Timeline Tracks" later in this chapter.

To name a timeline:

1. Select a timeline in the Project or Timelines tab of the Project window.

2. Choose Edit > Rename (**Figure 3.9**). The Rename Timeline dialog appears (**Figure 3.10**).

3. Type a new name in the box.

Or

1. Choose Window > Properties (**Figure 3.11**). The Properties palette opens.

2. Select a timeline. You can go to either the Project or Timelines tab of the Project window, or you can click in an empty space on a track in an active timeline.

3. Enter a new name for the timeline in the Name box in the Properties palette (**Figure 3.12**).

✔ Tip

- If you right-click on a timeline in the Project or Timelines tab, you can rename the timeline using the contextual menu that pops up.

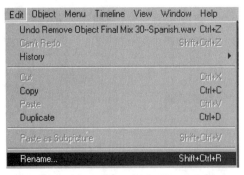

Figure 3.9 A timeline can be renamed by starting here...

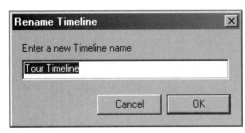

Figure 3.10 ...and typing in a new name here.

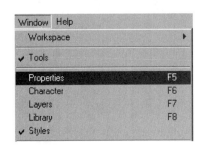

Figure 3.11 Or you can open the Properties palette for a timeline...

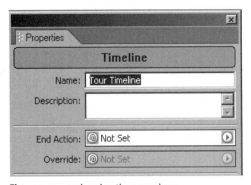

Figure 3.12 ...and assign the name here.

CREATING TIMELINES

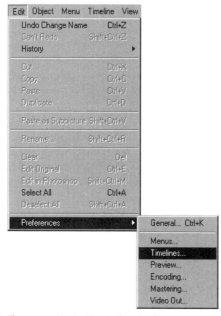

Figure 3.13 Navigating to the Timeline preferences through the Edit menu.

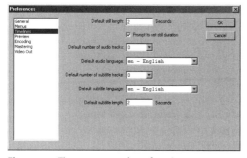

Figure 3.14 There are a number of settings you can adjust to customize your timelines.

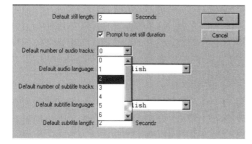

Figure 3.15 In this case, you can assign up to eight audio tracks as the timeline default.

To set the Timeline preferences:

1. Choose Edit > Preferences > Timelines (**Figure 3.13**).

   The Preferences dialog appears (**Figure 3.14**).

2. Establish default settings for new timelines using the pop-up menus (**Figure 3.15**).

3. Click OK to accept your selection.

✔ Tips

■ The settings chosen in the Preferences dialog are global—all subsequent new projects will retain these settings.

■ Once a timeline is created in a project, Encore DVD will write it to disc during final output. Make sure you delete all unwanted timelines. For example, if by mistake you have an "orphan" timeline pointing to an hour-long media file, it will throw your storage calculations off substantially.

■ A timeline can be created using any types of assets in any combination. For instance, an AVI file can be combined with an MP3 audio source and a WAV source, all on the same timeline. A timeline also can be created using only still-image files, or only audio files. (The video track will still be there, even if it's empty.)

CREATING TIMELINES

Working with Audio Tracks

Audio tracks on Encore DVD's timelines are somewhat different from audio tracks on, say, Premiere timelines. With Encore DVD, you can do very little in terms of manipulation. Your main concern is simply timing. Here are some considerations:

◆ Although you can have as many as eight tracks of audio, you can monitor only one track at a time (using the Speaker icon).

◆ The track itself can be stereo, mono, or even encoded with surround sound. However, within Encore DVD, you will have no control over the stereo or surround imaging (panning of sound); it will have to be already present in the audio asset when it is imported.

◆ Encore DVD also contains no tools with which to change audio levels or even to fade in or fade out. Again, all these things will have to be optimized before you import the audio asset.

To add audio tracks to the timeline:

◆ With a timeline open in the Timeline window, choose Timeline > Add Audio Track (**Figure 3.16**).

Or

◆ Right-click anywhere in the Timeline window's track panes and, in the contextual menu, choose Add Audio Track (**Figure 3.17**).

The new audio track will be added in sequential order (**Figure 3.18**).

✔ Tip

■ Only one audio track can be added at a time.

Figure 3.16 You can add an audio track from the Timeline menu...

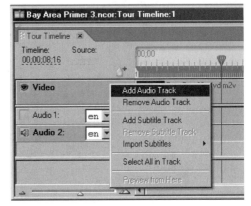

Figure 3.17 ...or on the timeline itself.

Figure 3.18 Each new audio track will be added sequentially to the track list.

Figure 3.19 Just as when adding an audio track, you can use the Timeline menu for removing a track...

Figure 3.20 ...or you can delete tracks on the timeline itself. Make sure you've selected the correct track to delete!

To remove audio tracks from the timeline:

1. Click anywhere on the Name area (e.g., "Audio 1") of the track you want to remove.

   The track is selected (the Name area is highlighted and the track name appears in bold).

2. Choose Timeline > Remove Audio Track (**Figure 3.19**).

Or

◆ Select a track as above, right-click in Name area of the audio track, and, from the contextual menu, choose Remove Audio Track (**Figure 3.20**).

   Both the audio track and any audio clip on it will be removed.

✔ Tips

■ You can remove only one audio track at a time.

■ When an audio track is deleted, all subsequent tracks "move up" in the timeline and are renumbered. (There can be no gaps; all audio tracks must be in the timeline in sequential order.) Conversely, when an audio track is added, it is always added as an empty track at the bottom of the timeline's track list.

■ For the most precision in removing tracks, make sure you have selected the track by clicking or right-clicking in the Name area. It's easy to inadvertently remove the wrong track.

Placing Assets on Timeline Tracks

Although the basic procedure for moving assets from the Project tab to timeline tracks is a simple drag-and-drop, there can be several variations, depending on what the original assets are. See the "Audio Drag-and-Drop Variations" sidebar for details.

Here are some general points to keep in mind:

◆ As noted earlier, when an asset is dragged to a track on a timeline, it is *copied* to the track. Once on a track, this copy of a video, audio, or still-image asset is referred to as a *clip*.

◆ There can only be one clip per track. You can't place two video or audio files on a track to create one longer timeline. This you must do in your video editor. (Slideshows and subtitles are the exception here. See the end of this chapter and Chapter 10 for more information.)

◆ Assets can be placed on any unoccupied track, whether or not the track is selected, by dragging and dropping.

◆ Encore DVD won't let you drag a video or audio asset onto a track that already contains a video or audio clip (**Figure 3.21**).

◆ Clips on tracks are color-coded as to type. Video clips are blue, still-image clips are pink, and audio clips are green. (Or perhaps periwinkle, rose, and avocado?) When deselected, a clip's color is light; when selected, it's dark.

Figure 3.21 You can't drag an asset onto an occupied track. The cursor changes into a "no" symbol.

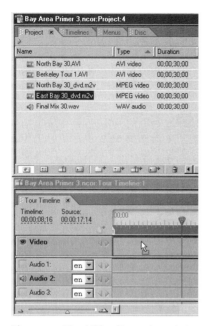

Figure 3.22 It's a bit hard to see here, but the highlighted asset is being dragged to the timeline's video track.

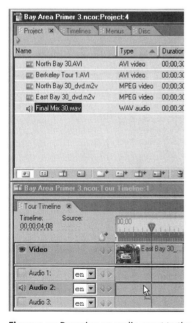

Figure 3.23 Dragging an audio asset to the timeline. With audio, you have more tracks to choose from.

To place a video or still-image asset on a timeline track:

1. Select a video or still-image asset in the Project tab.

2. Drag and drop it onto an unoccupied video track in a timeline (**Figure 3.22**).

✔ Tip

■ Video elements will always snap to the head of a timeline video track. They cannot move from that position.

To place an audio asset on a timeline track:

1. Select an audio asset in the Project tab.

2. Drag and drop it onto an unoccupied audio track in a timeline (**Figure 3.23**). The track onto which you drop the asset does not have to be selected in the Name area of the timeline.

✔ Tip

■ Initially, an audio clip will snap to the head of a timeline track. To move an audio track to a different position on the timeline, click and drag it with the mouse. (This only works if the audio clip is independent of and unrelated to the video clip on the timeline.) For greater precision while moving, place the Current Time Indicator or create a chapter point at the point in the timeline where you want to place the audio clip. You can then snap either the head or tail of the audio clip into position.

PLACING ASSETS ON TIMELINE TRACKS

To move an audio clip to another track:

1. Select a clip on an audio track (**Figure 3.24**).

2. Drag and drop the clip onto a different track (**Figure 3.25**). Drag the clip to the desired position on the track.

✔ Tips

- The track you drag to must be visible in the timeline.

- You can move only one audio clip at a time.

To remove a clip from a track:

- ◆ Right-click on clip in the Timeline window and choose Remove Audio Track from the contextual menu (**Figure 3.26**).

Or

- ◆ Select the clip in the Timeline window and press the Delete key.

✔ Tips

- Clips can be cut, copied, and pasted from one track to another within a timeline using standard Windows methods.

- Entire video, audio, and subtitle tracks can be cut/copied/pasted from one timeline to another within the same project, but they cannot be copied into another project.

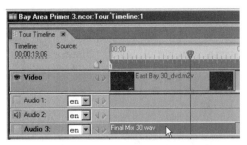

Figure 3.24 Moving an audio clip from track to track: before...

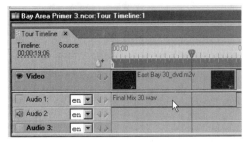

Figure 3.25 ...and after the move.

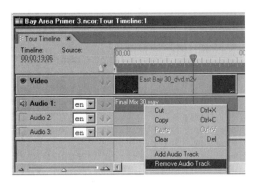

Figure 3.26 Removing a clip from a timeline track.

Audio Drag-and-Drop Variations

If your imported AVI, QuickTime, or MPEG-2 asset has *both* video and audio elements, Encore DVD will, by default, try to keep them together. It will *always* place the asset's video onto the timeline's video track if the track is unoccupied.

The track on which the audio ends up, however, depends on how you perform the drag-and-drop and how the timeline audio tracks are set up. These examples all assume that the video track is available (you can't drag assets onto a track if it already contains a clip).

Ready? Here goes:

◆ **If there is no audio track.** Encore DVD will automatically create an audio track during the drag-and-drop and place the audio element there.

◆ **Dragging to a specific audio track.** Drag the asset out of the Project tab and drop it onto the desired audio track. Encore DVD will place audio on this track and video on the video track. If there is a clip already on the audio track, Encore DVD stops the operation.

◆ **Selecting a specific audio track.** Select a specific audio track. Drag the asset out of the Project tab and drop it onto the video track. Encore DVD will place the audio on the selected track. If the selected audio track is occupied, Encore DVD will still place the *video* asset on the video track.

◆ **Dragging to the video track with no audio track selection.** Drag the asset out of the Project tab and drop it onto the video track. If there are no audio tracks selected, Encore DVD will create a new audio track at the bottom of the track list and place the audio there. There are only eight audio tracks available. If they are all occupied, Encore DVD will still place the asset's video on the video track, but the audio track will not be placed on the timeline.

PLACING ASSETS ON TIMELINE TRACKS

Managing Timelines

As revealed in Chapter 2, the Project and Timelines tabs contain a wealth of searchable information that can help you deal with the complexities of timelines.

The basics of timeline management, however, are quite straightforward.

To display a timeline:

◆ Double-click a timeline's icon in either the Project or Timelines tab.

Or

◆ Right-click the timeline's icon and choose Open (**Figure 3.27**).

The Timeline window appears, with the selected timeline displayed (**Figure 3.28**). Clicking any timeline's Close box (the *X* in the tab) will remove it from the Timeline window.

Figure 3.27 Opening a timeline from the Timelines tab...

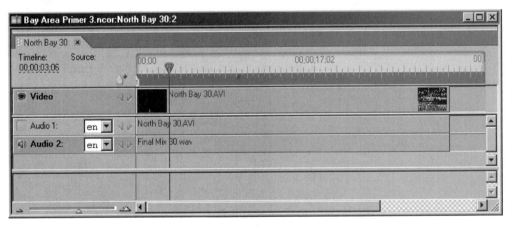

Figure 3.28 ...results in its appearance in the Timeline window.

MANAGING TIMELINES

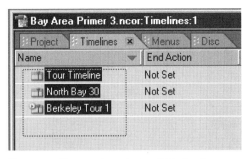

Figure 3.29 You can also select multiple timelines...

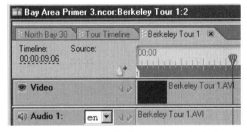

Figure 3.30 ...and they will all appear as tabs in the Timeline window.

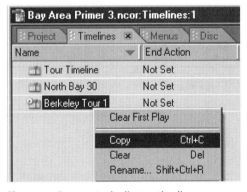

Figure 3.31 One way to duplicate a timeline...

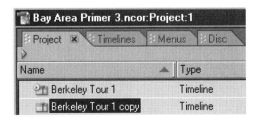

Figure 3.32 ...and here is the result.

To display multiple timelines:

1. Ctrl-click or Shift-click to select multiple icons in the Project tab or Timelines tab (**Figure 3.29**).

2. Double-click a timeline icon.

   All selected timelines will be displayed in the Timeline window as tabs (**Figure 3.30**).

✔ Tips

- You can also select one or more timelines in the Project or Timelines tab and press Enter on the keyboard to display them.

- A timeline can be rearranged in the Timeline window by selecting its tab and dragging it to a new position.

- You may want to make use of the Timeline Editing workspace template as well, as its screen layout has the Monitor window, the Timeline window, and all the other controls nicely laid out on the screen.

To duplicate a timeline:

1. Right-click on a timeline in the Project or Timelines tab and choose Copy from the contextual menu (**Figure 3.31**).

2. Right-click anywhere in the Project tab, and choose Paste.

   The copied timeline appears in the Project and Timelines tabs with the suffix *copy* added (**Figure 3.32**).

✔ Tip

- To copy multiple timelines, Ctrl-click or Shift-click to select multiple items and proceed as above.

MANAGING TIMELINES

To delete timelines:

1. Right-click on a timeline in the Project or Timelines tab and choose Clear from the contextual menu (**Figure 3.33**).

   A Delete Timeline Confirmation dialog appears (**Figure 3.34**).

   If you attempt to delete an asset that is associated with a timeline, you see a warning message (**Figure 3.35**). To successfully delete the asset, you must first delete the timeline.

2. Click OK.

✔ Tips

■ The activities mentioned here—creating, copying, and deleting—are all "undoable" and "redoable" through standard Windows commands and the Edit > History menu.

■ Encore DVD takes note of each timeline you create, copy, or delete, and it either adds or subtracts its duration from the bit budget. See the Appendix for more information.

Figure 3.33 One way to get rid of a timeline.

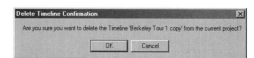

Figure 3.34 A chance to rethink the deletion before committing to it.

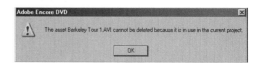

Figure 3.35 An asset that is being referenced by a timeline in the project cannot be deleted.

MANAGING TIMELINES

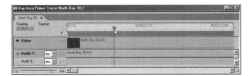

Figure 3.36 The Current Time Indicator can be grabbed and moved about the timeline.

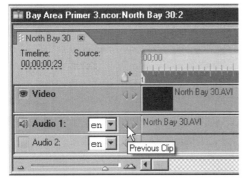

Figure 3.37 The Previous/Next Clip buttons allow you to cycle quickly through the clips lined up on your timeline tracks for previewing.

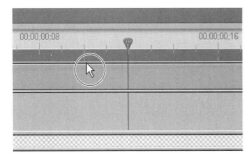

Figure 3.38 The cursor is pointing at I-frames, or GOP headers, which show up when your video source is MPEG-2.

Navigating in Timelines

Now that the process of managing timelines, tracks, and clips is a bit clearer, take a look at the navigational tools in the timeline:

◆ You can use the Current Time Indicator (CTI) to scroll around. (The CTI indicates your current position in the timeline.) Just grab it with the mouse and move around the timeline (**Figure 3.36**).

◆ To jump to a particular point on the timeline, click on that point in the Ruler bar. The CTI will jump to that point.

◆ To jump quickly between clips and tracks, you can use the Previous/Next Clip buttons in the Name section of the timeline tracks (**Figure 3.37**).

◆ If you have an MPEG-2 clip on the video track, the Ruler bar will display tick marks for I-frames (**Figure 3.38**). To jump to an I-frame in the timeline, click on it in the Ruler bar. (You'll learn more about I-frames later in the chapter.)

◆ To play the timeline, press the spacebar. Press it again to stop playback.

◆ To jog slowly through the timeline, position the mouse over the Timeline or Source counter until it turns into a directional arrow (**Figure 3.39**). Then move the mouse slowly back or forth to jog, releasing the mouse button to stop.

◆ To go to a particular timecode, select either the Timeline or Source timecode counter and type in the timecode point to which you want to go (**Figure 3.40**).

◆ To jump between the beginning and the end of a timeline, use the Home and End keys on your keyboard.

✔ Tips

■ The Timeline counter specifies the current location based on the timeline's timecode. The Source counter specifies the current location based on the clip's timecode.

■ The left and right keyboard arrows allow you to move around in the timeline, but the number of frames per keystroke varies. If zoomed in, you can jog frame by frame, even on an MPEG-2 clip. If zoomed out, a keystroke can jump up to 20 or 30 seconds.

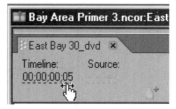

Figure 3.39 You can use the counters in the Timeline window to jog through your material.

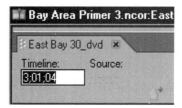

Figure 3.40 You can also go to a particular point by typing it into the counter.

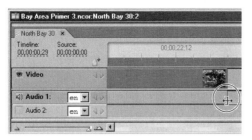

Figure 3.41 The Trim tool appears when you go near the edge of a track.

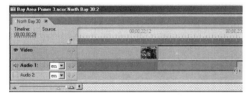

Figure 3.42 In this case, the end of a clip on Audio 1 is being extended by trimming.

Using the Timeline's Trim Tool

Encore DVD has a Trim tool that looks similar to the one you'll find in Premiere. However, because DVD authoring is a somewhat different process than "normal" editing, the Trim tool plays by somewhat different rules. Here are some of them:

◆ If the video and audio are "married" on the original source material, the Trim tool will always trim audio and video together, no matter what track you select.

◆ Video clips (with or without audio) always snap to the head of the timeline video track and remain there. You can trim the video track shorter, but though its duration changes, it will still start at the very beginning of the timeline track.

◆ "Independent" audio tracks can be trimmed much more freely—they aren't glued to the beginning of the timeline.

To trim the end of a video or audio track:

1. Move your pointer over the end of a track. It automatically turns into the Trim tool (**Figure 3.41**).

   If the Properties palette is open, it will display and update the properties (like the duration and out-point) of the clip you are trimming.

2. Grab the right edge of the track with the Trim tool and move it to the left to shorten the track, or to the right to extend it (**Figure 3.42**).

To trim the beginning of a video or audio track:

1. Move your pointer over the beginning of a track.

   The pointer automatically turns into the Trim tool.

2. Grab the left edge of the track with the Trim tool and move it to the right to shorten the track, or to the left to extend it.

   Note that the position of the video clip relative to the beginning of the timeline remains the same during a trim (**Figure 3.43**). The relationship of "independent" audio tracks to their position on the timeline is more flexible during trims (**Figure 3.44**).

✔ Tips

- You cannot trim (extend) beyond the length of the original asset.

- The Monitor window will display the position of the Trim tool while trimming, making it easy to see the frames you are working with while performing a trim. When the trim is complete, it will display the position of the Current Time Indicator.

Figure 3.43 It's a little hard to tell here, but the video track is being trimmed shorter. Its position relative to the beginning of the timeline will remain the same, even as its source footage is trimmed longer or shorter.

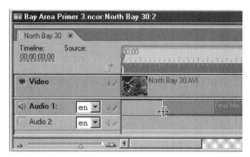

Figure 3.44 The clip on the Audio 1 track is being trimmed shorter, leaving a gap at the beginning of the timeline.

Making the Most of the Trim Tool

While the Trim tool in Encore DVD does not have nearly the sophistication of one you would find in an editing application, there are some ways to make it more effective.

◆ **Trim to the CTI.** Park the Current Time Indicator at the point you want to trim to (**Figure 3.45**). This will give you a target as you drag. Use the Trim tool to drag the edge of the track to the CTI.

◆ **Trim to a chapter point.** Chapter points also can be used as targets to aid in trimming. Place one at the point to which you want to trim, and drag the edge of the track to the chapter point (**Figure 3.46**). Delete the chapter point if it is no longer needed. (You'll learn more about chapter points later in this chapter.)

◆ **Zoom in on the timeline.** Use the Zoom slider and the scrollbar on the timeline to get zoomed in as close as possible. This will ensure that your tracks line up precisely after a trim operation.

◆ **Be patient while it updates.** It will take a second or so for the timeline to update after you complete a trim.

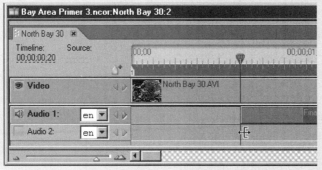

Figure 3.45 The clips on both the Video and Audio 1 tracks are being extended to the point where the Current Time Indicator is parked.

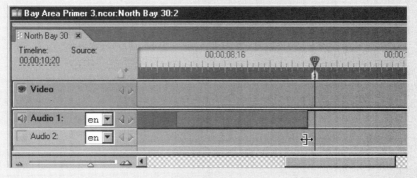

Figure 3.46 Here, the Audio 1 track is being trimmed to the chapter point.

USING THE TIMELINE'S TRIM TOOL

Viewing Timelines in the Monitor Window

Because you'll generally want to see picture playback as you work in a timeline, you'll be using the Monitor window extensively. Select Window > Monitor to open the Monitor window. For a quick refresher on its controls, see Chapter 1.

Here's an overview of what the Monitor window can do for you:

◆ The Monitor window will display the selected timeline in the Timeline window.

◆ The Monitor window can be resized and zoomed to and from full screen.

◆ The image inside the window can be displayed at selected settings between 25 and 200 percent (**Figure 3.47**).

◆ It has Play and Skip Forward/Backward keys built in (**Figure 3.48**).

◆ It has buttons you can use to create, and jump between, chapter points.

◆ It has a timecode counter, as on a timeline, but it can't be used to "go to" particular timecode points.

Figure 3.47 You can zoom in on the image inside the Monitor window, but the more the zoom, the fuzzier the image will be.

✔ Tip

■ When an MPEG-2 file is viewed in the Monitor window, the Skip Forward/Back controls are available. They can be used to jump between I-frames in the MPEG-2 video. These are usually 12 to 15 frames apart. When an AVI or other non-MPEG-2 file is viewed, the controls are grayed out.

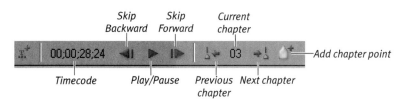

Figure 3.48 The controls of the Monitor window.

Figure 3.49 An example of a 16:9 image "squeezed" into a 4:3 Monitor window.

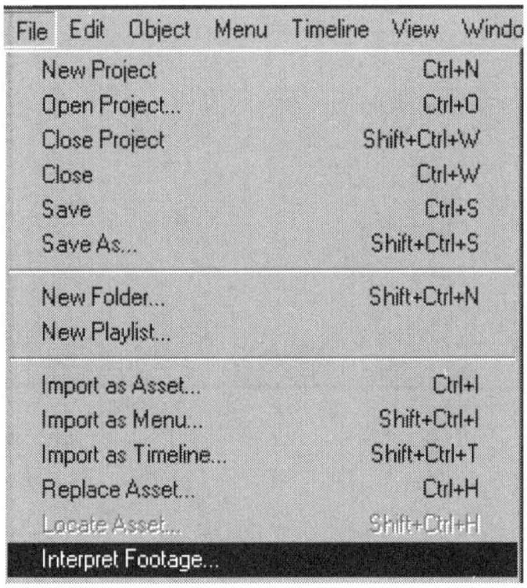

Figure 3.50 When a clip on a timeline seems to have an incorrect aspect ratio, the solution is for Encore DVD to (re)interpret the footage's pixel aspect ratio.

Monitor Window Aspect Ratio Adjustments

When displaying a video clip on a timeline, the aspect ratio of the Monitor window is determined by the pixel aspect ratio (remember the previous chapter?) of the clip. The Monitor window will automatically adjust its aspect ratio to accommodate different timelines with standard or widescreen content. If the Monitor window and a video clip have an aspect ratio mismatch, it may be because the clip was imported incorrectly. The mismatch can be fixed by "reinterpreting" the original footage's pixel aspect ratio.

When displaying still images, as in a slideshow, the Monitor window's aspect ratio is determined by the settings in the timeline's Properties palette. You can choose whether the timeline should be standard or widescreen and, if there is a mismatch, it can be fixed by rescaling one or more of the stills.

To correct an aspect ratio mismatch for a video clip on a timeline:

1. Determine that the Monitor window is not correctly displaying video on a timeline (**Figure 3.49**).

2. *Do one of the following:*

   ▲ Select the video asset in the Project window and choose File > Interpret Footage (**Figure 3.50**).

   ▲ Right-click on the video asset and choose Interpret Footage from the contextual menu.

   continues on next page

3. The Interpret Footage dialog appears (**Figure 3.51**).

The dialog gives you the choice of using the asset's "native" pixel aspect ratio (which may have been reported incorrectly on import) or changing the aspect ratio.

4. Select an alternate pixel aspect ratio from the pop-up menu (**Figure 3.52**). Click OK in the dialog that appears.

5. Close and reopen the Monitor window to reset its screen size and review the video clip's playback on the timeline (**Figure 3.53**).

Figure 3.51 The Interpret Footage dialog allows you to see the current pixel aspect ratio...

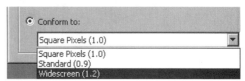

Figure 3.52 ...and presents you with options for changing it.

Figure 3.53 Once the new pixel aspect ratio is applied, you can view the results in the Monitor window. The image is now displayed correctly.

MONITOR WINDOW ASPECT RATIO ADJUSTMENTS

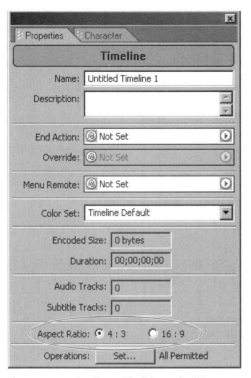

Figure 3.54 For timelines with slides and still images, you set the Monitor window's aspect ratio in the Properties palette.

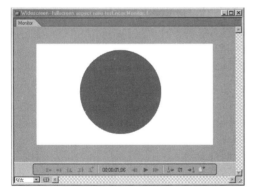

Figure 3.55 Correct display of a still image created in a 16:9 aspect ratio.

To correct an aspect ratio mismatch for a still image on a timeline:

1. Set the desired aspect ratio of a timeline in the timeline Properties palette (**Figure 3.54**).

   The Monitor window displays the selected aspect ratio.

2. Play the timeline and view it on the Monitor window (**Figure 3.55**).

continues on next page

Note if any still image clip is displayed incorrectly (**Figure 3.56**).

3. With the Properties palette open, click on a clip on the timeline.

   The Properties palette displays the properties of the selected clip (**Figure 3.57**).

4. Click on the pop-up menu for the Scale adjustment in the Properties palette and select from the following (**Figure 3.58**):

   ▲ *Do Nothing* maintains the original dimensions of the image and centers it in the Monitor window frame. If the image is larger than the frame, the frame crops it. If the image is smaller, it is surrounded by a black matte to fill the frame.

   ▲ *Scale And Crop Edges* proportionally scales the image up or down until it fills the frame. Any area that extends outside the frame is cropped.

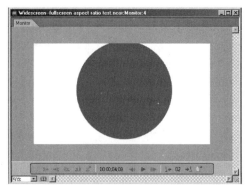

Figure 3.56 However, if an image created in a 4:3 aspect ratio is in the same timeline, it will need some adjustment to display properly.

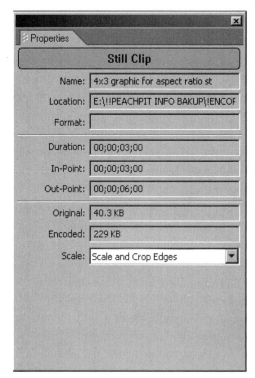

Figure 3.57 You can make changes to a clip in the clip's Properties palette.

Figure 3.58 Choose from three possible adjustments.

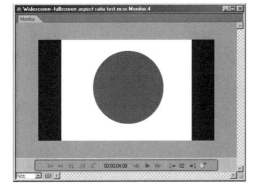

Figure 3.59 An example of what "Scale and Apply Matte" can do for a standard image in a widescreen world.

▲ *Scale And Apply Matte* proportionally scales the image up or down so that the entire image fits the frame. A black matte is applied as necessary to fill any blank area of the frame.

The clip is rescaled accordingly (**Figure 3.59**).

✔ Tips

■ The aspect ratio selections in the Properties palette are grayed out if there is a video clip on the timeline's video track.

■ You can select multiple clips on a timeline and apply a scaling adjustment to all of them.

■ When rescaling a still image, Encore DVD makes the adjustments to the clip on the timeline, leaving the original asset unchanged.

Working with Chapter Points

As I'll discuss in Chapter 5, a chapter point enables you to create a link to a timeline, allowing the viewer to click a button in a menu and play the timeline's content. Chapter points can be placed at various points in a timeline, allowing the viewer to jump to important scenes quickly. Here's what you need to know up front about them:

◆ Encore DVD automatically places a chapter point at the beginning of each timeline, which cannot be moved or deleted.

◆ The Add Chapter Point button in the Monitor window enables you to mark chapter points on the fly during playback.

◆ Chapter points cannot be added until there are video elements, audio elements, or still images on a track.

◆ Chapter points are associated with video and still clips on a timeline. If you move a still image clip, its chapter points will move with it. If you delete or trim a still or video clip on a track, you will also delete or trim away its chapter points.

◆ Chapter points are not tied to audio clips. Trimming, deleting, or moving audio clips will not change the position of any chapter points.

◆ Chapter points can only be placed at I-frames (a.k.a., GOP headers). Encore DVD automatically ensures that chapter points can only be placed on valid frames in the timeline. See the sidebar later in this chapter for more information.

◆ Encore DVD keeps chapter points in correct sequential order. If you add or delete a chapter point, or move one to a position between two existing chapter points, Encore DVD will renumber them all automatically.

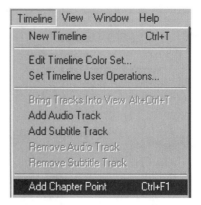

Figure 3.60 As always, there are several ways to get results in Encore DVD. You can add a chapter point through the Timelines menu...

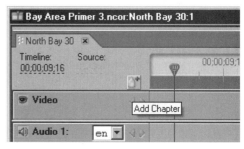

Figure 3.61 ...or you can add them in the Timeline window...

Figure 3.62 ...or you can add them on the fly in the Monitor window.

To add a chapter point:

1. Move the CTI in a timeline to the frame where you want to add a chapter point.

2. *Do one of the following:*

   ▲ Choose Timeline > Add Chapter Point (**Figure 3.60**).

   ▲ Click the Add Chapter Point button in the timeline (**Figure 3.61**).

   ▲ Click the Add Chapter Point button in the Monitor window (**Figure 3.62**).

A chapter point appears in the Timeline window and in the bottom pane of the Timelines tab (**Figure 3.63**).

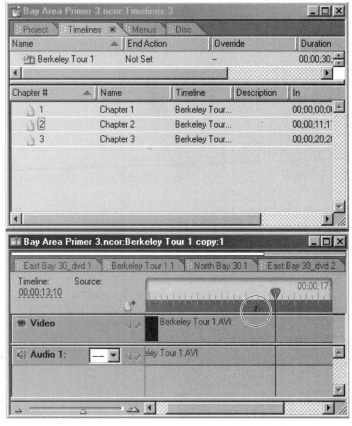

Figure 3.63 Once chapter points are added, they show up here.

To name a chapter point:

1. Select a chapter point by doing one of the following:

   ▲ Click it in the timeline in the Timeline window.

   The chapter point turns red (**Figure 3.64**.)

   ▲ Select the chapter point in the bottom pane of the Timelines tab in the Project window (**Figure 3.65**).

2. Choose Window > Properties if the palette is not already open (**Figure 3.66**).

3. Type the name of the chapter point in the Name box of the Properties palette (**Figure 3.67**).

4. If desired, type a description of the chapter point in the Description field.

✔ Tip

■ Naming chapter points makes a lot of sense. Creating a link between a button that says "Scene 5" is easier if the chapter point is also labeled "Scene 5."

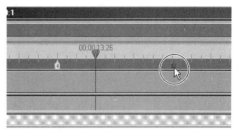

Figure 3.64 It's a bit hard to see here, but the chapter point has been selected and has turned red.

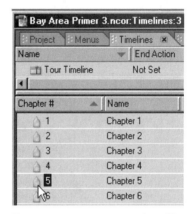

Figure 3.65 You can access and modify chapter points in the lower pane of the Timelines tab...

Figure 3.66 ...or you can open the Properties palette...

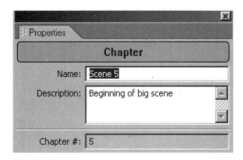

Figure 3.67 ...and type in a chapter point name there.

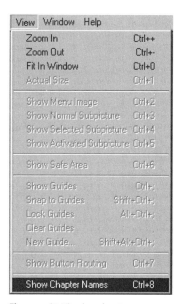

Figure 3.68 Viewing chapter names can be very helpful in organizing your chapter points. Here's one place to turn them on.

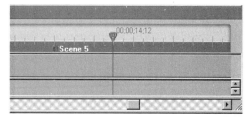

Figure 3.69 The chapter name appears close to the chapter point.

To show chapter point names:

◆ Choose View > Show Chapter Names (**Figure 3.68**).

Or

◆ Right-click on the Ruler in the Timeline window and select Show Chapter Names from the contextual menu.

Chapter names are displayed in the Timeline window (**Figure 3.69**).

✔ Tip

■ Chapter names can be toggled on and off by repeating these steps.

To move a chapter point:

1. Select a chapter point in the timeline.

2. Drag it to a new position on the timeline (**Figure 3.70**).

✔ Tips

■ For precise placement, the Monitor window will update as you move a chapter point.

■ You can also Shift-select or drag a marquee around multiple chapter points and move them as a group on the timeline.

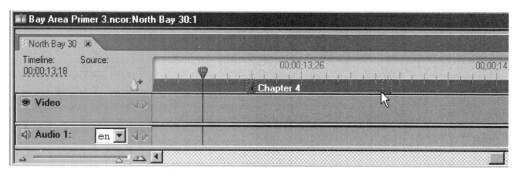

Figure 3.70 It's hard to see what's going on here, but the chapter point is being dragged to a new position.

To delete a chapter point:

◆ Right-click on a chapter point in the Timeline window and choose Delete Chapter Point from the contextual menu (**Figure 3.71**).

Or

◆ Click on a chapter point in the bottom pane of the Timelines tab and press the Delete key.

The chapter point is deleted.

✔ Tip

■ You can Shift-select or marquee-select multiple chapter points and delete them.

To navigate between chapter points:

Do one of the following:

◆ To jump to a chapter point, click the Ruler bar directly above that point.

◆ Click the Previous Chapter or Next Chapter button in the Monitor window (**Figure 3.72**).

◆ With the Chapter Points pane of the Timelines tab displayed, double-click on a chapter point to jump to it.

✔ Tip

■ If you want a different video frame to represent a chapter point in a button thumbnail, you can use the Set Poster Frame option. See Chapter 7 for more details.

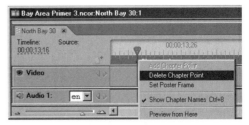

Figure 3.71 You can also dump chapter points you don't need anymore.

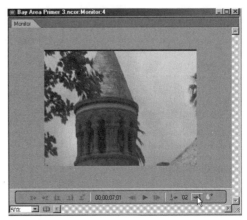

Figure 3.72 The Previous/Next chapter buttons in the Monitor window make navigation easier.

Chapter Points and Transcoding

You may have video assets in your project that are in AVI format. On the final DVD, your video assets will be encoded as MPEG-2. Here's how Encore DVD places chapter points on MPEG-2 and AVI material:

◆ **MPEG-2.** Chapter points must fall on I-frames, also known as reference frames or GOP headers. (More about this in Chapter 6.) If you have an MPEG-2 video track on the timeline, you'll notice the evenly spaced tick marks on the Ruler bar, indicating each GOP header. Any time you set a chapter point in MPEG-2 video, Encore DVD places it on the closest GOP header.

◆ **AVI.** Because AVI video contains all the frames of the original source, it is possible to move frame by frame in the timeline and to place chapter points on any frame (although, as the eventual destination is MPEG-2, Encore DVD will not let you place chapter points closer together than the MPEG-2 spec will allow). When the AVI footage is transcoded to MPEG-2, the chapter points remain exactly where you left them. Encore DVD just transcodes any frame with a chapter point associated with it as a GOP header.

Creating Slideshows

Although a timeline can only accommodate one track of moving video, you can edit together multiple still images on a video track. In terms of selecting and importing them, still images behave the same as any other asset, but once on the timeline, things change. Here are the basic facts about working with stills on a timeline:

◆ The duration of the still images is determined by the Timeline Preferences settings. You can set any length you wish as a default, and/or set a duration for each still image clip as you drag it to a timeline.

◆ When *adding* stills to a timeline from the Project window, Encore DVD does not permit gaps. The stills will all snap together.

◆ When *removing* stills from a timeline, Encore DVD does permit gaps. If you remove a still image, a "hole" is left behind, and the surrounding stills remain in place.

◆ You can move stills on the timeline and trim them to adjust their length.

◆ You can select multiple stills and/or audio tracks and move them on the timeline together.

◆ Each still is assigned a chapter point at its first frame as it is added to the timeline. As you move the stills around, the chapter point moves as well. If you change positions of stills on the timeline, Encore DVD automatically renumbers the chapter points to keep them in ascending order. If you've named the chapter point, the name remains unchanged.

To adjust the default length of still images:

1. Choose Edit > Preferences > Timelines (**Figure 3.73**).

   The Preferences dialog appears.

2. Type a new value in the Default still length box (**Figure 3.74**).

3. Click OK.

✔ Tips

■ Changing the default does not affect any existing stills on a timeline. It only affects the duration of stills added to the timeline after the default has been changed.

■ All subsequent new projects will retain the new default setting.

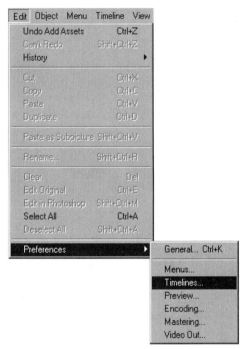

Figure 3.73 When adding subtitles, first you have to set the timeline preferences...

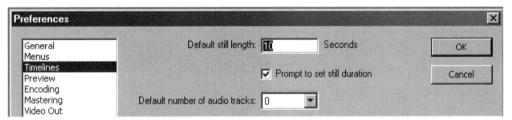

Figure 3.74 ...then you can establish a default length for subtitles created on the system.

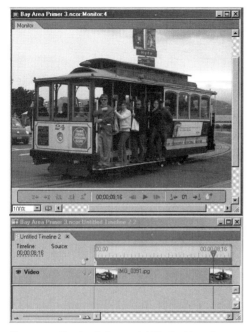

Figure 3.75 Here's what you might be looking at as you start building your slideshow.

To add a still image to a timeline video track:

1. Click on a timeline in the Timeline window to make it active.

2. Select a still image in the Project tab and drop it onto the unoccupied video track of the timeline.

   The image appears on the track, with its default duration. It is also displayed in the Monitor window (**Figure 3.75**).

✔ Tip

■ As part of the project's Timeline preferences, a dialog may appear each time a still image is added to the timeline which allows you to modify the duration of the still before adding it to the track (**Figure 3.76**).

Figure 3.76 You can confirm or change each subtitle clip's default duration whenever one is added to a timeline.

To add multiple still images to a timeline video track:

1. Click on a timeline in the Timeline window to make it active.

2. Select several still images in the Project tab and drop them onto the timeline's video track.

   The images are assembled on the video track (**Figure 3.77**).

   Note that there are chapter points automatically assigned to the beginning of each still.

✔ Tip

- Multiple stills will be assembled on the timeline according to the order they are displayed in the Project tab.

To add additional stills to a timeline:

1. Open a timeline with existing stills on it in the Timeline window.

2. Drag and drop a still from the Project tab onto the timeline.

   The new still is added to the *end* of the timeline (**Figure 3.78**).

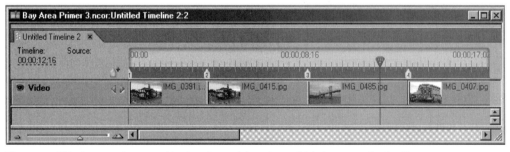

Figure 3.77 Slideshows can be created by dragging and dropping multiple images to the timeline.

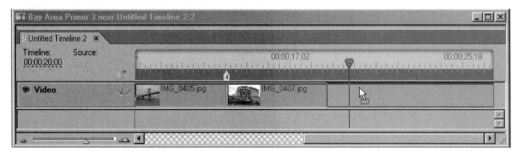

Figure 3.78 You can only add new stills to the end of an existing timeline.

To move stills in a timeline:

◆ Click to select a still and drag it to a new position on the timeline.

✔ Tips

■ When moving still images on the timeline, stills can be selected and moved individually or Shift-selected and moved in groups.

■ Stills can snap together (**Figure 3.79**) when you move them in a timeline, but they cannot overlap (**Figure 3.80**).

continues on next page

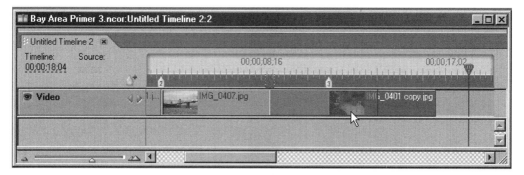

Figure 3.79 A bit subtle, but what's going on here is the snapping together of two video clips on the timeline.

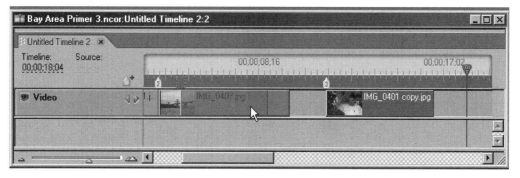

Figure 3.80 If you overlap two clips while dragging around in the timeline, even a little bit...

CREATING SLIDESHOWS

- If one still is dragged on top of another still, they will swap places on the timeline (**Figure 3.81**).

- Audio clips can be selected in addition to stills and can be moved with them (**Figure 3.82**).

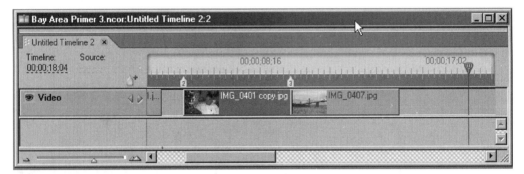

Figure 3.81 ...they will swap places.

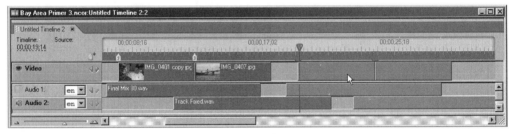

Figure 3.82 Multiple audio and still image clips can be ganged together and moved all over the timeline.

To remove stills from a timeline:

◆ Right-click on a still image and choose Clear from the contextual menu (**Figure 3.83**). The selected clip is deleted, and a gap is left behind (**Figure 3.84**).

✔ Tip

■ You can select multiple stills on a timeline and delete them. They need not be contiguous, and the remaining clips will stay in place.

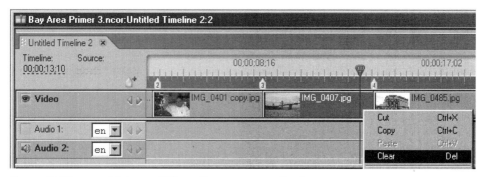

Figure 3.83 When you delete one still image from a group on a timeline...

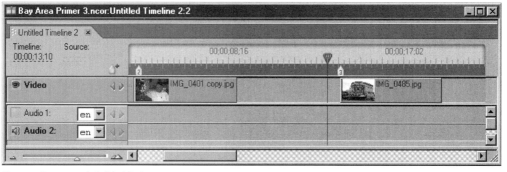

Figure 3.84 ...a gap is left behind.

To change the length of a still image:

1. Position your pointer over the edge of a still image on the timeline.

   The pointer turns into the Trim tool (**Figure 3.85**).

2. *Do one of the following:*

   ▲ Grab the edge with the Trim tool and shorten any clip (**Figure 3.86**).

   A gap will appear on the timeline as the clip's frames are trimmed away.

   ▲ Reposition clips to create gaps between them, and then use the Trim tool to extend or shorten a clip.

3. After trimming, manually drag clips back together to eliminate gaps.

✔ Tips

- You can trim to extend or shorten any still image clip on the track up to the edge of any surrounding stills (**Figure 3.87**). You cannot use the Trim tool to overlap clips.

- See the earlier sidebar on the Trim tool for other trim techniques.

Figure 3.85 Still images can be trimmed with the Trim tool.

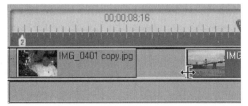

Figure 3.86 When you use the Trim tool to shorten a clip, a gap will be left behind...

Figure 3.87 ...and you can use the Trim tool to fill a gap, but you can't overlap clip edges while trimming.

WORKING WITH MENUS

Assuming that you've been working through each chapter in the order in which they appear, you've organized your disparate assets and created some timelines. Now you'll need to create some menus to link everything in your project together.

In menus, which are actually Photoshop files, you'll find some combination of four basic components:

- A *background,* which can be made of either still or moving images

- *Foreground objects,* such as text, logos, or other images

- *Buttons,* which are specialized objects you will use to link to timelines or other menus

- *Subpictures,* which are used to define the different states of a button (normal, selected, or activated)

These components are organized into layers and layer sets as you work with them in Encore DVD.

Although many Encore DVD users will design their menus in Photoshop, Encore DVD has a lot of menu-making capability built in. This chapter will focus on how you can use Encore DVD to create menus, starting with simple, static elements. For more advanced menu techniques, see Chapters 7 and 8.

Menu Basics

Chapter 2 discussed how to import menus. You can also create menus from scratch in Encore DVD, as I'll discuss here. The processes of creating, deleting, and modifying menus in Encore DVD are similar to those you use with when working with timelines. You'll use the Project and Menus tabs to access and manage your menus.

To create a menu in Encore DVD:

1. Select the Project tab or Menu tab of the Project window.

2. Choose Menu > New Menu (**Figure 4.1**), or click the Create a New Menu button at the bottom of the Project window (**Figure 4.2**).

 Encore DVD refers to the list of menus in the Library palette and opens the template currently set as the default (**Figure 4.3**).

Or

1. Select the Library palette.

2. Click the Menu Display toggle button on the Library palette (**Figure 4.4**).

 A list of menu templates appears. (You may want to deselect the other display toggle buttons in order to confine your view to menus.)

3. Choose a menu template from the list and click the New Menu button at the bottom of the palette (**Figure 4.5**).

 The selected template opens.

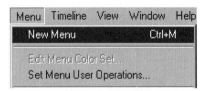

Figure 4.1 The classic approach to creating a new menu.

Figure 4.2 Another way to create a menu.

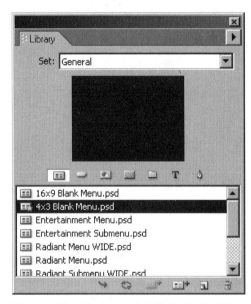

Figure 4.3 The default menu is indicated by the little star on the icon in the Library tab list.

Figure 4.4 Click the menu display toggle to show menus...

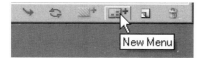

Figure 4.5 ...and then click the New Menu button to create one from your selection.

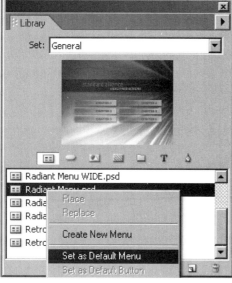

Figure 4.6 You can specify defaults for any of the items in the Library palette.

✔ Tips

- When using either of these methods, a new menu appears in both the Project and Menus tabs of the Project window, and the Menu Editor window automatically opens. To save effort in rearranging windows, you can enable the Menu Design workspace, or make and save one of your own. See Chapter 2 for more information on workspaces.

- The Library palette stores templates for menus, buttons, and backgrounds, and has a default selection in each of these categories. To change the default selection, right-click on the item you want to set as the default and choose Set as Default from the contextual menu that appears (**Figure 4.6**).

- Each menu template in the Library palette consists of at least a background layer—even the "blank" menus. This background layer can be covered over, but it cannot be deleted or modified. You'll see that its controls are grayed out when viewed in the Layers palette.

- Most of the menu templates included with Encore DVD were created with a standard 4:3 pixel aspect ratio. If you are working in a widescreen (16:9) project, you'll want to use menus created in the 16:9 aspect ratio. There's more about working with aspect ratios later in the chapter.

- If you create a menu in Photoshop and want to import it into Encore DVD, the process is basically the same as that for timelines outlined in Chapter 3. For more specifics on using Photoshop and Encore DVD, see Chapter 7.

To name a menu:

1. Select a menu in either the Project or Menus tab.

2. Choose Edit > Rename (**Figure 4.7**). The Rename Menu dialog appears.

3. Type a new name in the dialog (**Figure 4.8**).

Or

1. With the Properties palette open, select a menu in either the Project or Menus tab of the Project window.

2. Enter a new name for the menu in the Name box in the Properties palette (**Figure 4.9**). You can add a description here, too.

✔ Tip

■ If you right-click on a menu in the Project or Menus tab, you can rename it from the contextual menu.

Figure 4.7 The first step in the process of renaming a menu...

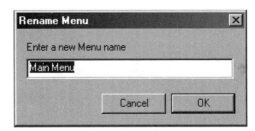

Figure 4.8 ...and here is the second step.

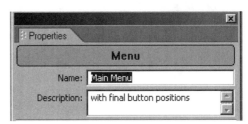

Figure 4.9 You can also change a menu's name in the Properties palette.

Figure 4.10 Opening a menu.

Figure 4.11 The menu, ready to go in the Menu Editor.

To display a menu:

◆ Double-click a menu's icon in either the Project or Menus tab.

Or

◆ Right-click a menu icon and choose Open (**Figure 4.10**).

The Menu Editor appears with the selected menu displayed (**Figure 4.11**). Clicking any menu's Close box (the *X*) removes it from the Menu Editor window.

MENU BASICS

To display multiple menus:

1. In the Project or Menus tab, select the menus you want to display (**Figure 4.12**).

2. Double-click a menu icon.

   All selected menus are displayed in the Menu Editor as tabs (**Figure 4.13**).

✔ Tips

- A menu can be rearranged in the Menu Editor window by selecting its tab and dragging it to a new position.

- Elements can be copied between menus in the Menu Editor.

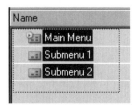

Figure 4.12 You can select a bunch of menus all at once.

Figure 4.13 Multiple menus appear as tabs in the Menu Editor.

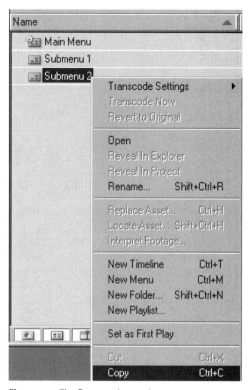

Figure 4.14 The first step in copying a menu.

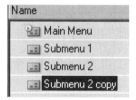

Figure 4.15 The copy is available in both the Menus and Project tabs.

To duplicate a menu:

1. Select a menu in the Project or Menus tab.

2. Right-click and choose Copy (**Figure 4.14**).

3. Right-click again in the Project tab and choose Paste.

   The copied menu appears in the Project and Menus tabs with the suffix "copy" added (**Figure 4.15**).

✔ Tip

■ Ctrl-click or Shift-click to copy multiple menus and proceed as above.

MENU BASICS

To delete a menu:

1. Right-click a menu in the Project or Menus tab and choose Clear from the contextual menu (**Figure 4.16**).

   A Delete Menu Confirmation dialog appears (**Figure 4.17**).

2. Click OK.

✔ Tip

- Creating, copying, and deleting are all undoable and redoable actions. Use the standard Windows commands and the Edit > History menu.

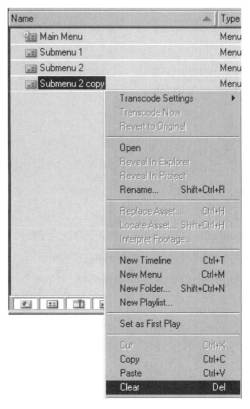

Figure 4.16 Deleting a menu from the project.

Figure 4.17 Encore DVD wants to make sure you're sure before deleting.

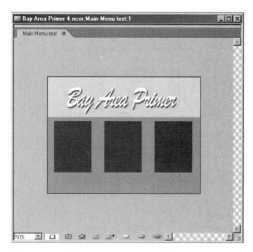

Figure 4.18 A typical menu, created in a 4:3 aspect ratio.

Figure 4.19 The aspect ratio for menus is deternined by these controls in the Properties palette.

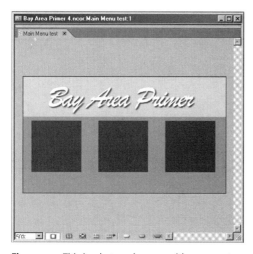

Figure 4.20 This is what can happen with an aspect ratio mismatch: a 4:3 menu stretched into a 16:9 widescreen aspect ratio.

To adjust the aspect ratio of a menu:

1. With the Properties palette open, open a menu in the Project or Menus tabs. The menu is displayed in the Menu Editor (**Figure 4.18**).

   The menu's aspect ratio is indicated at the bottom of the Properties palette (**Figure 4.19**).

2. Change the aspect ratio by clicking one of the buttons in the Aspect Ratio section of the Properties palette.

   The aspect ratio of the menu in the Menu Editor changes accordingly (**Figure 4.20**).

✔ Tips

- Encore DVD actually changes the pixel aspect ratio of the menu to fit the screen aspect ratio selected in the Properties palette.

- Keeping aspect ratios consistent in a project avoids jarring transitions between menus, timelines, and so on. Making an adjustment in the Properties palette does reformat a menu to a new aspect ratio, but there will be some compromises. The elements of a menu—the buttons, text, and the like—will appear somewhat "stretched" or "squeezed" when reformatted. For best results, create the menu in the aspect ratio you will be using in the project.

MENU BASICS

To view a menu on an external monitor:

1. Connect a DV device, such as a camera or a transcoder, to your computer via Firewire (for specifics, consult the user's guide for your particular device).

2. Choose Edit > Preferences > Video Out (**Figure 4.21**).

    The Preferences dialog appears.

3. Check the Show Menu Editor on DV Hardware option in the Preferences dialog (**Figure 4.22**).

4. Click Search to find available DV devices.

    Available devices appear in a list (**Figure 4.23**).

5. Select the device you want from the list and click OK.

    Encore DVD routes the output of the Menu Editor to the selected device.

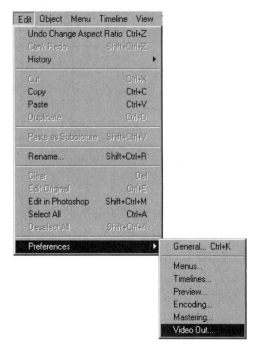

Figure 4.21 The setup for external viewing is in the project's Preferences menu.

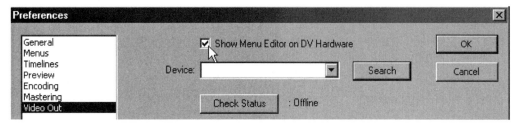

Figure 4.22 Checking this option gets it all started.

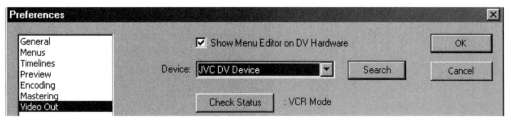

Figure 4.23 As soon as a DVD device is recognized, it appears in the list.

✔ Tips

- You may have to verify Encore DVD's connection to the DV device by clicking the Check Status button in the Video Out preferences window.

- Guides, button routing, and other overlays are not displayed on the external monitor.

- The DV device must be in VCR mode in order to receive the output of the Menu Editor.

- Viewing the Menu Editor output on a "real" video monitor is a very helpful feature that enables you to see how your menus will look to your audience. For best results, make sure your video monitor is set up properly.

- Not all DV devices are created equal. Anecdotal evidence suggests that the Video Out feature works well with a transcoder, such as the Canopus ADVC 100. Some DV cameras can only display the Menu Editor on their flip-out viewfinder monitor, which is not all that helpful in terms of determining what the menu will look like to the average viewer. Check for updates at www.adobe.com.

Working with the Library Palette

The Library palette plays a big role in menu building in Encore DVD. It comes standard with a number of useful templates, and is the place for you to store your own custom templates. It also helps manage the placement of elements in a menu, and has a lot of organizational tools to keep you well, *organized*.

When working in the Library palette, you'll be working with *Library sets,* groupings of items that you can customize to your needs, and using the various view toggle buttons on the Library palette to show or hide specific types of items in a particular set (**Figure 4.24**). Here's an overview of the different types of items you can find in a Library set (more detail on the more exotic items, such as buttons and layer sets, can be found later in the chapter).

◆ **Menus:** Photoshop files that may include several layers or two or more button layer sets.

◆ **Buttons:** Photoshop files that contain a layer set with layers that follow the layer-naming convention to indicate buttons, subpictures, thumbnails, and so on. (More on all this later in the chapter.)

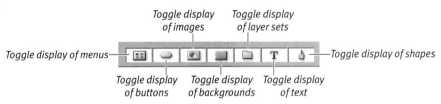

Figure 4.24 The Library palette view controls.

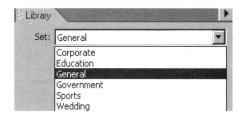

Figure 4.25 A list of default Library sets.

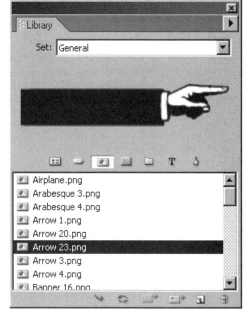

Figure 4.26 A preview image of the selected item is always displayed in the center of the Library palette.

◆ **Images:** Graphics or still images that you can use for menu backgrounds or for creating buttons.

◆ **Backgrounds:** A Photoshop file containing only a background layer.

◆ **Layer sets:** Photoshop files that contain no background layer and one layer set (without the naming convention that would classify it as a button).

◆ **Text:** Photoshop files containing one text layer and no background layers.

◆ **Shapes:** Photoshop files containing one vector layer and no background layers.

To display a Library set:

1. On the Library palette, click the pop-up menu arrow (**Figure 4.25**).
   The default Library sets appear.

2. Select a set from the list.
   The items available in the selected list are displayed in the Library palette (**Figure 4.26**).

To create a Library set:

1. Click the arrow for the flyout menu (**Figure 4.27**).

2. Choose New Set from the menu. The New Set dialog appears (**Figure 4.28**).

3. Name the set and click OK. The new set is added to the Library set list.

To delete a Library set:

1. Click the arrow for the fly-out menu (**Figure 4.29**).

2. Choose Delete Set. A warning dialog appears (**Figure 4.30**).

3. Click Yes to delete or No to exit the dialog.

To rename a Library set:

1. Click the arrow for the fly-out menu.

2. Choose Rename Set. The Rename Set dialog appears (**Figure 4.31**).

3. Type a new name and click OK.

✔ Tips

- The Library sets that are included with Encore DVD cannot be deleted or renamed.

- To display multiple types of items, you can Shift-click on multiple toggle display buttons.

Figure 4.27 Using the fly-out menu to access some options.

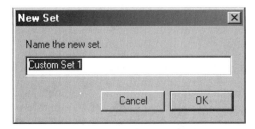

Figure 4.28 You can create a new set, and give it a new name.

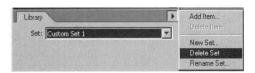

Figure 4.29 Back to the fly-out menu to delete a set.

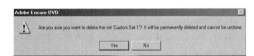

Figure 4.30 Again, Encore DVD wants to make sure before deleting.

Figure 4.31 You can rename a set that you've created, but not any of the default sets.

Figure 4.32 So, are you ready for several different ways to add your own items to the Library palette? Here's one...

Figure 4.33 ...and here's another...

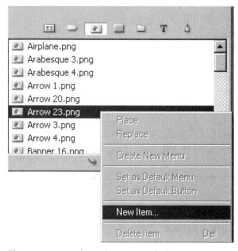

Figure 4.34 ...and another way to do it...

To add an item to the Library palette:

Do one of the following:

◆ Click the fly-out menu on the Library palette and choose Add Item (**Figure 4.32**).

◆ Click the Add Item button at the bottom of the Library palette (**Figure 4.33**).

◆ Right-click within the Library palette's item list and select New Item (**Figure 4.34**).

◆ Drag and drop a selected item from a folder on your computer into the Library palette's item list (**Figure 4.35**).

✔ Tip

■ Encore DVD will examine the new item and display it in the appropriate category. For instance, if you add a simple JPEG image into the Library palette, Encore DVD will store it as an image file, no matter what item type was displayed in the Library palette's list when you added the item. See the information about the different item categories earlier in this chapter.

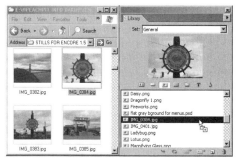

Figure 4.35 ...and one more: you can drag your items right into the Library palette.

WORKING WITH THE LIBRARY PALETTE

101

To delete an item from the Library palette:

Do one of the following:

◆ Select an item from the list, click the fly-out menu on the Library palette, and choose Delete Item (**Figure 4.36**).

◆ Select an item from the list and click the Delete Item button (the button with the trash can graphic) at the bottom of the Library palette (**Figure 4.37**).

◆ Right-click on an item in the list and select Delete Item (**Figure 4.38**).

◆ A warning dialog appears (**Figure 4.39**). Click OK in the Delete Item dialog.

✔ Tip

■ The items that are included as standard templates with Encore DVD cannot be deleted.

Figure 4.36 Here's a quick tour of the ways you can get rid of items in the Library that you don't want. You can use this method...

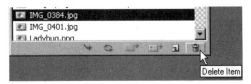

Figure 4.37 ...you can use the trash can...

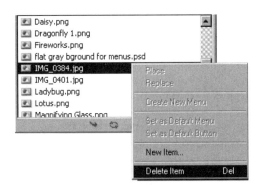

Figure 4.38 ...or you can right-click and get rid of the item here.

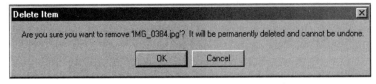

Figure 4.39 As usual, you are asked if you are sure about this.

Drag and drop placement from the Library palette into a menu:

◆ Select an item from the list, then drag and drop it onto a menu in the Menu Editor (**Figure 4.40**).

✔ Tips

■ You can also click on the preview image displayed in the Library palette and drop that into the Menu Editor.

■ The items will be placed where you drop them in the Menu Editor window. In the case of a Background item, however, Encore DVD automatically replaces any existing background in a menu with your selection, and centers it in the menu.

■ A good idea, no matter what method you use to assemble your elements into a menu, is to make use of the Lock function in the Layers palette. Your menu will consist of several layers, and as soon as you have a layer in the position you like you can apply a lock to prevent accidentally deleting it or bumping it out of place. Locking layers is discussed later in the chapter.

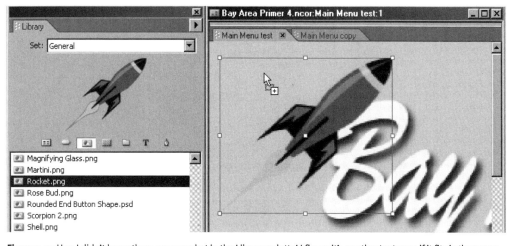

Figure 4.40 Hey, I didn't know there was a rocket in the Library palette! I figure it's worth a try to see if it fits in the menu.

Using the Place function in the Library palette:

◆ Select an item in the Library palette list and click the Place button (**Figure 4.41**).

Or

◆ With the Menu Editor selected, right-click on an item in the Library palette and select Place (**Figure 4.42**).

The item is added to the menu in the Menu Editor, according to item type:

▲ Buttons are aligned on the left edge of the Title Safe Guide (**Figure 4.43**).

▲ Menus, images, layer sets, text, and shapes are centered in the menu.

▲ A background item replaces the menu's current background.

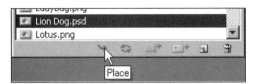

Figure 4.41 The Place function makes for precise placement. It's available here...

Figure 4.42 ...and can be found here as well.

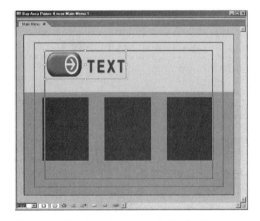

Figure 4.43 The Place function puts the first button in the upper left of the Safe Area grid.

Figure 4.44 If you keep hitting the Place button, it will continue adding buttons as neatly as possible.

✔ Tips

■ If you use the Place function multiple times, the selected items will be arranged according to item type. Buttons will line up in columns and rows, even if they are different shapes and sizes (**Figure 4.44**). Menus, images, layer sets, text, and shapes "pile up" in the center of the Menu Editor when the Place function is used repeatedly. (You can use the Layers palette to help sort them out, if you want. See the section, "Building a Menu with Objects and Layers" in the chapter.)

■ Double-clicking on an item in the Library palette will also place it in the Menu Editor.

Using the Replace function in the Library palette:

1. Select an object in the Menu Editor.

2. Select an item in the Library palette.

3. *Do one of the following:*

   ▲ Click the Replace button at the bottom of the Library palette (**Figure 4.45**).

   ▲ Right-click on an item in the Library palette and select Replace (**Figure 4.46**).

   The menu object is replaced with the item selected in the Library palette.

✔ Tips

■ Replace is not available for the Background item category. You can use either the Set Background button or the Place function to replace a background.

■ The replacement item is resized to fit the dimensions of the original object in the menu.

■ You can use the Replace function to swap items of different categories. Buttons, images, layer sets, text, and shapes can all be interchanged using the Replace function.

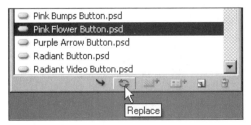

Figure 4.45 Replace allows for precision in replacing elements in a menu, and has a button at the bottom of the Library palette...

Figure 4.46 ...and of course it can be accessed by right-clicking in the Library palette, as well.

Figure 4.47 A quick look at the Layers palette, with a layer set opened up.

Building a Menu with Objects and Layers

As you've seen in the previous section, you can draw on the templates in the Library palette to create menus, and then alter the menus as needed. In addition to the process outlined in the previous section—adding items to the Library palette, then using them in a menu—you have many other options. You can select images, buttons, menus, and the like from elsewhere in your project or from any other folder on your computer or network and use them in a menu.

As you continue to design and customize your menus, you'll be using a trio of complementary tools: the Menu Editor, the Layers palette, and the Toolbox.

You'll rely on the Menu Editor to size and position the various onscreen objects that make up your menu. You'll use the Layers palette to determine how those objects stack up. The Layers palette also displays *layer sets*—layers within layers, organized in folders (**Figure 4.47**).

I use the terms *objects* and *layers* interchangeably here. They both refer to the images, buttons, and text that make up menus. When you are working in the Menu Editor, you see and manipulate objects on the screen. Those same objects appear as layers in the Layers palette. "Just like in Photoshop," you're probably thinking, and you're right. You can use the Menu Editor and the Layers palette interactively as you put your menus together, and you have tools similar to those in Photoshop to enable you to position, resize, and reorder the elements in your menu.

In the small, floating Toolbox you choose from two types of selection tools (**Figure 4.48**):

◆ The *Selection tool* (the black arrow) is the most commonly used tool in the palette. You use it to select entire layers and layer sets, and also to reposition and resize objects with the objects' selection handles.

◆ You use the *Direct Select tool* (the white arrow) to select and modify individual elements *within* layer sets. It would be used, for instance, to "break apart" the different elements in a button layer set so you can modify certain elements independent of the others.

Except in cases where you need to move individual elements in a layer set, it's best to use the Selection tool. There are times when menu choices will be unavailable to you if the Direct Select tool is active.

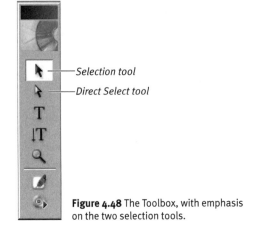

Selection tool

Direct Select tool

Figure 4.48 The Toolbox, with emphasis on the two selection tools.

✔ Tips

■ With this method, the item will be added as a layer on top of any existing background in the menu. To replace an existing background layer, see the information on using the Library palette and the Place function earlier in this chapter.

■ As you might expect, you can also select and drag multiple items into the Menu Editor with this method.

■ You can also drag and drop timelines and menus into the Menu Editor. These two types of items automatically become buttons in the menu and are assigned a default button shape. More information about this can be found in Chapter 5.

To add an object (or layer) to a menu:

1. Create or open a menu following the steps described earlier in the chapter.

2. Select an image file from the Project tab and drag it onto the Menu Editor (**Figure 4.49**).

   Or

◆ Navigate to a folder and select a one-layer image file or a Photoshop file with one or more layers. Drag and drop it onto the Menu Editor window.

   The selected item is now added to the menu, on top of any existing backgrounds or layers.

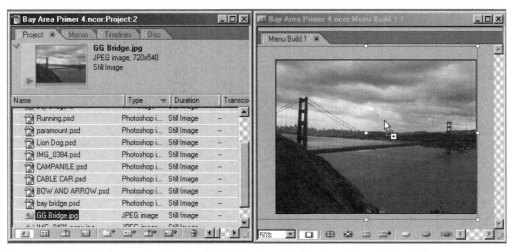

Figure 4.49 It's a bit hard to see, but this shot of the Golden Gate is being dropped into the Menu Editor.

To delete an object (or layer) from a menu:

1. Choose either the Selection tool or the Direct Select tool from the Tools palette. (See the earlier description of each to decide which tool to use.)

2. Use your chosen tool to select an object (or objects) in the Menu Editor.

3. Right-click and choose Clear (**Figure 4.50**).

Or

1. Select a layer (or layers) in the Layers tab (**Figure 4.51**).

2. Choose Edit > Clear to delete the selected layer(s).

Whether you use the Menu Editor or the Layers palette to delete objects and layers, the result is the same: Any items that were below the deleted item move up in the layer hierarchy, toward the foreground.

Figure 4.50 If the shot doesn't work, it's easy to get rid of it.

Figure 4.51 You can also get at an element in a menu in the Layers palette and then delete it.

Figure 4.52 Selection handles appear around selected objects in the Menu Editor.

Figure 4.53 Resizing and repositioning is a breeze in Encore DVD.

Figure 4.54 You can get very close to your material with the Zoom tool.

To move and resize an object:

1. In the Menu Editor, select the item to be modified.

   Selection handles appear around the object (**Figure 4.52**).

2. To use the selection handles, *do one or more of the following:*

   ▲ Click within the edges of the object and reposition it freely within the Menu Editor.

   ▲ Select and drag a handle to resize the object (**Figure 4.53**).

   ▲ Shift-drag a handle to proportionally resize the object.

   ▲ Alt-drag a handle to resize from the object's center point. (The center point maintains its position on the page.)

   ▲ Shift-Alt-drag to resize proportionally from the object's center point. (The center point maintains its position on the page.)

✔ Tips

- Use the zoom capabilities within the Menu Editor or the Zoom tool in the Tools palette to help as you make modifications (**Figure 4.54**).

- You can select multiple objects and move or resize them as a group in the Menu Editor.

- If the Direct Select tool is active, you may accidentally modify individual parts of a layer rather than the entire layer. Unless you specifically need to adjust individual items inside a layer set, use the Selection tool.

To align objects:

1. Choose Object > Align (**Figure 4.55**) and Select (or deselect) Relative to Safe Areas.

   With Relative to Safe Areas selected, the objects will be aligned relative to the Safe Area guides in the Menu Editor. With it deselected, the objects will be aligned relative to each other.

2. Using the Selection tool, Shift-select multiple objects in the Menu Editor (**Figure 4.56**).

3. Choose Object > Align again.

Figure 4.55 The Object menu enables you to rearrange the items in your menu.

Figure 4.56 Here are three objects in rather haphazard positions in the Menu Editor.

Figure 4.57 Some of the many alignment choices.

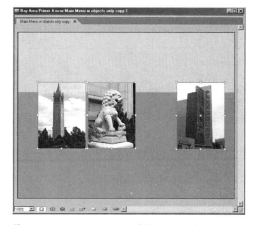

Figure 4.58 Step one accomplished. Now they need to be redistributed onscreen.

4. Select one of the options in the Align submenu (**Figure 4.57**).

▲ **Left** aligns the left sides of the selected objects to either the left side of the Title Safe area or the leftmost object.

▲ **Center** aligns the center of the selected objects to the center of the Title Safe area or to the center of a bounding box containing the selected objects.

▲ **Right** aligns the right side of the selected objects to either the right side of the Title Safe area or the rightmost object.

▲ **Top** aligns the top of the selected objects to either the top of the Title Safe area or the topmost object.

▲ **Middle** aligns the middle of the selected objects to either the center of the Title Safe area or the center of a bounding box that encompasses all the objects.

▲ **Bottom** aligns the bottom of the selected objects to either the bottom of the Title Safe area or the lowest object.

The objects align themselves along horizontal and vertical axes according to the option you choose in reference to the middle of the screen. In this example, the elements are aligned horizontally by their middle points (**Figure 4.58**).

BUILDING A MENU WITH OBJECTS AND LAYERS

To distribute objects evenly:

1. Using the Selection tool, Shift-select multiple objects or buttons in the Menu Editor.

2. Choose Object > Distribute and select one of the options from the submenu (**Figure 4.59**).

   The objects are evenly spaced onscreen, either vertically or horizontally, and in accordance with the Relative to Safe Areas option. **Figure 4.60** shows an example of horizontal distribution after alignment.

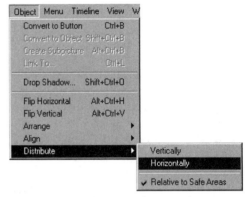

Figure 4.59 Redistributing can happen either up/down or side to side.

Figure 4.60 Now all the shots are evenly placed.

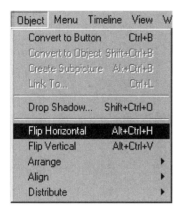

Figure 4.61 You can choose your flip options in the Object menu.

Figure 4.62 Here's a horizontal flip....

Figure 4.63 ...followed by a vertical flip.

To change an object's orientation:

1. Select one or more objects in the Menu Editor.

2. From the Object menu, choose a flip option (**Figure 4.61**).

   ▲ Choose Object > Flip Horizontal to flip an object 180 degrees horizontally (**Figure 4.62**).

   ▲ Choose Object > Flip Vertical to flip an object 180 degrees vertically (**Figure 4.63**).

✔ Tips

- Multiple objects must be on the same layer in the menu.

- Any type of object on a layer can be flipped. The background layer cannot be flipped.

To create alignment guides in the Menu Editor:

1. *Do one of the following:*

   ▲ Choose View > Show Guides (**Figure 4.64**).

   ▲ Click the Show Guides button at the bottom of the Menu Editor window (**Figure 4.65**).

   Any existing guides will be displayed in the Menu Editor.

Figure 4.64 There are two ways of showing guides in a menu. This is one...

Figure 4.65 ...and this is the other, located at the bottom of the Menu Editor.

Figure 4.66 One way of creating a new guide, via a menu...

Figure 4.67 ...and a second method, creating a guide from a button.

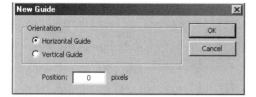

Figure 4.68 You specify a starting position for either vertical or horizontal guides in this dialog.

Figure 4.69 The guides are a bit hard to see here, but they're very handy for lining up elements in your menu.

2. *Do one of the following:*

▲ Choose View > New Guide (**Figure 4.66**).

▲ Click the New Guide button at the bottom of the Menu Editor window (**Figure 4.67**).

The New Guide dialog appears (**Figure 4.68**).

3. Select Horizontal or Vertical orientation, enter a position, and click OK.

A green line appears and is set at the onscreen pixel position specified.

4. Repeat these steps as necessary. You can have multiple guides in a menu (**Figure 4.69**).

BUILDING A MENU WITH OBJECTS AND LAYERS

To move a guide:

1. With the Menu Editor active, click either of the selection tools in the Toolbox (**Figure 4.70**).

2. Select a guide in the Menu Editor. The pointer will turn into a double-headed arrow (**Figure 4.71**).

3. Drag the guide to a new position and release.

To enable the Snap to Guide function:

◆ Choose View > Snap to Guides (**Figure 4.72**).

With Snap to Guides enabled, the edges and center points of selected objects (and the baseline of text objects) will snap to the guides in the menu. With it disabled, objects can be positioned freely.

Figure 4.70 The Toolbox selection tools, in close-up.

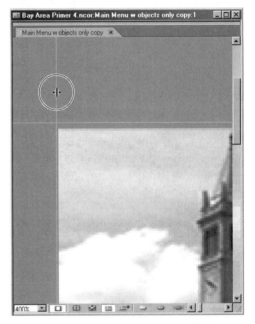

Figure 4.71 Again, it's a bit hard to see in this picture, but this guide is being moved by the double-headed arrow.

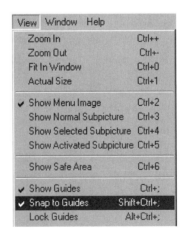

Figure 4.72 Turning on the Snap to Guides function.

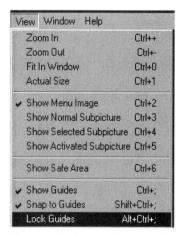

Figure 4.73 Lock Guides is very handy for preventing you from bumping your guides out of position.

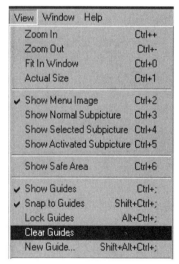

Figure 4.74 When you're done with your guides, this will get rid of them.

To lock menu guides:

◆ Choose View > Lock Guides (**Figure 4.73**).

With Lock Guides enabled, current guides cannot be moved or deleted. Choose View > Lock Guides again to unlock the guides.

To remove menu guides:

◆ *Do one of the following:*

▲ To remove a single guide, select it and drag it completely outside the Menu Editor window.

▲ To remove all guides, choose View > Clear Guides (**Figure 4.74**).

✔ Tips

■ Guides are visible only in the Menu Editor window. You do not see them when previewing or in the final DVD.

■ The guides you create are saved in the menu. They travel with the menu if you use the Edit in Photoshop feature, and any changes you make in either program are saved with the menu.

■ When placing guides, the pixel location you type in is relative to the Menu Editor screen, with the zero point being the top-left corner.

■ The pixel locations you specify when creating guides are relative to the menu, and will be calculated differently for different pixel aspect ratios. If you create guides in a square-pixel menu, their positions will not line up with guides created in a non-square pixel menu.

BUILDING A MENU WITH OBJECTS AND LAYERS

119

To arrange the layer order of objects:

1. *Do one of the following:*

   ▲ Using the Selection tool, select one or more objects in the Menu Editor.

   ▲ Select a layer in the Layers tab (**Figure 4.75**).

2. Choose Object > Arrange and select one of the options in the submenu (**Figure 4.76**).

   The selected object moves toward the foreground or background, according to the option you choose. **Figures 4.77** and **4.78** illustrate moving an object backward.

✔ Tip

■ You can also cut/copy/paste to rearrange layers in the Layers palette.

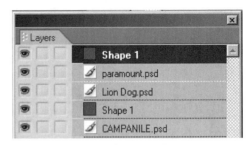

Figure 4.75 This layer needs to be lower in the list.

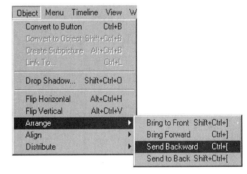

Figure 4.76 You can send a layer in several different directions from the Object menu.

Figure 4.77 This is the "before" example. The shape is obscuring the picture on the right.

Figure 4.78 This is the "after" example. The shape has been moved backward one layer, behind the picture.

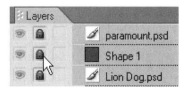

Figure 4.79 Locking a layer prevents deleting or changing it.

Figure 4.80 This is an example of locking layers inside a layer set.

To lock or unlock a layer:

1. In the Layers tab, click the Lock/Unlock column for any layer (**Figure 4.79**).

   A lock icon appears. The layer is now locked and cannot be altered or deleted.

2. To unlock a layer, click on the lock icon.

✔ Tips

- Each layer must be locked or unlocked individually.

- With layer sets, you can lock either the entire folder or the individual layer(s) inside the set (**Figure 4.80**).

To hide or show a layer:

1. In the Layers tab, click on the "eye" icon in the Hide/Show column for any layer.

   The eye icon disappears, and the layer is hidden (**Figure 4.81**).

2. To toggle a layer back to its show state, click in its Hide/Show column again.

   The eye icon is displayed, and the layer is shown (**Figure 4.82**).

Figure 4.81 Another "before-and-after" example. This is with the title layer hidden...

Figure 4.82 ...and this is the same menu, with the title layer returned to its "show" state.

121

To rename a layer:

1. *Do one of the following:*

   ▲ Right-click on a layer (a.k.a. an object) in the Menu Editor and choose Rename from the contextual menu (**Figure 4.83**).

   ▲ Select a layer in the Layers palette and choose Edit > Rename.

   ▲ Double-click on a layer in the Layers palette.

   The Rename Layer dialog appears (**Figure 4.84**).

2. Type in a new name and click OK.

   The new name appears in the Layers palette.

✔ Tip

■ Renaming does not affect any prefixes on a layer (prefixes are important to determine button status and subpicture settings).

To add a drop shadow to an object:

1. Using the Selection tool, select one or more objects in the Menu Editor.

2. Choose Object > Drop Shadow (**Figure 4.85**).

   The Drop Shadow dialog appears.

Figure 4.83 Renaming a layer from the Menu Editor.

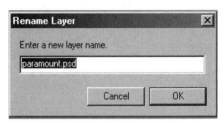

Figure 4.84 The Rename Layer dialog.

Figure 4.85 Selecting the Drop Shadow option.

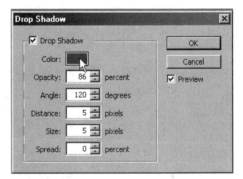

Figure 4.86 Step one in choosing a color for the drop shadow.

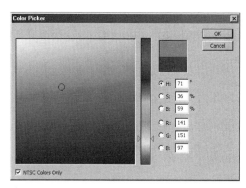

Figure 4.87 Creating a drop shadow color in the Color Picker. Note the NTSC Colors Only check box.

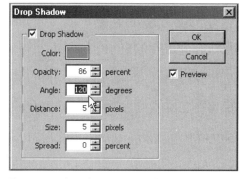

Figure 4.88 The other controls in the Drop Shadow dialog.

Figure 4.89 Here's a close-up of the final result.

3. To pick a color for the drop shadow, click the Color swatch (**Figure 4.86**).

The Color Picker appears (**Figure 4.87**).

4. Use the controls to modify the color and click OK to accept the changes.

5. Use the other controls in the Drop Shadow dialog to modify parameters of the drop shadow (**Figure 4.88**).

The drop shadow is applied to the object (**Figure 4.89**).

✔ Tips

- Drop shadows can be applied to any object, including text and layer sets.

- You can also apply a drop shadow (and many other edge and surface treatments) with the Styles palette. However, treatments applied via the Styles palette cannot be modified within Encore DVD. Their parameters are only adjustable in Photoshop.

BUILDING A MENU WITH OBJECTS AND LAYERS

To change the color of a shape object:

1. In the Layers palette, locate the layer that has the shape you want to modify (**Figure 4.90**).

2. Double-click on the color chip in the layer. The Color Picker appears.

3. Select a new color in the Color Picker and click OK (**Figure 4.91**).

   The shape color will be updated with your color selection (**Figure 4.92**).

Figure 4.90 The rectangle shape on the left (behind the tower) is selected...

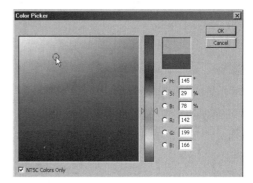

Figure 4.91 ...and a new color for the shape is chosen in the Color Picker.

Figure 4.92 Here's the result of the color change.

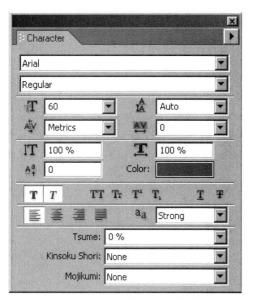

Figure 4.93 The Character palette, showing just a few of its attributes.

Working with Text

As you would expect from the folks who brought you Illustrator, the Character palette is quite a sophisticated typography tool. Without going over every feature here, I'll give you the basics of entering and modifying text in a menu. For an overview of the Character palette controls, see Chapter 1.

To enter text horizontally:

1. Use the Character palette to set the desired text attributes (**Figure 4.93**).

2. Choose the Text tool from the Toolbox (**Figure 4.94**).

continues on next page

Figure 4.94 To enter horizontal text, choose the Text tool.

3. *Do one of the following:*

- ▲ Click in a menu (the insertion point appears) and begin typing freely (**Figure 4.95**).

- ▲ Click and drag in a menu to define a bounding box for type (**Figure 4.96**).

  When the bounding box is set, text will be constrained by the box and will wrap around within the box (**Figure 4.97**).

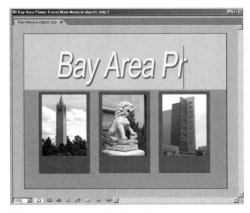

Figure 4.95 An example of *free* text entry.

Figure 4.96 Drawing a bounding box for text.

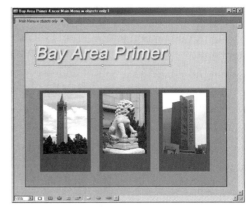

Figure 4.97 The text is now constrained by the bounding box.

Figure 4.98 Choosing the Vertical Text tool...

Figure 4.99 ...and getting sideways with it.

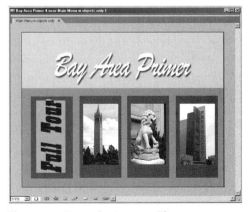

Figure 4.100 Drag-selecting to modify text.

To enter text vertically:

1. Choose the Vertical Text tool from the Toolbox (**Figure 4.98**).

2. Choose from the options described in the previous section to enter text freely or within a bounding box (**Figure 4.99**).

To select and modify text elements:

1. In the Menu Editor, open the menu containing the text you want to modify.

2. With the appropriate text tool selected, drag to select the text you want to modify (**Figure 4.100**).

3. Make your changes.

   You can retype the text, cut it, copy it, or paste it. You can also change any of its attributes, using the controls in the Character palette.

✔ Tip

■ You can select and modify text as a block using several methods. You can use the Selection tool to select one or more text elements in the Menu Editor, or select one or more text layers in the Layers palette, and then use the selection handles to resize or reposition the block. Or you can choose the Menu Editor's Object menu and select any of the available options to arrange, align, or distribute the text block. Or you can adjust any of the available attributes in the Character palette.

Working with the Styles Palette

The Styles palette is very similar to the Library palette in terms of how it is designed and organized. The main difference is that, although the purpose of the Library palette is to store, organize, and apply various items that can be used to *make* a menu, the Styles palette comes equipped with prebuilt drop shadows, bevels, gradients, text effects, and so on that can be applied to objects/layers in a menu. Like the Library palette, the Styles palette organizes the various styles in sets and allows you to add your own custom styles to the styles that come standard on Encore DVD.

There are three different categories of these predefined effects in the Styles palette: *Image, Text,* and *Shape.* Any of these types can be applied to a layer or object in a menu. (They behave somewhat differently when working with layer sets. More on that later in the chapter.)

In fact, because the Styles palette has the same structure as the Library palette, I'll introduce you to the basics of the Styles palette and then jump into using styles with menus. If you have any operational questions about displaying/creating/deleting or adding items to style sets, check back to the Library palette section earlier in the chapter.

To display a style set:

1. On the Styles palette, click the pop-up menu arrow (**Figure 4.101**).

   The default style sets are displayed.

2. Select a set from the list.

   The items available in the selected list are displayed in the Styles palette.

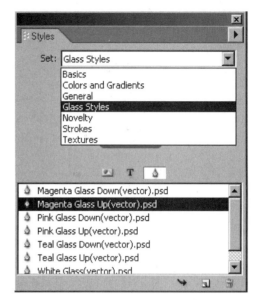

Figure 4.101 Here's just one example of all the style treatments available.

Figure 4.102 And you can use the Apply Style button at the bottom of the Styles menus as well.

To apply a style to a menu:

◆ *Do one of the following:*

▲ Click on the preview image in the Styles palette and drop it onto an object in the Menu Editor.

▲ Double-click on an item in the Style palette list.

▲ Click the Apply Style button at the bottom of the Styles palette (**Figure 4.102**).

▲ Select the preview image or an item from the Styles palette list and drag and drop it onto an object in the Menu Editor (**Figure 4.103**).

The style is applied to the selected element in your menu.

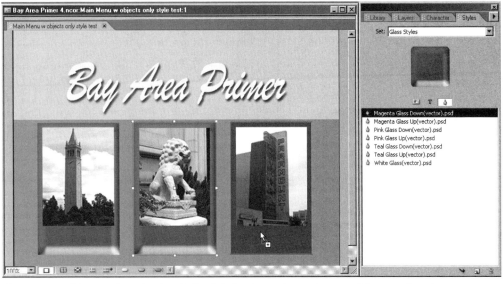

Figure 4.103 In this example, a glass bevel effect is being dropped onto elements of the menu from the Styles palette.

✔ Tips

- Styles with a plus sign (+) in their name in the Styles palette can be combined with other styles from the palette (**Figure 4.104**). Other styles cannot be combined—each one replaces the one that preceded it when applied to an object in a menu.

- The style you apply to a menu object is attached to that object. If the object moves or is changed, the style also moves or is changed.

- A very useful feature in the Styles palette is found in the Images section of the General Styles set. It's the ability to clear any styles that you've applied to a menu item (**Figure 4.105**). Because many of the styles are additive, it's very nice to remove unwanted style effects easily.

- When applying a style from the Image category to a layer set, the style is applied to all layers in a set. The Text category styles only affect text objects/layers, and the Shape category only affects shape layers. Style palette selections do not affect button highlights (subpictures).

Figure 4.104 Some image effects are additive—you can just keep "piling them on" to a selected item.

Figure 4.105 When you get a style or two applied that you want to get rid of, you can delete them with the Clear function.

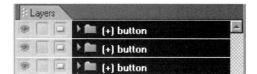

Figure 4.106 (+) is the little prefix that does so much.

Working with Buttons and Layer Sets

So far, you've been working with discrete objects, arranging their order and position in a menu, and applying styles to them. Layer sets, however, are *groups* of objects on a layer, which can be moved and modified *as a group*. They are stored in a folder that is accessible through the Layers palette. If necessary, the layer set can be opened up and the individual components adjusted or replaced. Again, if you're a Photoshop user, this is familiar territory.

Buttons are a special type of layer set. They are the most important part of your menu, because you'll use them to link together the other parts of your DVD's content.

The prefix (+) denotes a button layer set (**Figure 4.106**). This prefix enables Encore DVD to assign the set button-specific attributes, such as links and button-highlight colors (a.k.a. subpictures), which are part of the layer set.

As you'll see in this section, you can convert objects (layers) into buttons and vice versa. Using the Direct Select tool and the Layers palette, you can also get inside button and layer sets to make modifications.

✔ Tip

■ I'll show you the basics of what you can do in Encore DVD, but in order to have the most control over all your layers it's best to use Encore DVD's Edit in Photoshop feature to make any extensive adjustments. Photoshop's Layers palette is much more flexible. More on that in Chapter 7.

To modify objects in a layer set using the Direct Select tool:

1. Choose the Direct Select tool in the Tools palette.

2. Select an object in the Menu Editor that is part of a layer set.

   The object's selection handles are displayed (**Figure 4.107**).

3. The selection handles can be used to reposition and resize the object as described earlier in the chapter (**Figure 4.108**).

   Although the layer is modified, the other elements in its layer set are unaffected.

✔ Tip

- To change text within a layer set, use the Toolbox's Direct Select tool to select the text and then choose one of the text tools from the Toolbox to retype the text.

Figure 4.107 By using the Direct Select tool, the button and the text have been separated, so that...

Figure 4.108 ...the button can be resized without affecting the text.

Figure 4.109 An exploded view of a layer set.

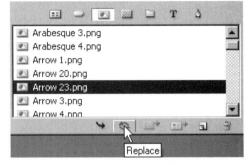

Figure 4.110 Selecting an item in the Library palette and using the Replace function.

Figure 4.111 The button image has been replaced by this hand graphic.

To replace a layer within a layer set:

1. Open a layer set to display its contents (**Figure 4.109**).

2. Select a layer in the layer set.

3. Select an item from the Library tab and click the Replace button (**Figure 4.110**). The layer is replaced with the new item (**Figure 4.111**).

✔ Tips

- While it is possible to replace a layer by copying and pasting an image asset from the Project tab, using the Library palette's Replace function makes the process much easier. (You can add an image to the Library tab via its Add Item function.)

- Layers within layer sets can be moved elsewhere in the Layers tab by using standard cut/copy and paste methods.

- To rearrange the order of layers in a layer set, choose Object > Arrange and select one of the options in the submenu. The selected object moves toward the foreground or background, according to the option you choose.

To add a button from a template to a menu:

1. With a menu active in the Menu Editor, select the Library tab.

2. Select a button from the list and drag and drop it into the Menu Editor (**Figure 4.112**).

   By default, the button is displayed in the Menu Editor with selection handles (**Figure 4.113**).

3. Select a handle to reposition or resize the button as outlined in "To move and resize an object," earlier.

Figure 4.112 Dragging and dropping a button template into the Menu Editor.

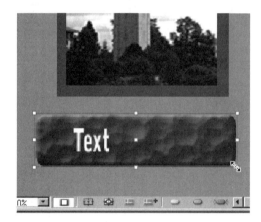

Figure 4.113 The button can then be repositioned and resized.

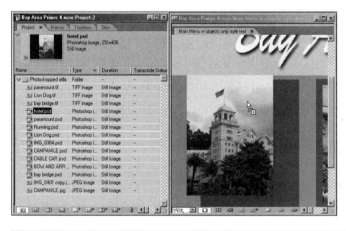

Figure 4.114 Assets can also be dragged out of the Project tab.

Figure 4.115 An object can be converted into a button with this menu selection.

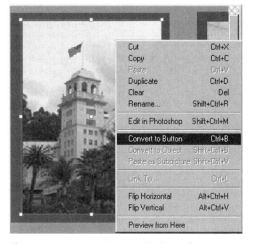

Figure 4.116 A conversion can also be performed with a right-click on the object itself.

Figure 4.117 The item is now a button layer set.

To create a button from an image file:

1. With a menu active in the Menu Editor, *do one of the following:*

   ▲ Select an image file asset from the Project tab and drag and drop it onto the Menu Editor window (**Figure 4.114**).

   ▲ Navigate to a folder and select an image file and drag and drop it onto the Menu Editor window.

   ▲ Select an image from the Library tab and drag and drop it onto the Menu Editor window.

2. Select the image in the Menu Editor and choose Object > Convert to Button (**Figure 4.115**).

   Or

   ◆ Right-click on the image in the Menu Editor and choose Convert to Button from the contextual menu (**Figure 4.116**).

   The image has now been converted to a button layer set, with a (+) prefix denoting that it is a button. These attributes can be seen in the Layers palette (**Figure 4.117**).

✔ Tips

■ When an object is converted to a button, Encore DVD automatically creates a subpicture. There's more detail on subpictures later in the chapter.

■ To convert an object or layer from a button back to an object, choose Object > Convert to Object (**Figure 4.118**). It remains a layer set, but the (+) prefix is deleted.

■ Alternatively, you can use the button/object column in the Layers palette to toggle back and forth between objects and buttons (**Figure 4.119**).

■ In order to modify a drop shadow in a layer set, you must use the Layers palette and/or the Direct Select tool to select the item within the layer set that has a drop shadow applied to it. Selecting the layer set as a whole will not allow you to modify the drop shadow.

To convert text to buttons:

1. Choose a selection tool from the Tools palette and select the text block. Size and position the text if necessary.

2. Choose Object > Convert to Button.

   The text is now a button layer set with the (+) prefix added, as can be seen in the Layers palette.

Figure 4.118 If you need to convert a button into an object, this is the place to do it.

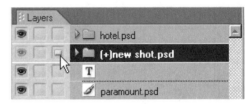

Figure 4.119 It's a bit subtle, but the arrow is pointing at a button icon. This turns on and off the attributes of a button layer set.

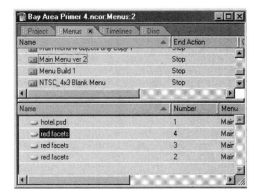

Figure 4.120 Here's another way to select a button: this time in the lower pane of the Menus tab.

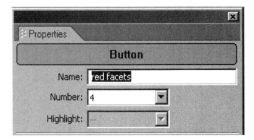

Figure 4.121 The button—ready to be named—in the Properties window.

To name a button:

1. With the Properties window open, *do one of the following:*

   ▲ Use the Selection tool to select a button in the Menu Editor.

   ▲ Select a button in the Layers tab.

   ▲ Select a button in the bottom pane of the Menus tab (**Figure 4.120**).

   Any of these methods will display the properties of the selected button in the Properties window.

2. Select the Name box and type a new name (**Figure 4.121**).

Working with Subpictures

When you create a button in a menu, you will most likely want it to have the proper highlights to indicate when it is in its normal (unselected), selected, or activated states. These highlights are created by graphic overlays called subpictures. Each subpicture shape can have three colors assigned to it, with opacity controls for each color as well. Those color and opacity values are managed by the menu's color set (**Figure 4.122**).

A little background on subpictures and color sets and how they work:

◆ A subpicture is a 2-bit color overlay, which occupies a layer in a button layer set (**Figure 4.123**).

◆ Subpictures are limited to solid colors and sharp edges—no color gradients and no feathering.

◆ You can create a button without a subpicture, but it makes navigating a menu more difficult. Without highlighting to indicate a button's state, the viewer will be unsure which button, if any, is selected.

◆ The button templates in Encore DVD have a subpicture included. If you create custom buttons out of text and other objects, you can create a subpicture to go along with them.

◆ In Encore DVD, the subpicture shape is defined by the shape of the button image it is associated with (**Figure 4.124**). You can also assign a different shape to a subpicture.

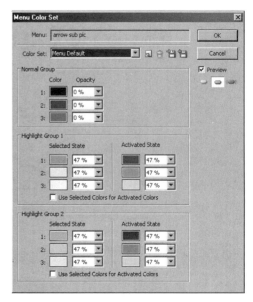

Figure 4.122 A quick look at the color set for this project.

Figure 4.123 The track with the =1 prefix is the subpicture for this layer set.

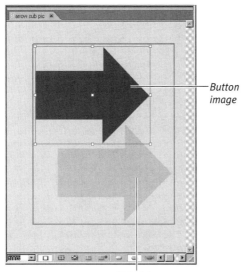

Button image

Subpicture

Figure 4.124 An example of a button and its subpicture. The Direct Select tool was used here to separate the two elements.

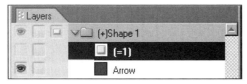

Figure 4.125 One subpicture layer. The (=1) indicates that the Color 1 controls in the Menu Color Set dialog will apply to this layer.

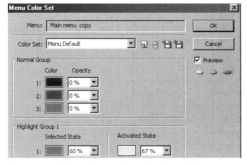

Figure 4.126 The Color 1 values for the subpicture layer's Normal and Highlight Group 1 states.

In order to understand how subpicture colors work in creating button highlights, you need to understand the relationship between color sets and layer sets.

For the basic button in Figure 4.124, there is one subpicture layer, denoted by the (=1) prefix (**Figure 4.125**). This means that its color values and opacity will be determined by the Color 1 settings in the Menu Color Set dialog. As you can't see color differences in this book, I'll point out the adjustments made to the opacity settings.

In the Menu Color Set dialog, note the Color 1 opacity setting for this button's subpicture. In its Normal (unselected) state, the opacity is 0%, so there will be no highlight color visible at all (**Figure 4.126**).

For the button's selected and activated states (Highlight Group 1), its subpicture, and therefore its highlight, have values set to 60% and 67% respectively. **Figures 4.127–4.129** show what it looks like in the Menu Editor.

What we have here is *one* button, *one* subpicture shape, *one* color, mapped to *one* set of controls in the Color Set window, and those controls manage the color settings for the *three* button highlight states. Got all that?

You can add a little more complexity right in the Menu Color Set window, because you can assign two different groups of highlights to the selected and activated states of various buttons in a menu. This allows more visual variety in a menu. For instance, the main navigation buttons, such as Play Intro or Scene Select, can have a bolder highlight color scheme than a secondary navigation button, such as Next or Return.

You can also add more complexity when you design your menus in Photoshop, because you can create subpicture layers designated as (=2) and (=3), to route to the Color 2 and Color 3 controllers in the Menu Color Set dialog.

In addition, each of these layers can have their own shape or mask applied to control the color highlight. In Photoshop, you can also design subpicture layers with objects that "pop on" or "pop off" for the different highlight states when you adjust the opacity settings in the menu's color set. More about that in Chapter 7.

Figure 4.127 The same button as before, reunited with its subpicture layer. This is the unselected state...

Figure 4.128 ...and the selected state...

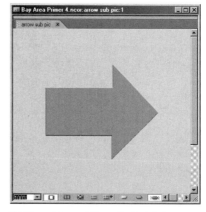

Figure 4.129 ...and the activated state.

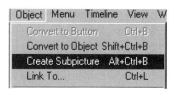

Figure 4.130 You can create a subpicture for a button.

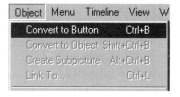

Figure 4.131 If you are starting with an object, you can make it into a button first.

Figure 4.132 You can also apply a subpicture to button text with the Properties palette.

To create a subpicture:

◆ Select an object in the Menu Editor and *do one of the following:*

   ▲ If the selected object is a button, choose Object > Create Subpicture (**Figure 4.130**).

   ▲ If the selected object is an image file, choose Object > Convert to Button (**Figure 4.131**). Then choose Object > Create Subpicture as above.

   ▲ If the selected object is text, choose Object > Convert to Button. Then choose Object > Create Subpicture as above.

✔ Tips

■ To verify that a subpicture was in fact created, you can use the Show Subpicture Highlights button on the bottom of the Menu Editor window to view the different colors attached to each subpicture state, or you can check the Layers palette for the telltale (=1) prefix in a layer's name.

■ For button text, you can also use the Properties palette to create a subpicture (**Figure 4.132**).

■ When you create a subpicture in Encore DVD, only the subpicture layer #1, with the (=1) prefix, is created. Some of the button templates in Encore DVD have more than one subpicture layer. If you need to add a subpicture layer or change the number of a layer, it must be done in Photoshop, using the Edit in Photoshop function. Once in Photoshop, the subpicture layer can be renamed or more layers added. See Chapter 7 for more information.

Working with Color Sets

You can have as many color sets in a project as you like, and you can save and reuse color sets in different projects. Each menu references only one color set at a time, and each color set can have up to 15 colors (plus one opacity setting for each color) you can customize for the different button states.

Some facts and suggestions about color sets:

◆ Encore DVD has a default color set, which you can use or modify.

◆ For menus imported from Photoshop, Encore DVD calculates an Automatic color set, based on the colors chosen for the subpictures in Photoshop. This menu cannot be modified.

◆ You can make changes to some or all of the color sets in a project via the Properties palette.

◆ It's generally best to design one color set for all the menus in your project. Consistency will help your viewers navigate through the menus without being distracted or confused.

◆ To help maintain consistency, Encore DVD "remembers" the last color set used, and applies that as a default for subsequent new menus.

◆ It's also common to use the same highlights for both the selected and activated states of a button, as a color change on activation can sometimes be a distraction to the viewer.

◆ The opacity settings in color sets can be used to "pop-on/pop-off" menu elements to indicate different button states.

The controls for these functions are in the Menu Color Set dialog.

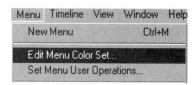

Figure 4.133 Preparing to edit the project's color sets.

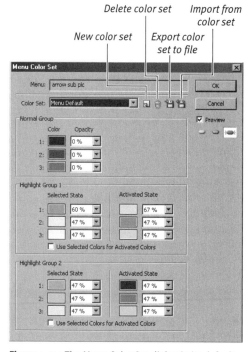

Delete color set   Import from color set

New color set   Export color set to file

Figure 4.134 The Menu Color Set dialog in its default display.

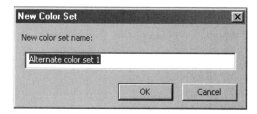

Figure 4.135 The New Color Set name dialog.

To view a color set:

1. Choose Menu > Edit Menu Color Set (**Figure 4.133**).

   The Menu Color Set dialog appears with the currently active color set displayed (**Figure 4.134**).

2. To select an alternate color set, use the pop-up menu in the upper pane of this window.

   In a new project, the only color set available for a new menu will be Menu Default.

To create a new color set:

1. Choose Menu > Edit Menu Color Set.

   The Menu Color Set dialog appears with the currently active color set displayed.

2. Click the Create a New Color Set button.

   The New Color Set dialog appears, with a copy of the current color set as the default name.

3. Keep the current name or type a new name in the New Color Set dialog (**Figure 4.135**).

4. Click OK.

   The color set file is saved and incorporated into your project file (.ncor).

✔ Tips

- Although you *can* modify the Menu Default color set, it is a good idea to copy it and modify the copy.

- Color sets saved as above are not available to other projects.

To adjust the colors in a color set:

1. Follow the steps above to open the Menu Color Set dialog and either create a new color set or open an existing one.

2. Select the color swatch for any of the color groups in the Menu Color Set dialog (**Figure 4.136**).

   The Color Picker appears (**Figure 4.137**).

3. Use the controls to modify the color. The box in the upper right displays the original color in the bottom pane and the new color you are picking in the top pane.

4. Click OK.

   The modified color appears in the color swatch you selected.

5. Click the pop-up menu for opacity and select the amount of opacity for the highlight (**Figure 4.138**).

6. Follow steps 3 to 5 for the other color groups.

7. Click OK to commit changes and close the Menu Color Set dialog.

Figure 4.136 Getting ready to modify a color in a color set.

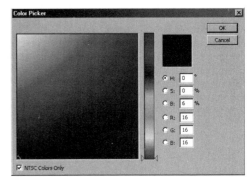

Figure 4.137 The Color Picker. Note that NTSC Colors Only is checked to keep colors within "legal" limits for TV display.

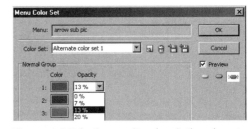

Figure 4.138 Selecting opacity values in the color set.

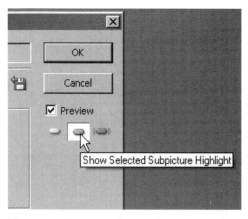

Figure 4.139 You can preview the changes you make to the color set while you make them.

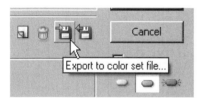

Figure 4.140 Preparing to export the current color set.

Figure 4.141 Save the color set file to a folder you can locate again when you want to reuse it.

✔ Tips

- The Preview check box in the Menu Color Set dialog allows you to see the changes you make reflected in the menu that's displayed in the Menu Editor window (**Figure 4.139**).

- Check the NTSC Colors Only check box in the Color Picker to avoid colors that will be too saturated to display well on a TV.

To export a color set:

1. Choose Menu > Edit Menu Color Set.

2. Click the Export to Color Set File button (**Figure 4.140**).

   The Save Color Set File dialog appears (**Figure 4.141**).

3. Name the color set file and select a folder.

4. Click Save to save the color set to the folder.

✔ Tips

- Exported color sets are available to other projects.

- It's a good idea to create a specific folder to save your color sets in and be consistent in saving to that folder.

To import a color set:

1. Choose Menu > Edit Menu Color Set.

2. Click the Import from Color Set File button (**Figure 4.142**).

   The Import Color Set File dialog appears (**Figure 4.143**).

3. Navigate to the desired color set file and click Open.

   The selected color set file is displayed in the Menu Color Set dialog.

To delete a color set:

1. Choose Menu > Edit Menu Color Set.

2. Select a color set in the Color Set pop-up menu and click the Delete Color Set button (**Figure 4.144**).

   The Delete Color Set confirmation dialog appears (**Figure 4.145**).

3. Click Yes to confirm.

✔ Tip

■ The Menu Default color set and any Automatic color sets cannot be deleted.

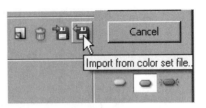

Figure 4.142 Importing a color set.

Figure 4.143 Locating and getting ready to import a color set file.

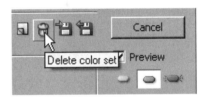

Figure 4.144 Preparing to delete the active color set.

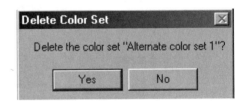

Figure 4.145 Confirming the color set deletion.

Figure 4.146 A menu's current color set is displayed in the Properties palette.

Figure 4.147 You can choose another color set in the project from the list in the Properties palette.

To apply a color set to a menu:

1. With the Properties palette open, select a menu from the Project tab, Menus tab, or Menu Editor window.

   The menu properties are displayed in the Properties palette (**Figure 4.146**).

2. Select the Color Set pop-up menu in the Properties palette, and choose a color set from the pop-up list (**Figure 4.147**).

✔ Tip

- You can select multiple menus from the Project or Menus tab, then use the Color Set pop-up menu in the Properties palette, as above, and Encore DVD will apply the chosen color set to all the selected menus.

5

LINKING

This is where it all comes together. You now get to determine the connections between each menu, button, and timeline in your project. In this chapter, you'll learn how to orchestrate the following actions:

◆ What happens when the viewer inserts the DVD into the player. This is called *first play*.

◆ What happens when the viewer clicks a button on a menu. This is called a *link*.

◆ What happens when a timeline finishes playing, or when a menu times out. This is called an *end action*.

◆ What happens when you need to give the viewer an optional path through a series of menus and timelines. This is called an *override*.

◆ What happens when you want to give the viewer the ability to see several timelines play in a sequence. This is called a *playlist*.

Encore DVD offers several different ways of connecting these *actions* to their proper *destinations*. Of course, to successfully author an interesting, easy-to-navigate DVD, you'll be both planning before you begin and experimenting as you go, but this chapter will give you a good foundation in the techniques of creating and modifying the links that hold your project together.

About Linking

Once you've created the pieces that will make up your final product—the timelines, menus, buttons, and so on—you'll be connecting them with *links*. To get an idea of how these connections work, take a look at **Figure 5.1**. There are fundamentally three kinds of *actions* that you can connect to four kinds of *destinations* as you build your DVD. (This gets much more elaborate with playlists and motion menus and DVD remote controls, as you'll see later on, but bear with me for now—the basic procedures are the same.)

The Properties palette is the place to manage and modify these links. The tools you'll be using in the Properties palette are the pop-up menus and what is called the *pickwhip*. This may sound like an unexpected excursion into kinkiness, but they're really just the means to link the various parts of your project together. (Hope you're not too disappointed.)

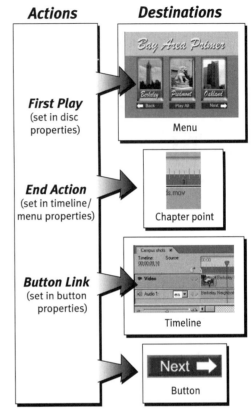

Figure 5.1 Some Encore DVD actions and the types of destinations they can link to.

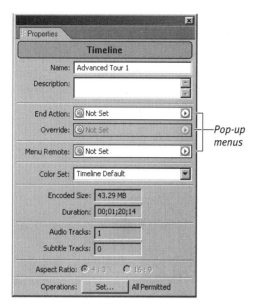

Figure 5.2 The Properties palette offers several pop-up menus to choose from.

Figure 5.3 The pickwhip, up close in its "coiled" state.

When you use the Properties palette to display the properties of a menu, timeline, button, or disc, you'll see several pop-up menus offering different types of actions (**Figure 5.2**).

Next to each pop-up menu, you'll also notice a small "coil" icon (**Figure 5.3**). That's the pickwhip. You can use a pop-up menu to *navigate* to a destination, or you can use the pickwhip to click, drag, and *point* to it.

An alternative, and very intuitive, method for creating links is to simply drag a timeline, menu, or playlist from the Project window and drop it onto a menu. In one step, you can create a button and a link to a destination. If you need to make any changes, you can use the controls available in the Properties palette. More details on all these methods later in the chapter.

Some Advice on Workflow

After you sketched out your project on that cocktail napkin, you probably then created a precise flowchart of how all the pieces were going to link together...or at least you have it in your head. Here are some general guidelines for building links in Encore DVD that will keep the navigational flow of your DVD, well... *flowing*.

For example, let's say you have a simple project—maybe a main menu, a couple of secondary menus (aka "submenus"), and a few timelines that need to link up coherently:

- You should create a button that links the main menu to each submenu.

- You should create a button that links each submenu back to the main menu (this one is easy to forget). Alternatively, you can set an end action for a submenu to return to the main menu, but using a button to do this puts the viewer in control.

- You can give the viewer the means to quickly jump back to the last thing he or she did. Encore DVD has options such as Return to Last Menu and Resume to help them go back a step (more information on these two options later in the chapter.)

- You can use buttons to link every menu to every other menu but don't have to. (You can just have a button in each submenu that returns to the main menu, and the viewer can choose a new menu from there.)

- Each button must have a link to *something*: a menu, a specific button in a menu, a time-line, or a specific chapter point in a timeline. (Again, it's very easy to create a button and forget to link it to a destination.)

- Each chapter point you want to access must have a button it is linked to.

As you'll see later, there are various ways in which to put the above structure together, including some shortcuts. Encore DVD will check all the links in your project before you build the final disc, but these guidelines apply to any Encore DVD project, and if you keep them in mind, you'll have greater confidence that your DVD's navigation will make sense, and you'll have to do fewer "fixes" before burning to disc.

Figure 5.4 Setting the destination for a First Play.

Figure 5.5 The First Play item now has a First Play icon attached.

Figure 5.6 Using the pop-up menu method to set a First Play for the disc.

Setting a First Play

Encore DVD lets you specify a menu or timeline for First Play, which will appear when the DVD first starts playing in the drive. In commercial DVDs, this is usually the familiar FBI Warning. If you don't specify a destination for First Play, Encore DVD will set the First Play to either the first menu or timeline created in the project or imported into the project.

If you have an introductory movie you want the viewer to see first, set a timeline as First Play. If you want the viewer to see a menu right away, set a menu as First Play. Also see the sidebar "Destinations and Defaults" later in this chapter.

To specify a menu or timeline as First Play:

1. Select a menu in the Menus or Project tab, or a timeline in the Timelines or Project tab.

2. Right-click on the menu or timeline icon and choose Set as First Play from the contextual menu (**Figure 5.4**).

   The First Play icon is added to the selected menu or timeline (**Figure 5.5**).

   In this example, the main menu will begin playing when the DVD is inserted.

Or

1. With the Properties palette open, select the Disc tab in the Project window.

   The disc's properties are displayed in the Properties palette.

2. *Do one of the following:*

   ▲ Click the First Play pop-up menu in the Properties palette and select a timeline or menu from the list (**Figure 5.6**).

continues on next page

SETTING A FIRST PLAY

▲ If the selection is not available in the pop-up menu's list, select Specify Other. From the Specify Link dialog (**Figure 5.7**), choose a chapter point, timeline, menu, or button.

The selection appears in the Target box. Click OK to confirm and close the dialog.

▲ Click the pickwhip icon in the First Play pop-up menu and drag it to the timeline or menu you want (**Figure 5.8**).

With any of these methods, the selected menu or timeline appears in the Disc Properties First Play menu as a destination (**Figure 5.9**).

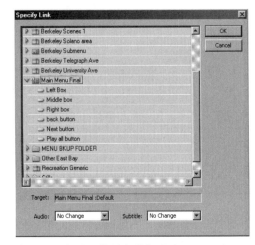

Figure 5.7 The Specify Link dialog helps you navigate over a wider area to establish links.

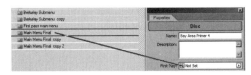

Figure 5.8 Using the pickwhip method to set a First Play for the disc.

✔ Tips

■ Setting a First Play is not mandatory. If you don't specify anything as First Play, Encore DVD will remind you of this fact when you preview the project from the beginning and when you check the project's links. If you have no First Play, then your DVD will do nothing when it's inserted into the DVD player. The viewer will have to use the player's remote control to initiate playback.

■ If you choose a video as First Play, keep it short, because the viewer has to sit through the video before getting to a menu. Depending on how you've set up your navigation, it may be difficult to exit the video early and get to a menu, which might irritate your audience.

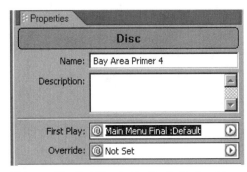

Figure 5.9 The First Play destination is displayed in the Properties palette.

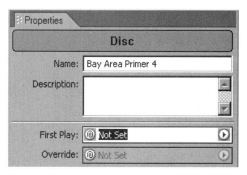

Figure 5.10 First Play has been deleted.

To clear a First Play:

◆ Right-click on the current First Play selection and choose Clear First Play from the contextual menu.

Or

1. With the Properties palette open, display the Disc properties as described earlier.

2. Click the First Play pop-up menu and select Delete.

   The First Play pop-up menu now displays Not Set (**Figure 5.10**).

✔ Tip

■ You can also simply make a new First Play selection, without having to clear the old one.

SETTING A FIRST PLAY

Selecting from a Pop-up Menu

When you click a pop-up menu in the Properties palette, there are several selections you can make.

Here are the selections available in the pop-up menu list and what they do:

◆ **Cut/Copy/Paste/Delete.** These apply to the item you have set as a destination in a pop-up menu. When there is no destination selected, Not Set is displayed.

◆ **Destination list.** This pop-up displays a list of up to 20 recently opened timelines and menus—with the most recent at the top—from which to select. You can also select specific chapter points or buttons as destinations for links.

◆ **Link Back to Here.** The source and destination for the link are the same.

◆ **Stop.** Default for both timelines and menus. A timeline stops after it finishes; a menu is inactive until there is viewer interaction.

◆ **Specify Other.** Used to expand the search for destinations beyond the 20 displayed in the pop-up menu's Destination list.

◆ **Resume.** Used as a button link to take the viewer a step back to where they accessed the current menu.

◆ **Return to Last Menu.** A timeline end action or menu remote link that returns the viewer to the last menu viewed.

Setting an End Action

End actions can be applied either to time-lines or menus. In a timeline, the end action determines what happens when the timeline finishes playing. The default end action is Stop. (When the timeline finishes, it stops and the screen goes black.) You'll likely want to use the end action to link the timeline to another timeline or menu instead.

For menus, the default end action is also Stop. The menu simply remains on the screen until the viewer interacts with it by clicking a button. You can replace this with an end action that will automatically time out the menu if there is no viewer interaction.

To set an end action for a timeline:

1. With the Properties palette open, select a timeline.

2. Click the End Action pop-up menu and select the menu or timeline you want the current timeline to link to when it finishes playing (**Figure 5.11**).

   Or

◆ Click the pickwhip icon in the pop-up menu and point to the item you want the current timeline to link to when it finishes playing (**Figure 5.12**).

With either method, the selected item appears in the End Action pop-up menu as a destination.

Figure 5.11 Navigating to the timeline's end action from the pop-up menu.

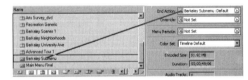

Figure 5.12 Pointing to the timeline's end action with the pickwhip.

Why Use an End Action?

Here's a scenario: Suppose you were creating a disc to use at a trade show or kiosk, and wanted it to play back a series of timelines continuously. You,d probably want a menu to appear first, with the ability to click a button to start the initial playback of your timelines. By setting an end action in each timeline that links it to the next, you can create a sequence of timelines that will play over and over, unattended. That's an example of a useful *timeline* end action.

You may also want to establish a *menu* end action to make sure the DVD didn't get "stuck" on a menu—if, for example, no one in your trade show booth remembers to push "play" on the main menu at the beginning of the day. By setting the appropriate end action, after a few moments of being displayed, the menu would automatically begin playback of the linked timelines on its own.

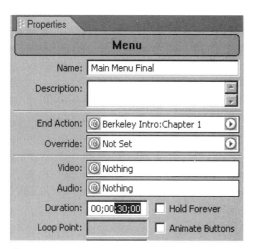

Figure 5.13 Setting the duration of a menu before it executes its end action.

Figure 5.14 Setting the end action of a menu with the pop-up menu.

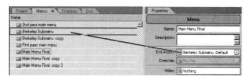

Figure 5.15 Setting the end action of a menu with the pickwhip.

To set an end action for a menu:

1. Select a menu from a tab in the Project window and open its Properties palette.

2. Double-click the Duration box to select it.

3. Type in the amount of time you'd like the menu to stay on the screen before it executes the end action (**Figure 5.13**).

   Note that the Hold Forever option should be deselected.

4. Click the End Action pop-up menu and select the menu or timeline to which you want the current menu to link when the duration you've specified expires (**Figure 5.14**).

   Or

◆ Click the pickwhip icon in the pop-up window and point to the item to which you want the current menu to link when the duration expires (**Figure 5.15**).

With either method, the selected item appears in the End Action pop-up menu as a destination.

✔ Tips

■ If you'd rather have Encore DVD hold the menu and wait for viewer action, rather than executing an end action after a set time, click the Hold Forever check box in the Properties palette.

■ There are extra options for motion menus. See Chapter 9 for more information.

To clear an end action:

◆ In the Properties palette for a timeline, right-click on the End Action pop-up menu and choose Delete from the contextual menu.

Linking Buttons

The way you set up your button links determines how your DVD works. The buttons and links you create are the means by which the viewer can get at all that great content locked up on the disc. As usual, the following sections cover the mechanics of linking. It's up to you to design and test a strategy to make your links work together smoothly and logically.

Destinations and Defaults

Timelines contain chapter points, and menus contain buttons. Encore DVD makes it easy for you to link to any of these four things. You will always have the option—and several ways of exercising it—to link to a specific chapter point or button. If you don't specify, however, and link only to a timeline or menu, Encore DVD will automatically link to a default chapter point or button within that timeline or menu.

In timelines, the default chapter point is Chapter 1, which is always the chapter point at the beginning of the timeline.

In menus, the default button is button number 1, which is the first button you created in the menu. This button will be highlighted when you access the menu. If you want, you can change the number of any button in the menu, or specify a different button as the default, or you can turn off the default-button feature entirely.

Figure 5.16 Though it's a bit hard to see here, this is the journey of a timeline on its way to becoming a button in a menu.

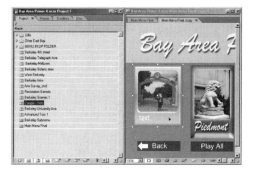

Figure 5.17 Here's a rough result of dragging a timeline or menu into an active menu. Encore DVD assigns the default button shape for the new material.

✔ Tips

- You can also drop an element onto an existing button in the Menu Editor. The button is automatically linked.

- To modify a button created in this way, you can use the pickwhip and/or the pop-up menus in the Properties palette, as described on the next page.

Drag-and-Drop Linking

You can select several different types of items from one of the Project window tabs and then drag and drop your selection into the Menu Editor. This method provides easy, quick ways to put together buttons and links in a menu.

To drag and drop items into the Menu Editor:

1. Open the Menu Editor, if it is not already open.

2. *Do one of the following:*

   ▲ Select a timeline or menu in one of the Project window tabs.

   ▲ Select a playlist from the Project tab (more about playlists later in this chapter).

   ▲ Select a button from the lower pane of the Menus tab.

   ▲ Select a chapter point from the lower pane of the Timelines tab.

   ▲ Select multiples of any of the above.

3. Drag and drop your selection into the Menu Editor (**Figure 5.16**).

   A button is created, using the current default button template selected in the Library palette (**Figure 5.17**). The button's link is automatically set to the timeline, menu, or other element from which it was created.

4. Resize and reposition the newly dropped elements as necessary.

Linking Using Pop-up Menus

You use pop-up menus to navigate to a destination rather than pointing (as you do with the pickwhip).

To link a button with the pop-up menu:

1. Open the Properties palette, if it is not already open.

2. *Do one of the following:*

   ▲ Double-click on a menu in the Project or Menus tab.

   The menu opens in the Menu Editor and its properties are displayed in the Properties palette. Select a button in the Menu Editor (**Figure 5.18**).

   ▲ Select a menu in the Menus tab and, in the lower pane of the Menus tab, select a button from the list (**Figure 5.19**).

   With either method, the button properties appear in the Properties palette.

3. Click the Link pop-up menu in the Properties palette.

4. From the Link menu, select a destination—it could be a timeline, menu, chapter point, button, or playlist (**Figure 5.20**).

   Your selection appears in the Link pop-up menu as a destination.

✔ Tip

■ Only the 20 most recent items appear in the menu list, so you may need to use the Specify Other option to widen your search for a destination.

Figure 5.18 Selecting a button in the zoomed-in Menu Editor.

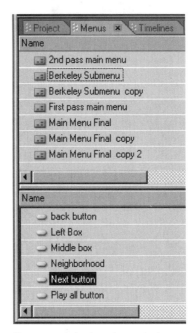

Figure 5.19 Selecting a button in the bottom pane of the Menu Editor.

Figure 5.20 A destination selected.

Linking Using the Pickwhip

If you use the pickwhip, you have a number of target choices. You can point and link to

◆ A timeline in the Timelines or Project tab

◆ A menu in the Menus tab or Properties palette

◆ A button in the lower pane of the Menus tab

◆ A chapter point in the lower pane of the Timelines tab

◆ A chapter point in the Timeline window

◆ A playlist in the Project tab

Because the mechanics of linking to each type of destination with the pickwhip are so similar in all of these cases, I'll just give one example and let you extrapolate.

To link a button to a chapter point:

1. Follow steps 1 and 2 of the previous method.

2. When the button properties are displayed in the Properties palette, do one of the following:

   ▲ Click the pickwhip icon in the Link menu and point to a chapter point on an active timeline in the Timeline window (**Figure 5.21**).

Figure 5.21 Using the pickwhip to point to a chapter point on a timeline in the Timeline window.

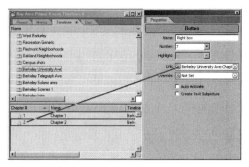

Figure 5.22 Linking to a chapter point in the bottom pane of the Timelines tab, using the pickwhip.

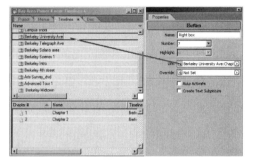

Figure 5.23 Linking to a timeline in the top pane of the Timelines window, using the pickwhip.

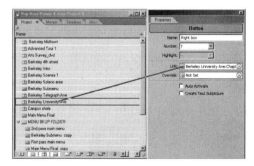

Figure 5.24 Linking to a timeline in the Project tab, using the pickwhip.

▲ Click the pickwhip icon in the Link menu and point to a chapter point in the bottom pane of the Timeline tab (**Figure 5.22**).

▲ Click the pickwhip icon in the Link menu and point to a timeline in the top pane of the Timelines window (**Figure 5.23**).

▲ Click the pickwhip icon in the Link menu and point to a timeline in the Project tab (**Figure 5.24**).

After you make your selection, the pickwhip "recoils," and the selected chapter point appears in the Link pop-up menu as a destination.

✔ **Tip**

■ Using the Menu Editor to select a button will give you the most flexibility with the pickwhip: You'll be able to point to items in various tabs. When you select a button in the lower pane of the Menus tab, for instance, you can't use the pickwhip to point to a timeline in the Project or Timelines tab, because when you select a different tab, its properties replace those of your selected button in the Properties palette.

Setting Overrides

When you are creating links, not only can you choose the destination of the link, you can also choose an optional override setting, which—guess what?—*overrides* the link destination's normal end action.

Overrides allow you to plan two different paths through the same material on the DVD. You can think of an override as an *alternative* end action. Overrides save Encore DVD (and you) from having to make and manage copies of menus and timelines to accommodate two different navigational paths.

Consider this scenario:

For the Bay Area Primer project used as an example in this book, you might need two viewing options:

Option 1: The viewer watches a series of highlight videos (timelines) about a particular Bay Area city, played in a particular order. At the end of the highlight series, the viewer is returned to the main menu.

Option 2: The viewer views each highlight video individually. When each video finishes playing, the viewer is returned to the main menu, where he or she can choose to view one or all of the videos as his or her next choice.

Option 1 can be accomplished by:

◆ Creating a Play All button in the main menu that links to the first highlight video you want to present.

◆ The end action for each video links to the next video. The last highlight video's end action returns viewers to the main menu.

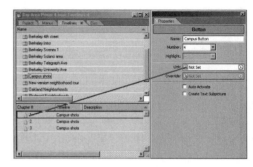

Figure 5.25 Creating a link destination.

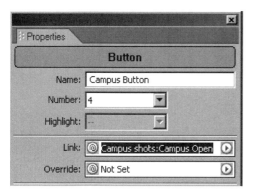

Figure 5.26 The link destination is displayed.

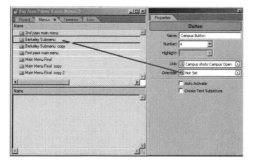

Figure 5.27 Creating an override.

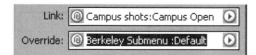

Figure 5.28 The override destination is displayed.

Option 2 employs overrides to link the same material in a different way:

◆ In the main menu, you create a play button for each individual highlight video. You set the *link* for each play button to each video's timeline. You set the *override* for each button to link back to the main menu. Here's how.

To set an override for a link:

1. Open the Properties palette, if it is not already open.

2. Select a button, either by selecting it in the Menu Editor or any other Encore DVD method.

3. When the button's properties are displayed in the Properties palette, use any of the pop-up or pickwhip methods to create a link (**Figure 5.25**).

   The link destination is displayed in the Link pop-up menu (**Figure 5.26**).

4. Click the Override pop-up menu and, using the pop-up or pickwhip method, select an override destination (**Figure 5.27**).

   The override destination is displayed in the Override pop-up menu (**Figure 5.28**).

   When the button is activated, it will execute its link. The previously programmed end action of the destination timeline or menu will be overridden and redirected to a new destination.

✔ Tip

■ Overrides can also be set for First Play in the Disc properties.

Creating Playlists

Playlists are similar to overrides, and more flexible, so you may find yourself using them rather than overrides. Essentially, a playlist goes beyond overrides in that it allows you to put together a *group* of timelines as one destination, and have them play sequentially. Here are the other salient details that define playlists:

◆ Playlists are created and stored in the Project tab, just like menus, timelines, and so on.

◆ You add and delete timelines to a playlist via the playlist's Properties palette.

◆ Timelines play in order, starting from the top of a list displayed in the playlist Properties. To change the order, you can drag and reposition timelines in the list.

◆ You can specify which chapter point in each timeline should be used as the starting point for playback.

◆ You can choose playlists as a link or end action destination from other elements in your project.

◆ Unlike overrides, you need to set only one end action for the whole group of timelines, not each one individually.

◆ You can chain playlists together by programming an end action in each playlist that points to the next in the chain.

◆ Playlists play all the timelines in their list, and can't be interrupted, except by the DVD remote control.

◆ As you'll find out in the next chapter, you can set different audio and subtitle tracks for timelines that are accessed via a playlist.

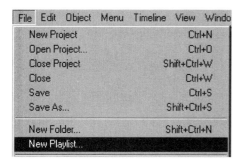

Figure 5.29 One method for creating a playlist from the File menu...

Figure 5.30 ...and an alternative method.

Figure 5.31 Encore DVD will prompt you to name your playlist.

To use the same example as in the *Setting Overrides* section earlier, you could fulfill Option 1—sequential playback of time-lines—by creating a Play All button that links to a playlist with each highlight video's timeline in it. The playlist's end action would take the viewer back to the original menu. Then, for option 2—individual playback—each timeline would be linked to its own button and each timeline would have an end action to return to the menu.

To create a playlist:

1. *Do one of the following:*

   ▲ Choose File > New Playlist (**Figure 5.29**).

   ▲ Click the Create a new Playlist button at the bottom of the Project tab (**Figure 5.30**).

   The New Playlist Name dialog appears (**Figure 5.31**).

2. Type a name for the playlist and click OK. The playlist appears in the Project tab.

To add timelines to a playlist:

1. Open the Properties palette, if it is not already open.

2. Select a playlist from the Project tab. The playlist is displayed in the Properties palette (**Figure 5.32**).

   The active area of the playlist in the Properties tab is called the Playlist Inspector.

3. *Do one of the following:*

   ▲ Use the pickwhip in the Playlist Inspector to point to a timeline in the Project tab (**Figure 5.33**).

   You can also point to a chapter point in the lower pane of the Timelines tab or to a chapter point in the Timeline window.

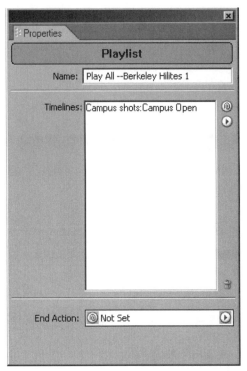

Figure 5.32 The new playlist appears in the Properties palette.

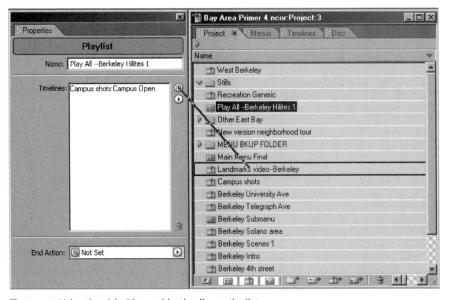

Figure 5.33 Using the pickwhip to add a timeline to the list...

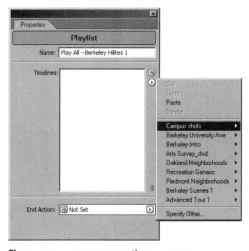

Figure 5.34 ...or you can use the pop-up menu...

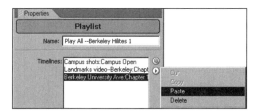

Figure 5.35 ...or you can copy/paste items into the Playlist Inspector.

Figure 5.36 And of course, you can get rid of material easily, too.

▲ Use the pop-up menu in the Playlist Inspector to navigate to a timeline or chapter point (**Figure 5.34**).

▲ Select a timeline in the Project tab, right-click and choose Copy, and then choose Paste from the pop-up menu in the Playlist Inspector (**Figure 5.35**).

The selected timeline is added to the bottom of the list in the Playlist Inspector.

To delete timelines from a playlist:

1. Select one or more timelines in the Playlist Inspector.

2. Select Delete from the Playlist Inspector's pop-up menu (**Figure 5.36**).

   Or

◆ Click the Delete (trash can) button at the bottom of the Playlist Inspector's window.

The selected timeline is removed from the playlist.

To reorder timelines in a playlist:

1. Select a timeline in the Playlist Inspector.

2. Drag it to a new position in the Playlist Inspector list.

CREATING PLAYLISTS

To add an end action to a playlist:

◆ *Do one of the following:*

▲ Click on the pickwhip in the End Action section of the Playlist Inspector and point to a destination such as a timeline or menu (**Figure 5.37**).

▲ Click the pop-up menu in the End Action section of the Playlist Inspector and select a destination from the list (**Figure 5.38**).

The timelines in the playlist will play in sequence. At the end of the last timeline in the sequence, the end action will be executed.

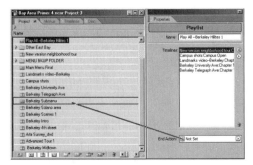

Figure 5.37 The pickwhip can be used to create an end action....

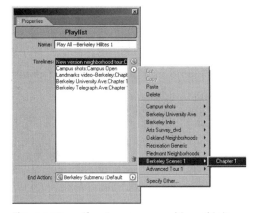

Figure 5.38 ...or if you're more menu-driven, this is the place.

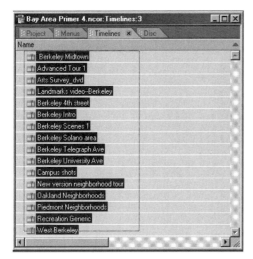

Figure 5.39 Multiple items can be selected in the project...

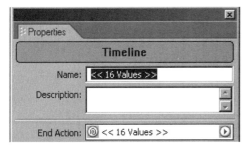

Figure 5.40 ...the Properties tab is intelligent enough to do more than one thing at a time.

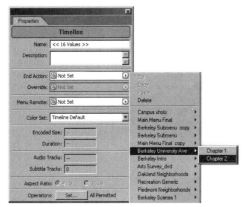

Figure 5.41 A new destination for the selected items can be found.

Changing Multiple Links

You can use the tabs in the Project window in combination with the Properties palette to manage and modify the links you create. As you may remember from Chapter 2, the various tabs are chock-full of data to help you organize your project, and much of that data is about links, end actions, and the like.

As you work on more complex projects, you can use the global view provided in the Project window tabs to see the relationships between all of the elements in your project. You can then make changes to multiple items simultaneously, again in combination with the Properties palette.

For instance, if you have a set of timelines that all have end actions returning them to the main menu, and you want them all to return to the Scene Select menu instead, you can make that change to all the timelines at once. Or, if an override is set for several different menus and you now wish to cancel it, you can cancel it for all the menus in one step.

To make changes to multiple menus, timelines, or buttons:

1. Select several menus, timelines, or buttons in one of the Project window tabs (**Figure 5.39**).

   The properties for the selected items are displayed in the Properties palette.

2. Use the pop-up menu or pickwhip to select a new destination for the action or link (**Figure 5.40**).

   The new selection is displayed as a destination in the pop-up menu of the Properties palette (**Figure 5.41**).

   The change is also reflected in the appropriate columns in the Project window tabs.

PREVIEWING AND FINISHING

6

In this chapter, you'll learn how to work with the Project Preview window so you can test all those links you created in the previous chapter. You'll also learn how to program new links—between the buttons, menus, timelines, and so on of your project and the real-world controls of a DVD player.

You'll also learn how to perform final checks on your project that will help guard against any rude surprises when you write to disc. The four types of output from Encore DVD are covered. And, at the end of the chapter, you'll find a short overview of the different DVD formats and the things to consider when choosing a disc format for your project.

As you move closer to the final phase of burning your DVD, you'll find that you have as many options to choose from as in any other part of the process. Many of the choices you'll make now were actually determined way back in the planning and asset-gathering phases of the project. Decisions on disc type and capacity, on desktop burning or mass-production of discs, on whether to include copy protection—all these things come together now. There's a lot to cover, but just take a deep breath and dive in.

About the Preview Window

The Project Preview window allows you to see the interaction of all the pieces of your project. Its control panel simulates all the functions of a DVD player's remote control (**Figure 6.1**). Because this window is so important in understanding how your final DVD will work, I'll go over its interface in some detail.

◆ **Status area.** For *timelines,* this area displays the name of the timeline, the current chapter point, and the current timecode position. For *menus,* it displays the name, the highlighted button, and the duration of the menu. The disc icon indicates whether the video file for a currently playing timeline is an MPEG-2 file (green) or is non-transcoded (red). Encore DVD will have to transcode any "red" files before writing them to the final DVD.

◆ **Display area zoom.** Specifies the magnification of the preview.

◆ **Render current motion menu button.** Renders files for playback of motion menus (see Chapter 9 for more details).

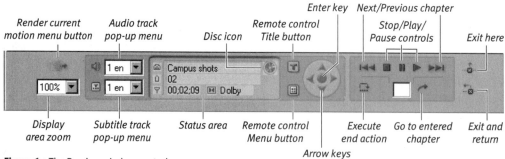

Figure 6.1 The Preview window controls.

◆ **Audio track pop-up menu.** Enables audio track selection and displays the current audio track.

◆ **Subtitle track pop-up menu.** Enables subtitle track selection and displays the current subtitle track.

◆ **Remote control Menu button.** Previews the function of the Menu button on a DVD remote control.

◆ **Remote control Title button.** Previews the function of the Title button on a DVD remote control.

◆ **Arrow keys.** These move the cursor between buttons.

◆ **Enter key.** Enables button activation.

◆ **Stop/Pause/Play controls.** Stops, pauses, or plays the current chapter.

◆ **Next/Previous chapter.** Skips to the next or previous chapter point in a timeline.

◆ **Go to entered chapter.** Specifies the chapter to preview in a timeline.

◆ **Execute end action.** Plays the end action selected in the Properties palette.

◆ **Exit here.** Exits the Preview window and returns to the currently displayed timeline or menu.

◆ **Exit and return.** Exits the Preview window and returns you to the project, closing the Preview window.

Previewing a Project

Now that you know how to navigate in the Preview window, take a look at your project.

To preview a project:

◆ Choose File > Preview.

The Project Preview window opens (**Figure 6.2**). You can use any of the navigation or transport controls to test your project from the beginning.

Or

◆ Right-click on a menu, timeline, button, chapter point, or playlist in another window and choose Preview from Here in the contextual menu (**Figure 6.3**).

The Preview window opens at the point you selected. You can now use any of the navigation or transport controls to test your project, starting at that point.

✔ Tips

■ The Preview from Here function can be a *great* timesaver, especially in a larger project. You won't need to watch huge amounts of footage or climb through many layers of menus just to preview a small change deep in your project.

■ If you don't have a First Play set, Encore DVD will display a warning message (**Figure 6.4**). As the dialog indicates, you may continue with your previewing.

■ Unlike the Monitor window you use to play timelines, the Preview window must be closed before you can resume work on your project.

Figure 6.2 The Project Preview window opens.

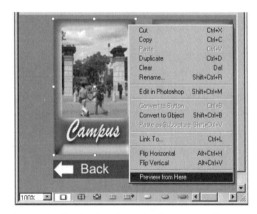

Figure 6.3 The Preview from Here function can be a huge timesaver.

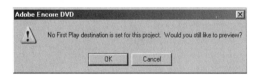

Figure 6.4 Encore DVD will warn you if you have no First Play established.

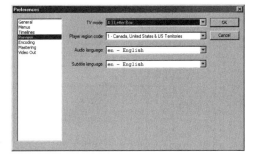

Figure 6.5 The Preview Preferences dialog.

Figure 6.6 Make sure your aspect ratio matches your source material.

Setting the Preview Preferences

You may need to make changes in your project's Preview preferences, depending on your source material. For instance, the default aspect ratio for previewing is 4:3. If you have a wide-screen project, you can change the setting in the Preferences menu. Although your choice of aspect ratio will play the biggest part in how you use the Preview window, the Preferences menu is also where you make choices in terms of the regions and languages you're working in while designing and creating your DVD. I'll cover the regions later in this chapter, and the languages in Chapter 10.

To set the Preview aspect ratio:

1. Choose Edit > Preferences > Preview.

   The Preferences dialog appears (**Figure 6.5**).

2. Click the button for the TV mode menu and choose the aspect ratio you want (**Figure 6.6**). Click OK.

   The Preview window will now display your project in the aspect ratio you've selected.

✔ Tips

- Preview settings are not confined to a particular project. You'll have to change the settings again if the next project you open requires a different aspect ratio.

- Your choice of Player region code in the Preview dialog must match the region code in the Project settings for the Disc tab. If there's a mismatch, you'll get an error message and the Preview window won't open.

Setting User Operations Controls

As you build your DVD, you may want to impose some limits over what a viewer can and can't do with the DVD player's remote control. An example might be a timeline video that you really want a viewer to pay attention to—perhaps you've set up an important video for First Play and want to make sure the viewer can't skip over it or fast-forward through it. This is where Encore DVD's User Operations controls come in. You can embed controls into timelines, menus, and disc functions via the Properties palette. For a quick overview of the types of actions you can control through the User Operations settings, see the sidebar.

To modify User Operations settings:

1. Select a timeline or menu, or click on the Disc tab to bring up the appropriate Properties palette (**Figure 6.7**).

2. Click the Set button at the bottom of the Properties palette (**Figure 6.8**).

   The User Operations dialog appears (**Figure 6.9**).

3. *Do one of the following:*

   ▲ Click All to enable all user operations.

   ▲ Click None to disable all user operations.

   ▲ Click Custom and then enable or disable selected operations.

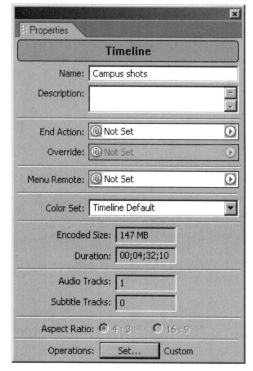

Figure 6.7 Once again, time to visit the Properties palette...

Figure 6.8 ...to make changes to User Operations for a timeline, menu, or disc.

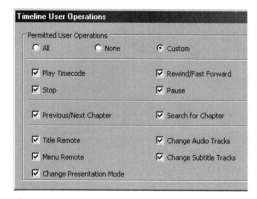

Figure 6.9 The User Operations dialog.

✔ Tips

■ Turning off user operations in the Disc tab disables that operation for all menus and timelines. If you have a function enabled at the disc level, you can turn it on and off in specific timelines and menus as you go.

■ Disabling Play Chapters also disables the Search for Chapter operation.

■ The user operations that you set for timelines and menus are maintained in any copies you make of them.

The user operation status is displayed as a column in the Menus and Timelines tabs.

User Operations Settings

I'll skip over the obvious controls, such as stop, pause, and play in this list, and describe the more notable or unusual controls. Also, note that the user operations that you can affect differ somewhat, depending on whether you are modifying the properties for a timeline, a menu, or a disc function.

◆ **Play timecode.** Allows the user to enter a timecode on the remote control to go to in a timeline.

◆ **Previous/Next chapter.** Allows selection of the previous or next chapter with the remote buttons.

◆ **Search for Chapter.** Allows chapter points to be accessed via the remote control.

◆ **Title Remote.** Enables the Title button on a remote control.

◆ **Menu Remote.** Enables the Menu button on a remote control.

◆ **Change Audio track.** Enables the Audio Track button on a remote control.

◆ **Change Subtitle Tracks.** Enables the Subtitle Track button on the remote control.

◆ **Change Presentation Mode.** Enables the viewer to change the aspect ratio of the DVD player.

◆ **Resume.** In a menu, allows the viewer to jump back to the previous timeline by using the Menu key on the remote control.

◆ **Arrow and Enter Keys.** Enables the arrow and enter keys on a remote control.

◆ **Play Timeline.** Allows a viewer to access a timeline with the remote control.

◆ **Play Chapter.** Allows the viewer to directly access a chapter anywhere on the disc by typing in its title and number.

◆ **Search for Chapter.** Allows the viewer to directly access a chapter in the current title by typing in its number.

SETTING USER OPERATIONS CONTROLS

Setting the Title Button Link

DVD players have three primary remote controls (**Figure 6.10**): the Title button, the Menu button, and the arrow buttons.

The Title button is generally used by the viewer to return to the beginning of the DVD. It is usually linked to the main menu of the DVD.

Figure 6.10 A very basic DVD remote control setup.

To set the link for the Title button:

1. With the Properties palette open, select the Disc tab in the Project window.

   The Disc properties are displayed in the Properties palette.

2. *Do one of the following:*

   ▲ Click the Title Button pop-up menu and select a timeline or menu from the list (**Figure 6.11**).

   ▲ Click the pickwhip icon in the Title Button pop-up menu and drag it to the timeline or menu you want (**Figure 6.12**).

   With either method, the selected menu or timeline appears as a destination in the Disc Properties Title Button menu (**Figure 6.13**).

✔ Tips

■ Only the 20 most recent items appear in the menu list, so you may need to use the Specify Other option from the pop-up menu.

■ If you have no First Play set in your project, you can link a menu or timeline to the Title button. When the DVD is inserted in the player, a blank screen is displayed. The viewer can click the Title button on the DVD remote to begin viewing.

Figure 6.11 Setting the Title Button link using the pop-up menu method.

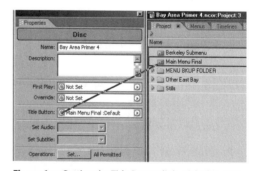

Figure 6.12 Setting the Title Button link, pickwhip style.

Figure 6.13 The Title Button link is set.

Figure 6.14 Setting the Menu Button (Menu Remote) link in the pop-up manner...

Setting the Menu Button Link

The viewer uses the Menu button to interrupt playback of a timeline and return to the previous menu. Unlike the Title button, which is only set once, the Menu button link is set in the Properties palette of each timeline.

To set the link for the Menu button:

1. With the Properties palette open, select a timeline in the Project or Timelines tab.

   The properties of the selected timeline appear in the Properties palette.

2. *Do one of the following:*

   ▲ Click the Menu Remote pop-up menu and select the menu or timeline you want to be accessed when the Menu button on a remote control is pressed (**Figure 6.14**).

   ▲ Click the pickwhip icon in the pop-up menu and point to the item you want to be accessed when the Menu button on a remote control is pressed (**Figure 6.15**).

✔ Tip

■ A great shortcut is to choose Return to Last Menu from the Menu Remote pop-up menu. This saves the effort of searching for and specifying a particular menu in the list.

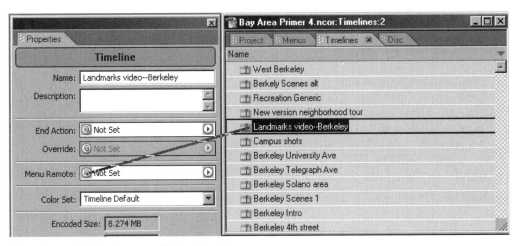

Figure 6.15 ...and doing the same with the pickwhip.

Setting Button Routing Preferences

DVD-player remote controls are sprouting more and more buttons and functions, but their ability to select buttons on the screen is still generally limited to a series of vertical and horizontal movements with four arrow keys.

To help you make the most of DVD remote-control capabilities, Encore DVD has some automatic routing patterns available in its project preferences settings (**Figure 6.16**). For most projects, the default button-routing settings will be satisfactory, but they can be adjusted to meet your needs.

Here's what you should know about using and modifying the automatic routing preferences:

◆ When you open the preferences settings for menus, the Preferences dialog presents you with four check box choices and two pop-up menus. The various combinations of these selections allow you to control the routing and wrapping of a remote control's arrow key movements among your onscreen buttons. The default setting is for all the check box selections to be in their active—checked—state.

◆ If you happen to uncheck the Route up/down selection, you disable the up and down arrow keys on a user's remote control. He or she won't be able to use those keys to navigate your menus. Unchecking the Route left/right selection yields similar results—it disables the left and right arrow keys on a DVD player's remote control (none of these sound like good ideas, do they?).

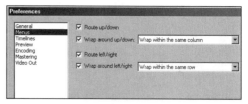

Figure 6.16 Setting automatic button routing patterns.

Figure 6.17 The default routing: left to right, then wrapping to the beginning of the same row.

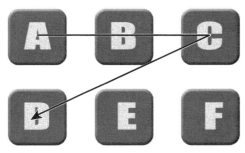

Figure 6.18 Moving left to right, but then wrapping to the next row.

Figure 6.19 Routing top to bottom, then wrapping back to the top of the same column.

Figure 6.20 Routing top to bottom, but then wrapping to the next column.

◆ The Wrap around check boxes control what happens when you reach the end of a row or column with the remote control's arrow keys. With one or both of the Wrap around selections turned off (unchecked), you are stopped when you reach the end of a row or column (or both). With the selections turned on (checked), you can "overshoot" the end of a row or column, and you will be returned ("wrapped around") to the beginning of the row or column.

◆ The final variable controls the type of wrap that is applied. The pop-up menus on the Wrap around selections allow you to select whether your movement will be wrapped around to the beginning of the same column or row, or to the beginning of the next column or row.

For a graphic example of how these routing selections work, see **Figures 6.17** to **6.20**.

To select an automatic routing preference:

1. Choose Edit > Preferences > Menus.
   The Menu Preferences dialog appears.

2. Select the routing and/or wrapping preferences from the Menu Preferences dialog (**Figure 6.21**).

3. Click OK.

✔ Tips

- The settings you establish in the Menu Preferences can be enabled or disabled by the state of the Automatically Route Buttons option in a menu's Properties palette.

- Generally, if you allow the user to wrap to the next column or row, it allows them to use one button to access all buttons on the menu. If you wrap back to the same column or row, they have to use two buttons. Unless you have a good reason for the latter, the former is a better alternative.

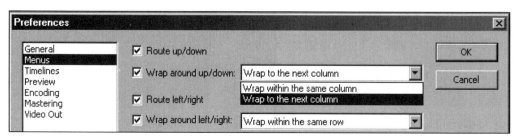

Figure 6.21 Selecting a new setting to control the wrap-around characteristics in a menu.

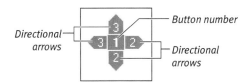

Figure 6.22 A close-up of the Routing icon, a close cousin of the pickwhip.

Customizing Button Routing

There may be times when automatic routing patterns don't allow the viewer to navigate the buttons as you've laid them out in your menu. This situation can come up when button placement does not follow a simple left/right and up/down grid.

In situations like this, you can override the automatic button routing-and-wrapping settings and set a specific path through your buttons. The tool you use to manually set the button routing pattern is the Routing icon, found in the Menu Editor. It's easy to use, working something like the pickwhip tool in the Properties palette (**Figure 6.22**).

To customize button routing:

1. With the Properties palette open, open a menu from the Project window.

   The Menu Editor opens and the menu properties are displayed in the Properties palette (**Figure 6.23**).

continues on next page

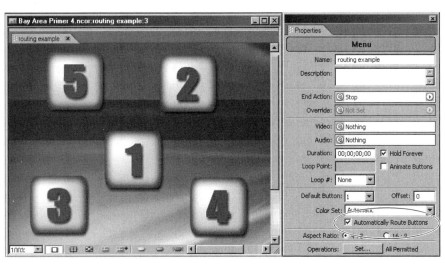

Figure 6.23 First stop in customizing the button routing pattern for a menu.

185

2. Deselect the Automatically Route Buttons option in the Properties palette.

3. In the Monitor window, click the Show Button Routing button (**Figure 6.24**).

In the Menu Editor, a routing icon is displayed for each button (**Figure 6.25**).

4. Click on an arrow (up, down, right, or left) on a button's routing icon, and drag to the button you want to be next in the routing order when the user presses that arrow key on the remote (**Figure 6.26**).

In this example, the routing has just been set so that, from button 1, a remote control's down arrow key would take the user to button 3. (Or, also from button 1, a right arrow key selection would take you to button 4, an up arrow key would go to button 2, and a left arrow key would take you to button 5.) The routing pattern for each button can be seen when the routing icon is displayed (**Figure 6.27**).

5. Repeat the previous step until you have set the routing pattern for all the buttons you want to change.

Figure 6.24 Turning on the Show Button Routing display in the Menu Editor.

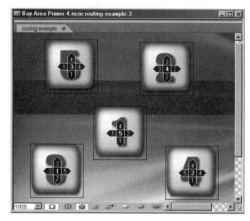

Figure 6.25 Each button has a routing icon displayed.

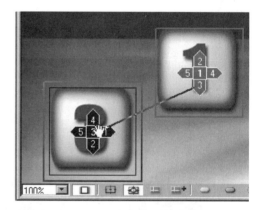

Figure 6.26 Just as with the pickwhip, you can establish custom routing patterns with a click and a drag.

Figure 6.27 Each button's routing pattern can be displayed.

Using the Auto Activate Function

The typical design of a menu requires that button activation take two steps: the viewer first navigates with the arrow keys on a remote control to select a button, then presses Enter on the remote control to activate it. You can, however, set a button to activate as soon as it is selected.

To set a button to Auto Activate:

1. With the Properties palette open, open a menu from the Project window.

   The Menu Editor opens and the menu's properties are displayed in the Properties palette (**Figure 6.28**).

continues on next page

Figure 6.28 The first step in setting Auto Activate for a button.

2. Using the Selection tool in the Menu Editor, click the button you have selected for auto activation (**Figure 6.29**).

3. In the Properties palette, set the button's link with the pickwhip or pop-up menu and click the Auto Activate option (**Figure 6.30**).

   The button will now execute its link as soon as it is selected with a remote control's navigation keys. The user needn't press the Enter key.

✔ Tip

- The Auto Activate function can also be used to streamline movement through menus. If you have several menus that can be navigated with a Next button, you could set that button to Auto Activate, so the viewer can move to the next menu as soon as Next is selected, rather than requiring use of the Enter command on the remote control each time.

Figure 6.29 Selecting the button that will have Auto Activate enabled.

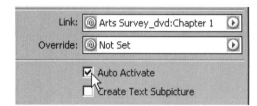

Figure 6.30 The button's link is set and the Auto Activate setting is enabled.

About Transcoding

As you may recall from Chapter 2, transcoding is the process Encore DVD uses to convert your project's non-MPEG-2 video assets (QuickTime and AVI files) into MPEG-2 files, which it then writes to disc. Encore DVD also must put any other non-DVD-compliant assets into a DVD-compliant form. Assets that are already in MPEG-2 format do not have to be transcoded.

The transcoding process is a bit complex, but you don't have to deal with the complexity unless you want to. Here are your options:

◆ Transcoding can be managed by Encore DVD automatically, for users unfamiliar with management of MPEG and audio compression parameters.

◆ For more experienced users, Encore DVD provides DVD-compliant transcode presets, customized for several different quality and storage settings. Or you can fully customize and save your own transcoding settings.

◆ Also, for more experienced users, Encore DVD offers the ability to apply filters for noise reduction and de-interlacing of video fields as "pre-encode" tasks, to give more control over the picture quality within Encore DVD's transcoding process.

◆ You can select and transcode assets at any time during the project, or let Encore DVD transcode assets when it builds the DVD.

✔ Tip

■ Transcoding presets and custom settings can be applied to each individual asset at any time. If a transcoded version of a file is available, Encore DVD uses that version for authoring, previewing, and building. If no transcoded version is available, Encore uses the original file for authoring and previewing, and will transcode the files as necessary when building the DVD.

ABOUT TRANSCODING

Transcoding Assets

The Project tab has several columns describing the transcode status, file size, and so on of your assets (**Figure 6.31**). Assets in the Project tab will have one of the following designations in the Transcode Settings and Transcode Status columns:

◆ **Automatic.** This is the default setting for all non-DVD-compliant video and audio assets (file types such as AVI, WAV, etc.). Encore DVD will determine optimal transcoding settings based on the number, length, and file sizes of your assets, and the available disc space. See the Appendix for bit-budget information.

You can specify a transcode preset to replace the default setting for any asset at any time.

◆ **[*Transcode preset name*].** If you select a preset from the project's preferences settings or a custom transcode setting, the setting name will appear in the Transcode Settings column.

Name	Transcode Settings	Transcode Status ▼	Size	Type	Bitrate
🔊 Final Mix--Alt..wav	Automatic	Untranscoded	2.884 MB	WAV audio	0.2 Mbps
🔊 Spanish Final mix.wav	Automatic	Untranscoded	12.47 MB	WAV audio	0.2 Mbps
🔊 Spanish Overvu.wav	Automatic	Untranscoded	34.71 MB	WAV audio	0.2 Mbps
🔊 East Bay 30.wav	Automatic	Untranscoded	2.884 MB	WAV audio	0.2 Mbps
🔊 Neighborhoods vo.wav	Automatic	Untranscoded	34.71 MB	WAV audio	0.2 Mbps
🔊 Berkeley Theme.wav	Automatic	Untranscoded	12.47 MB	WAV audio	0.2 Mbps
🔊 East Bay 30.wav	Automatic	Untranscoded	2.884 MB	WAV audio	0.2 Mbps
🔊 Alternate mix.wav	Automatic	Untranscoded	34.71 MB	WAV audio	0.2 Mbps
🔊 Final Mix Spanish.wav	Automatic	Untranscoded	12.47 MB	WAV audio	0.2 Mbps
🎞 Berkeley Intro.AVI	Automatic	Untranscoded	1 GB	AVI video	8.4 Mbps
🎞 Recreation Generic.mov	NTSC DV Low quality 4M...	Transcoded	478.7 MB	Video file	4.2 Mbps
🎞 Berkeley Scenes 1.mov	NTSC DV Low quality 4M...	Transcoded	596.8 MB	Video file	4.2 Mbps
🎞 Berkeley Neighborhoods.mov	NTSC DV Low quality 4M...	Transcoded	1.013 GB	Video file	4.2 Mbps
🎞 Advanced Tour 1.mov	NTSC DV Low quality 4M...	Transcoded	298.5 MB	Video file	4.2 Mbps
🎞 Arts Survey_dvd.m2v	N/A	Don't Transcode	8.042 MB	MPEG video	5.8 Mbps
🎞 Arts Survey_dvd-001.m2v	N/A	Don't Transcode	11.61 MB	MPEG video	5.9 Mbps
▷ 📁 MENU BKUP FOLDER	N/A	--	--	Folder	--
▷ 📁 Other East Bay	N/A	--	--	Folder	--
▷ 📁 Stills	N/A	--	--	Folder	--

Figure 6.31 Note all the different flavors of transcoding shown in the Project tab.

- ◆ **Don't Transcode.** This designation is assigned to those assets that are already DVD-compliant. You can override this setting and specify Automatic or another transcode setting if you wish. However, Encore will then retranscode the asset, which may degrade quality, so avoid this if possible. Retranscoding to squeeze assets onto a very full disc would be one (rare) reason to change this setting.

- ◆ **Transcoded.** This is the designation for those assets already transcoded into a DVD-compliant format. You can return these assets to their original file formats, if you wish.

- ◆ **N/A.** This is displayed for items such as menus, timelines, and still image files that don't require transcoding.

✔ Tips

- ■ When Encore DVD transcodes a file, the asset in the Project tab now "points" to the transcoded copy of the asset (stored in the project's Transcodes folder). As long as you retain the original source, you can right-click and choose Revert to Original to point back to the original source. This can be useful if you want to change the settings and "re-transcode" an asset from its original source.

- ■ The Project and Timelines tabs and the Properties palette also have information about size of your assets, both before and after transcoding.

To assign a transcode setting to an asset:

1. In the Project tab, right-click the asset you want to transcode and choose a transcode preset from the contextual menu (**Figure 6.32**).

2. The selected preset now appears in the Transcode Settings column for that asset (**Figure 6.33**).

✔ Tip

■ The Transcode presets will be displayed only for assets that require transcoding. If you select an asset that has Transcoded, Don't Transcode, or N/A in its Transcode Settings column, the preset selections will be grayed out in the contextual menu.

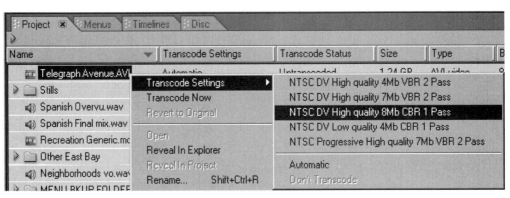

Figure 6.32 Choosing a transcode preset from the list...

Figure 6.33 ...puts it in the settings column for the selected clip.

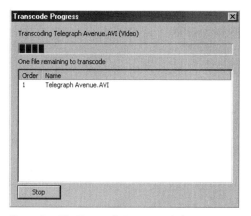

Figure 6.34 The Transcode Progress window.

To transcode an asset:

◆ In the Project tab, right-click the asset you want to transcode and choose Transcode Now from the contextual menu.

The Transcode Progress window appears (**Figure 6.34**).

When the transcoding process is complete, the asset's Transcode Settings column says Transcoded (**Figure 6.35**).

✔ Tips

■ The Transcode Now function will be grayed out if the asset does not require transcoding.

■ You can select several assets and transcode them simultaneously. Each can have a different transcode preset, if you wish.

■ You can cancel the transcoding process by clicking Stop in the Transcode Progress window.

■ Transcoding assets is a background function, so you can continue working in Encore DVD while assets are being transcoded. The exception to this is during the import of QuickTime files and/or files with progressive video (see the sidebar). Transcoding of these files occurs on import, and is not a background function.

TRANSCODING ASSETS

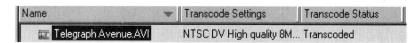

Figure 6.35 The end result of the transcode process.

A Note on Progressive Video

As you may recall from way back in Chapter 2, the DVD spec can accommodate a large number of frame rates. In addition to the plain vanilla NTSC rate of 29.97 fps (frames per second), you can use NTSC sources which have a frame rate of 24, 23.976, or 23.98 fps. These video variants use *progressive* rather than *interlaced* frames. (For convenience, I'll lump the various progressive frame rates into the category that is commonly known as *24p*: 24 progressive frames per second.) To very briefly describe the difference, in traditional TV, each frame consists of two fields. Each field has half of the video information. In one field, the odd lines in a TV screen are scanned. In the other field, the even lines are scanned, and this *interlaced scan* happens so fast (about 1/60th of a second for each field) that the human eye blends them together into a single picture.

Film and computer screens work with *progressive* frames—all of the picture information in a frame is presented all at once rather than in two interlaced halves. As you probably know, some video cameras and TV screens can now operate in either interlaced or progressive modes. Without getting into all the pros and cons of each mode, the general idea is that progressive frames have more detail and resolution, which is why the 24p format is becoming more common. Here's what you need to know for your DVD project:

◆ Even if your source material is 24 progressive frames per second, the DVD standard still insists that it be written to disc in such a way that it can be displayed at the standard NTSC TV rate of 29.97 interlaced frames per second.

◆ To conform to this standard, Encore DVD will transcode any 24p source video immediately upon import. You will be given a choice of transcode presets (more about these in this chapter), and no matter which one you choose, Encore DVD will automatically store the 24p source in a way that will enable it to work in *both* an older DVD player/TV set combination that can only play interlaced video, *and* a newer DVD player/TV set that can play progressive video. How does that work? Again, very briefly, while the DVD standard is designed to support the millions of existing interlaced TV sets and DVD players, it also employs "Flags" embedded into the video file that enable a progressive-capable DVD player to re-create and play the source's original 24 progressive frames.

◆ So, although it is good to be aware of whether your sources originate in a progressive or interlaced format, the bottom line for working with Encore DVD is that it can accommodate both, and even allows you to mix them together in the same project.

◆ While there are fewer frame rate variants in PAL and the specifics of how the progressive video frames are "flagged" is different, in general, the interlaced/progressive discussion in this chapter applies to PAL projects in Encore DVD, as well.

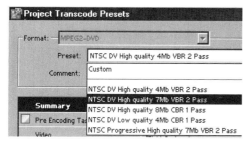

Figure 6.36 There are several default presets to choose from in Encore DVD. (PAL projects have PAL presets.)

Working with Transcode Presets

There are many custom transcoding options available in Encore DVD, and there are a couple of approaches to dealing with these options:

◆ You can select an existing transcode preset from a list in the project preferences.

◆ You can modify the parameters of a transcode setting, and save and recall, or delete, these custom transcode presets.

See the next sidebar for information on the video and audio parameters that can be modified and the controls you can use to adjust them.

To view the parameters of a transcode preset:

1. Choose File > Transcode > Edit Project Transcoding Presets.

   The Project Transcode Presets dialog appears.

2. Choose a preset from the Preset pop-up menu (**Figure 6.36**).

   All the preset's parameters appear in the Summary window (**Figure 6.37**).

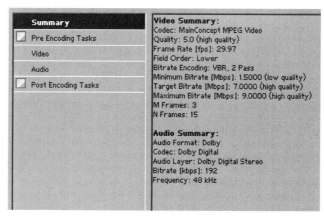

Figure 6.37 Here is a summary of the parameters of the selected preset.

To create a custom transcode preset:

1. Choose Custom from the Preset pop-up menu in the Project Transcode Presets dialog.

2. Choose either Video or Audio to bring up the appropriate parameter controls.

   The parameter controls appear (**Figure 6.38**).

3. Modify the parameters as needed.

4. Click OK.

   The Choose Name dialog appears (**Figure 6.39**).

5. Type a name for the custom preset and click OK.

✔ Tips

- Default presets cannot be modified, saved, or deleted. If you have one selected and begin adjusting parameters, Encore DVD automatically changes the selection to Custom (although it does not change the information in the default preset's description field—you will have to do that yourself).

- When working with progressive video sources, Encore DVD transcodes the asset on import into the project. (See the sidebar for more information on progressive and interlaced video sources.)

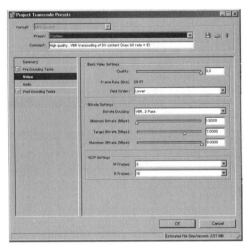

Figure 6.38 The video parameters, ready for adjustment.

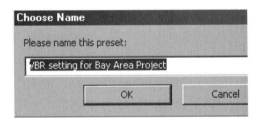

Figure 6.39 After you have created a custom preset, you can name and save it.

- By default, Encore DVD employs a preset optimized for progressive video. It can mix different progressive frame rates in the same project, and transcodes each one independently. If you import several assets with different progressive frame rates, then cancel the transcode process for one of them, Encore DVD will continue transcoding the other assets.

  In NTSC projects, Encore DVD can accommodate video assets in 24, 23.976, and 23.98 progressive frames per second.

- Assets that are not in use and are set to Automatic can't be transcoded using the Transcode Now function. (Because they haven't yet been put on timelines, Encore DVD isn't able to estimate how these assets will fit in with all the others in its bit budget.) You need to either place each asset on a timeline or apply a transcode preset to it before using Transcode Now.

- To save a custom preset, you can also use the Save Preset button in the Project Transcode Presets window (**Figure 6.40**).

  Transcode presets are saved by default to the Documents and Settings folder on your C drive.

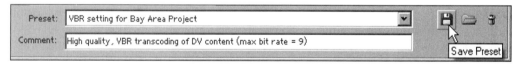

Figure 6.40 Another method for saving a custom preset.

197

Transcode Preset Parameters

You have a great deal of control over transcoding settings via the Transcode Preset dialog. Have a look at the options available for both video and audio (**Figures 6.41** and **6.42**).

The parameters you can adjust to balance the quality of your project against your storage requirements include the following:

Preset options for video

◆ **Quality.** Determines the quality of the transcoding. Quality levels range from 1 to 5, with higher numbers representing better quality—and increased transcoding time.

◆ **Frame Rate.** Displays the output frame rate for either NTSC or PAL format.

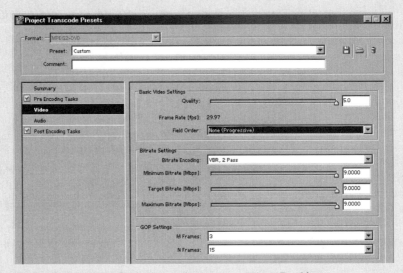

Figure 6.41 The controls for the transcode preset parameters. For video…

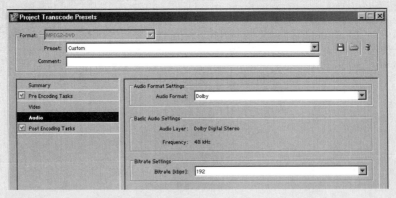

Figure 6.42 …and for audio.

Transcode Preset Parameters *(continued)*

◆ **Field Order.** Specifies the field order for both interlaced and progressive scan media.

◆ **Bitrate Encoding.** Specifies the type of compression: constant bit rate (CBR) or variable bit rate (VBR). Also establishes whether VBR will be 1 pass or 2. "2-pass" encoding means that the computer will analyze the video stream twice for greater precision in the encoding process (which will, obviously, take about twice as long).

◆ **Bitrate Controls.** VBR only. Specifies minimum, maximum, and target values for encoding. While the maximum bit rate can be set to 9.0 Mbps, setting it at this level is not recommended, as it will tax the capabilities of DVD players, while not necessarily improving picture quality.

◆ **M Frames.** Specifies the number of predicted frames between reference frames in a GOP (group of pictures, in MPEG).

◆ **N Frames.** Specifies the GOP size, in frames.

Preset options for audio

◆ **Audio Format Settings.** Specifies the codec used to compress the audio. The options in the Audio Format Settings pop-up menu are:

▲ **Dolby.** Dolby Digital. The most common encoder for DVD-Video. Supports surround sound.

▲ **MPEG.** MPEG-1, Layer II stereo format.

▲ **PCM (Pulse-Code Modulation) Audio.** Uncompressed audio format, resulting in large files. Supports surround sound.

◆ **Bitrate.** Specifies the audio output bitrate for Dolby and MPEG formats.

Note that NTSC DVDs must use either the PCM Audio or Dolby Digital format. They cannot contain only MPEG audio.

✔ Tips

■ In most cases, the default settings available in Encore DVD will deliver all the quality you'll need. However, you may find it useful to create a preset with a particular data rate in some situations. If you want to go deeper, Encore DVD offers a lot of custom controls, and you should feel free to experiment with them. However, don't try to use them in a real-world situation until you are confident with your "compressionist" skills.

■ Dolby Digital audio is the only compressed format that must be available on DVD players shipped in the United States. MPEG audio is usually supported, but not universally. If you have to compress to fit the audio on the disc, use Dolby Digital.

WORKING WITH TRANSCODE PRESETS

To export a transcode preset:

1. Alt-click on the Save Preset button in the Project Transcode Presets window.

   The Export Preset dialog appears (**Figure 6.43**).

2. Navigate to the folder you want and then name and save the preset.

To import a preset:

1. In the Project Transcode Presets window, click on the Import Preset button (**Figure 6.44**).

   The Import Preset dialog appears (**Figure 6.45**).

2. Navigate to the location of the preset, select it, and click Open.

   The Choose Name dialog appears (**Figure 6.46**).

3. Type a name for the preset and click OK.

   The preset is added to the list in the Project Transcode Presets window.

Figure 6.43 You can also choose to export a preset to a particular location.

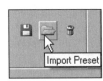

Figure 6.44 Presets can be imported into a project as well by clicking this button, then...

Figure 6.45 ... navigating to a folder, and...

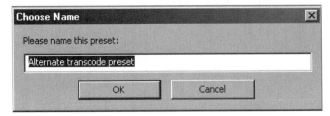

Figure 6.46 ... naming the imported preset.

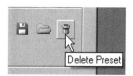

Figure 6.47 To dump a preset, just click on the trash can...

To delete a custom preset:

1. In the Project Transcode Presets window, select the preset you want to delete.

2. Click the Delete Preset button (**Figure 6.47**).

   The Delete Preset dialog appears (**Figure 6.48**).

3. Click OK to confirm the deletion.

✔ Tip

- To delete all custom presets, simply Ctrl-Alt-click the Delete Preset button. Click OK to confirm the deletion.

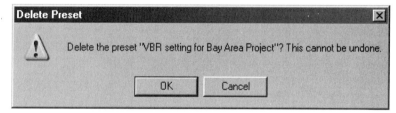

Figure 6.48 ...and confirm that you want to get rid of it.

Using Pre- and Post-Encoding Tasks

Another set of parameters you can adjust in the transcode presets are pre- and post-encoding tasks. These are, as you might surmise, changes you can make to an asset either before or after it is transcoded. These tasks are accessed through the project's Transcode Presets window.

In the pre-encode category, you have two choices:

◆ **Video Noise Reduction.** This task enables you to apply a noise-reduction filter to your video before it is transcoded to MPEG-2. A generic thumbnail is displayed to allow you to apply different levels of noise reduction and get an idea of the results in terms of picture sharpness—the more noise reduction applied, the softer the picture (**Figure 6.49**).

Figure 6.49 A look at the interface for applying noise reduction as a pre-encode task.

◆ **De-interlace.** This setting gives Encore DVD the task of "pulling apart" interlaced fields of a video asset prior to transcoding to MPEG-2 (**Figure 6.50**).

Both these tasks are intended to allow you to optimize picture quality as the asset is transcoded into MPEG-2. This optimization comes at a price—the transcoding will take appreciably longer. For best results, test these settings on a short piece of representative video to make sure you have the look you want and then apply the appropriate setting to the asset you'll use in the project.

In the post-encoding task category, you can instruct Encore DVD to create a text log file with information about the transcoded asset and store it with the asset in the project's Transcodes folder. In the post-encode dialog, you can choose what kind of information you'd like included in the log file.

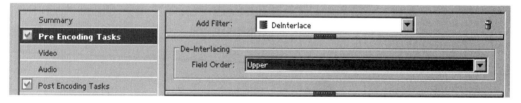

Figure 6.50 A close-up of the de-interlace task controls.

To set up a pre-encoding task:

1. Choose File > Transcode > Edit Project Transcode Presets.

2. Select the transcode preset you want to add a task to from the pop-up menu (**Figure 6.51**).

3. Check the Pre Encoding Tasks selection (**Figure 6.52**).

   The Pre Encode settings pane appears (**Figure 6.53**).

4. *Do one of the following:*

   ▲ From the Add Filter pop-up menu, choose Noise Reduction.

   ▲ From the Add Filter pop-up menu, choose De-Interlace.

   The appropriate controls for the selected filter appear.

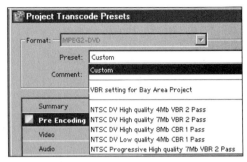

Figure 6.51 To set up a pre-encoding task, first select a transcode preset...

Figure 6.52 ...then put a checkmark in the task selector...

Figure 6.53 ...and the Pre-Encode settings pane appears.

USING PRE- AND POST-ENCODING TASKS

Figure 6.54 You can set a level for noise reduction with a slider in the settings pane.

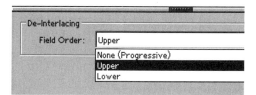

Figure 6.55 The parameters for de-interlacing are just a click away.

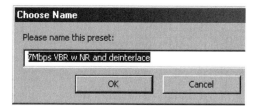

Figure 6.56 Name the preset and remember to indicate any tasks you've embedded in it.

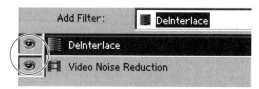

Figure 6.57 You can turn either of these filters on or off with the "eye" selector.

5. Set a level for the Video Noise Reduction task by moving the slider in the settings pane (**Figure 6.54**).

The scale extends from minimum to maximum noise reduction on a scale of 0–100. The video thumbnail at the bottom of the main pre-encoding task pane updates to show the approximate effect of the selected level of noise reduction.

6. Select the parameters for De-Interlace by clicking the pop-up menu (**Figure 6.55**). Set the field order that is appropriate for the asset.

Choose None if your asset is from a progressive video source. Choose upper or lower field order if your asset is from an interlaced video source.

7. Click OK. The Choose Name dialog appears (**Figure 6.56**).

8. Type a name for the custom transcode preset plus filter settings you've created and click OK.

This will now appear in the list of transcode presets in your project.

✔ Tips

■ You can apply either or both filters to an asset. Select which filter is active by clicking its display/hide "eye" selector (**Figure 6.57**).

■ The settings pane actually consists of three smaller panes, displaying the filter selection pop-up, the filter adjustment contols, and the thumbnail. You can resize any of the panes by clicking and dragging with the mouse.

To set up a post-encoding task:

1. Follow steps 1 and 2 of the previous task.

2. Check the Post Encoding Tasks selection (**Figure 6.58**).

   The Post Encoding settings pane appears (**Figure 6.59**).

3. Click the Log File Details button (**Figure 6.60**).

4. From the list, check the details to include in Encore DVD's log file for that transcode preset.

5. Click OK.

   The Choose Name dialog appears.

6. Follow step 8 from the previous task.

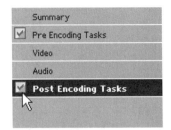

Figure 6.58 The first step in establishing post-encoding tasks...

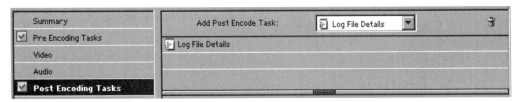

Figure 6.59 ...brings up step two, the Post Encoding settings pane.

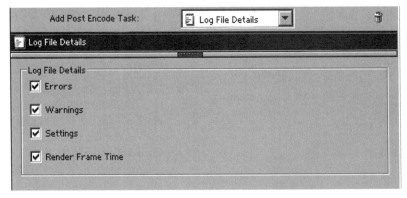

Figure 6.60 You can select what information you want to have displayed in a log.

✔ Tips

- You can apply both pre- and post-encoding tasks to an asset, if you'd like.

- Be sure to note in the name of the presets you create what pre- and post-encoding tasks you've embedded.

- The log file that is created as part of the Log File Details task looks something like **Figure 6.61**. It is stored with the transcoded file in Encore DVD's Transcoded folder.

- While at the moment there are only a few pre-and post-encoding tasks available, it sure looks like there is a lot of room in the settings pane to add capability in the future.

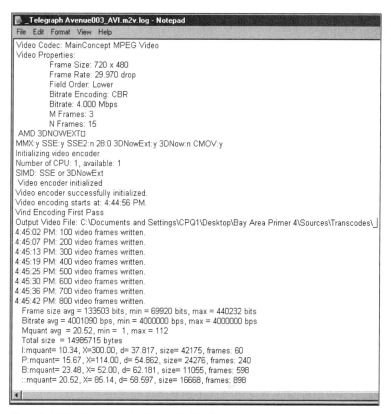

Figure 6.61 Here's an example of an actual log file.

Checking a Project

After going through all the work in the previous chapters, it is almost time to burn your project to DVD. But first, you'll want to make sure that all the pieces in your project really are going to work together as planned. Encore DVD's Check Project function will analyze your project to make sure there are no problems that will interfere with building the final DVD. You don't need to wait until the end of the project to do this; you can run Check Project at any time. Check Project looks for errors and problems in the following categories:

◆ **Button Links.** Checks for links that are not specified or that point to missing timelines, buttons, or menus.

◆ **End Actions.** Checks for invalid or un-set end actions.

◆ **Overrides.** Checks for invalid override links.

◆ **First Play.** Checks that a first play action is present and valid.

◆ **Title Remote.** Verifies that the title remote selection in the Properties palette for Menus and for the disc is set and valid.

◆ **Menu Remote.** Verifies that the menu remote selection in the Properties palette for timelines is set and valid.

◆ **Orphans.** Searches for menus or timelines created in the project, but without any links to them. (Finding and eliminating orphan timelines is especially important, as they will still be included—and will take up valuable space—when Encore DVD writes the project to disc.)

◆ **Playlists.** Checks that all playlists are populated and valid.

◆ **Button Overlap.** Identifies buttons that overlap in menus, which makes it difficult for the viewer to make a clear selection.

◆ **Total Size Of Menus.** The DVD spec has a limit of 1 GB per menu "class." Menus created with different aspect ratios or with different audio formats are separated into distinct classes. Check Project warns you if you go over this limit in your menu size.

◆ **Disc Capacity.** Checks that the size of the project matches the capacity of the selected disc.

◆ **Timeline Bitrate Too High.** Identifies timelines in which the combined video, audio, and subtitle bit rates will exceed the DVD limit. To reduce the bitrate, you can either lower the data rate by modifying the transcoding preset of the timeline or remove tracks or clips from the timeline. (More about this in the Appendix).

◆ **Chapters and Trims.** If Encore DVD had to make any adjustments to chapter point placement or trims as it transcoded a timeline's video asset to MPEG-2, it will be reported here.

◆ **Subtitle Text Overflow.** Identifies subtitle text that is truncated in the subtitle text box and will not appear on screen. You can modify the specified text to fit it all in the text box or increase the size of the box to fit the text.

CHECKING A PROJECT

To check a project:

1. Choose File > Check Project (**Figure 6.62**). The Check Project dialog appears (**Figure 6.63**).

2. Click Start.

   Encore DVD performs a check on all categories selected in the dialog and lists any problems found in the bottom pane of the Check Project dialog (**Figure 6.64**).

✔ Tip

- By default, Encore DVD will check all the categories for possible problems. To save time, you can deselect any categories you do not want to check. For instance, if you have no playlists or subtitles in your project, Encore DVD does not have to perform a check on them. However, Adobe recommends that you leave this dialog in its default state, just so you don't miss any potential problem.

Figure 6.62 Time to run a check on the project.

Figure 6.63 The Check Project dialog, ready to start.

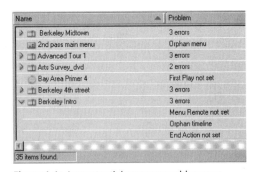

Figure 6.64 Any potential errors or problems are listed in the bottom pane.

CHECKING A PROJECT

Fixing Links

Once Encore DVD has identified problematic links, you'll want to go in and fix them.

To fix a broken or unset link:

1. Select the menu, button, or timeline listed in the Check Project dialog.

2. Open the Properties palette (**Figure 6.65**). The name of the problematic link is displayed in red in the Properties palette.

3. Using the pop-up menu or pickwhip, select a valid destination for the link (**Figure 6.66**).

continues on next page

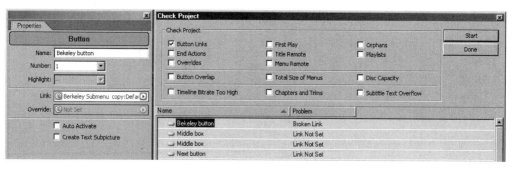

Figure 6.65 The Properties palette for a broken link is opened.

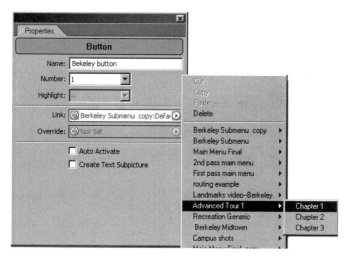

Figure 6.66 Fixing the broken link by navigating to a valid destination.

FIXING LINKS

The link's destination is updated in the Properties palette and the Project window tabs (**Figure 6.67**).

4. Repeat the process until all of the broken links or links not set are corrected.

5. Click Done.

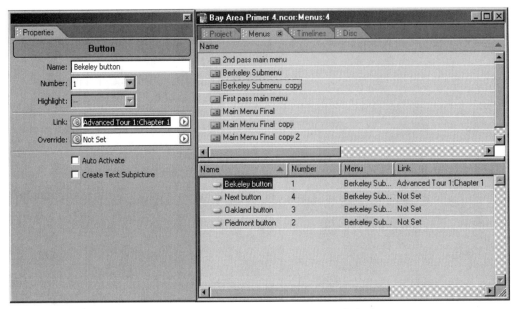

Figure 6.67 The valid link can now be seen in the Properties palette and the tab database.

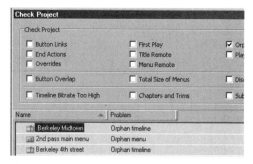

Figure 6.68 Check Project can also locate orphan timelines and menus.

Figure 6.69 A button has been selected to link to an orphan timeline.

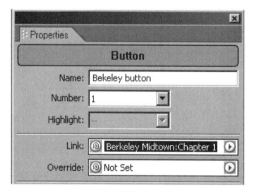

Figure 6.70 Now that everything is lined up, the former orphan is displayed in the button's Link pop-up menu.

To fix orphan timelines and menus:

1. In the Check Project dialog, click the box for Orphans (**Figure 6.68**).

2. Click Start.

   If orphans are detected, they are displayed in the dialog.

3. Determine which item in the project (button, timeline, or menu) should link *to* the orphan.

4. With the Properties palette open, select the item in a Project window tab.

   The item is displayed in the Properties palette (**Figure 6.69**).

5. Using the pickwhip or the pop-up menu in the Properties palette, select the orphan as a destination.

   The former orphan's name appears as a destination in the pop-up menu (**Figure 6.70**).

6. Repeat the process until all the orphans are properly linked.

7. Click Done.

✔ Tip

- Encore DVD will include orphaned items when it builds your project to disc. This can take up valuable space, especially in the case of orphaned timelines, so it is a good idea to find and fix any orphaned items before you finish your project.

Preparing for Final Output

By now, you've done all the work outlined in the previous chapters. You've previewed the project, fixed any bad links, and made sure your orphans have been successfully adopted. You've also set your transcoding options (or left them in their default settings).

There are just a few more things to do before you build your final DVD-compliant file. For best results, you'll want to check your project settings in the Disc tab and adjust them if necessary.

You also can add other files to your DVD—related documents, images, software applications—that will be accessible on a PC via Windows Explorer.

To check and adjust disc parameter settings:

1. Select the Disc tab in the Project window (**Figure 6.71**).

2. Verify that the disc name is correct. Select the name box and type a new name if necessary.

3. Click the Project Settings button. The Project Settings dialog appears (**Figure 6.72**).

4. Confirm that the disc size (and side, if you are creating a dual-sided disc) in the Disc Information pane is correct. Click on the pop-up menu and choose a new size if necessary (**Figure 6.73**).

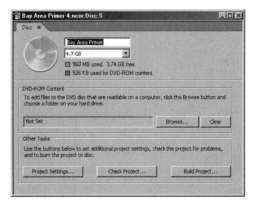

Figure 6.71 Getting ready to perform the last checks before building the disc.

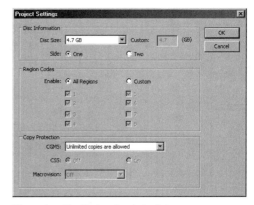

Figure 6.72 The Project Settings dialog.

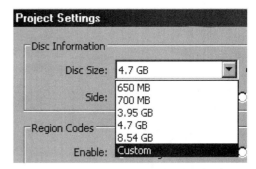

Figure 6.73 Verifying that the disc size is correct.

Figure 6.74 Checking the region code settings.

Figure 6.75 Checking the copy protection options.

5. Confirm that the region code matches the region in which your DVD will be distributed (**Figure 6.74**).

You can use region coding to restrict playback of your DVD to certain DVD players in certain countries. This allows you to control the legitimate distribution of your DVD and reduce piracy. Region coding is part of the DVD spec, which is why it is available here, but unless you are producing Hollywood-level content, you can pretty well ignore this and leave the All Regions setting selected.

6. Confirm your copy protection settings.

You can protect your DVD from being copied by choosing one of the types of copy protection available here.

With CGMS, you allow copies of your DVD to be made but set a limit on how many. CSS and Macrovision, respectively, prevent digital and analog copying of your DVD (**Figure 6.75**).

✔ Tips

- Encore DVD assigns a default name of DVD Volume to the disc. Assigning a specific name to the disc is recommended—it will be the name that is displayed when you build your final disc. You can also name the disc and add descriptive notes and comments about the disc in the Properties palette.

- Copy protection and region coding can *only* be used on discs that were saved as files to be replicated by mass production. Neither of these features can be encoded onto your disc with desktop DVD burners.

PREPARING FOR FINAL OUTPUT

215

Adding DVD-ROM Content

In addition to the video, audio, and image assets you have included in your DVD, you can add documents or other files that can be read only by a computer, not by a DVD player.

To add or archive DVD-ROM content:

1. Select the Disc tab in the Project window.

2. Click the Browse button in the DVD-ROM content pane.

   The Browse for Folder dialog appears (**Figure 6.76**).

3. Locate the content you want to add and click OK.

   The selected content appears in the DVD-ROM Content pane of the Disc tab (**Figure 6.77**).

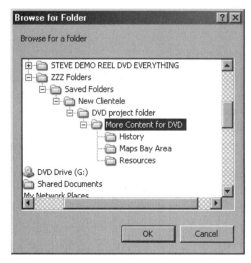

Figure 6.76 Locating the folder with the DVD-ROM content to include on the DVD.

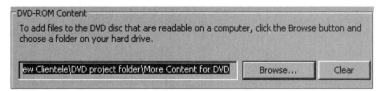

Figure 6.77 The selected folder appears in the DVD-ROM Content pane.

Figure 6.78 The available disc space updates to reflect any additional files added.

✔ Tips

■ The content you add will be accessible only via Windows Explorer.

■ Plan ahead and gather your content for inclusion on the DVD into one folder. The DVD-ROM Content pane can only reference one location at a time.

■ When you add DVD-ROM content, note the available disc space information on the top pane of the Disc tab (**Figure 6.78**). It will update to reflect any DVD-ROM content you add.

■ Encore DVD's bit budget will also take account of the space taken up by DVD-ROM content, which will affect accordingly the application's automatic transcode settings for the video and audio assets on the DVD.

Region Code Key

From www.dvddemystified.com/dvdfaq:

1 = U.S., Canada, U.S. Territories

2 = Japan, Europe, South Africa, and Middle East (including Egypt)

3 = Southeast Asia and East Asia (including Hong Kong)

4 = Australia, New Zealand, Pacific Islands, Central America, Mexico, South America, and the Caribbean

5 = Eastern Europe (Former Soviet Union), Indian subcontinent, Africa, North Korea, and Mongolia

6 = China

7 = Reserved

8 = Special international venues (airplanes, cruise ships, and so on). See the map at www.unik.no/~robert/hifi/dvd/world.html.

Making a DVD Disc

Now's the time to actually perform the final output and either burn a disc on your desktop or prepare a file that can be replicated for mass production.

There are four output options to choose from: Make DVD Disc, Make DVD Folder, Make DVD Image, and Make DVD Master.

You use the Make DVD Disc option to burn the production to your DVD recorder for playback on DVD players, PCs, or game consoles. See the sidebar for a discussion on burners and disc formats.

To make a DVD disc:

1. Choose File > Build DVD > Make DVD Disc.

   The Save Project dialog appears (**Figure 6.79**).

2. Click Save and Continue (or Save As, and name the saved copy). Encore DVD performs a Check Project function. If problems are encountered, a warning appears (**Figure 6.80**).

3. *Do one of the following:*

   ▲ Click Ignore and Continue to proceed to the next step.

   ▲ Click View to see the list of problems Encore DVD encountered.

4. If View is clicked, the Check Project dialog appears with the list of problems displayed (**Figure 6.81**).

5. *Do one of the following:*

   ▲ Follow the steps outlined earlier in the chapter to fix links, reunite orphans, and so on.

   When finished, start the Make DVD process over again from Step 1 above.

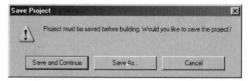

Figure 6.79 You can either save your current project or make a copy before moving on to building the DVD.

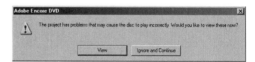

Figure 6.80 Encore DVD runs a check and reports on any potential problems.

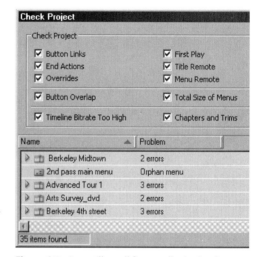

Figure 6.81 As you'll recall from earlier in the chapter, here's the Check Project dialog after it has scanned for problems and found a few.

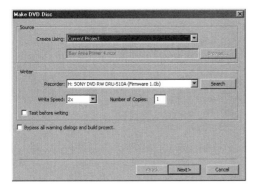

Figure 6.82 The Make DVD Disc dialog.

Figure 6.83 The Make DVD Disc: Summary window appears. This is the last stop before building the disc.

▲ Move on to the next step without fixing the reported problems by clicking Continue Build in the Check Project dialog.

6. The Make DVD Disc dialog appears (**Figure 6.82**). You have several options from which to choose in the following menus and windows:

▲ **Create Using.** Current Project appears by default. If you click the pop-up menu, you also can choose either DVD Volume or Disc Image as the file type, then browse for either file on your hard drive and write it to disc.

▲ **Recorder.** Specifies the DVD burner attached to your system, and which you will use to burn the project to disc. You also can use Search to scan and select another attached DVD burner.

▲ **Write Speed.** Click the pop-up menu to select from the write speeds available on the DVD burner.

▲ **Number of Copies.** Type the number of copies of the project you want to write to disc in the current session. If you ask for multiple copies, Encore DVD will prompt you to insert a new disc when each disc is complete.

▲ **Test before Writing.** If you check this box, Encore DVD will test the writing process, report any problems, and suspend the process if necessary. If no problems are detected, Encore writes to disc automatically.

7. Click Next.

The Make DVD Disc: Summary window appears (**Figure 6.83**).

continues on next page

MAKING A DVD DISC

8. Click Build.

Two progress bars appear to display the progress of transcoding assets and building the disc (**Figure 6.84**). The build can be cancelled by clicking Stop.

✔ Tips

- You can control the Check Project process by deselecting categories you don't want checked and then clicking Start on the Check Project dialog. However, because the Check Project dialog will display errors only for selected categories, it's a good idea to run at least one check with all the categories selected.

- You can also bypass all warning dialogs and build the project by checking the appropriate box in the Make DVD Disc dialog.

- The time it takes to burn a DVD depends on the speed of the recorder and the amount of data. A 2x DVD burner, running at 22 Mbps, can write a full 4.7G DVD in about 30 minutes. A 4x burner will take approximately 15 minutes.

- As with CD-ROM burning, DVD burning requires a steady stream of data to be successful. For this reason, it's best not to use the computer for other tasks when rendering or burning.

- Technology has progressed to the point where if you've successfully burned several discs, you probably can assume that you don't have to test before writing, which takes as much time as the burn itself.

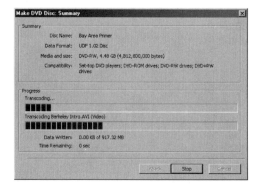

Figure 6.84 The transcoding process is tracked and updated with the progress bars.

MAKING A DVD DISC

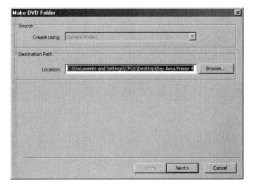

Figure 6.85 The Make DVD Folder dialog. These dialogs are all looking rather familiar at this point, aren't they?

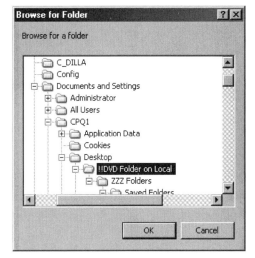

Figure 6.86 Searching for a likely place on a hard drive to write the DVD folder.

Making a DVD Folder

This selection allows you to build a "virtual DVD" in a folder on your hard drive. You can use this to check your project for quality or for playback on a PC.

To make a DVD folder:

1. Choose File > Build DVD > Make DVD Folder.

   You may need to save your project and/or view a list of errors that Encore DVD encountered. Follow the steps described in the "Making a DVD Disc" section.

   The Make DVD Folder dialog appears (**Figure 6.85**). The Create Using selection will be set to Current Project and cannot be changed.

2. In the Destination Path pane, click Browse.

   The Browse for Folder dialog appears (**Figure 6.86**).

   continues on next page

3. Navigate to and select the location where the DVD folder will be written and click OK.

The selected location appears in the Make DVD Folder dialog (**Figure 6.87**).

4. Click Next.

The Make DVD Folder: Summary window appears (**Figure 6.88**).

5. Click Build.

The build process can be monitored and managed as described in the last section.

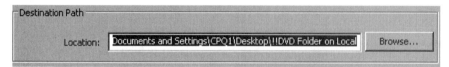

Figure 6.87 The destination folder is confirmed.

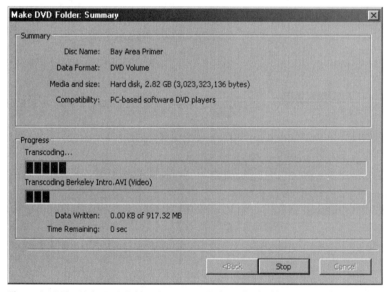

Figure 6.88 The Make DVD Folder: Summary window. The build process is displayed the same way in all the Summary windows.

Making a DVD Image

This selection builds a DVD image on a hard drive. The image can then be used to create multiple DVD copies of your project or can be taken to a disc replication facility for mass duplication. Many replicators utilize digital linear tape (DLT) rather than a disc image to make copies. (Check with the replicator first.)

To make a DVD image:

1. Choose File > Build DVD > Make DVD Image.

As in the previous procedures, the Save Project and warning messages may appear.

The Make DVD Image window appears (**Figure 6.89**).

2. Follow the steps in the section "Making a DVD Folder" to change the source or destination entries and build the image.

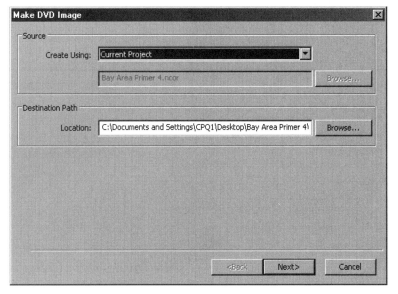

Figure 6.89 The Make DVD Image dialog.

Making a DVD Master

This option is used to write to a DLT, which can then be taken to a facility for mass replication. The DLT drive needs to be connected to the Encore DVD computer to use this option. You can't create the file and then later connect the drive and write the tape.

Increasingly, replicators are accepting recordable DVDs as their data source. Be sure to determine what source your replicator accepts as early as possible.

To make a DVD master:

1. Choose File > Build DVD > Make DVD Master (**Figure 6.90**).

   As before, the Save Project dialog and warning messages may appear.

   The Make DVD Master dialog appears (**Figure 6.91**).

2. Follow the steps under "Making a DVD Folder" to change the source or destination entries and build the image.

✔ Tip

■ Generally, you'd use this option to write a copy of your project to DLT tape in order to take it to a professional facility for replication. There are many details to take into account, from the make and model of the DLT drive you'll buy, borrow, or rent (though Encore DVD should be able to support any drive you attach) to the point in your content where you'll arrange a program break (if you're writing your final program to dual-sided discs). Consult both the Encore DVD User Guide and the replication facility for details before hooking up a DLT drive.

Figure 6.90 The starting point for creation of a DVD master.

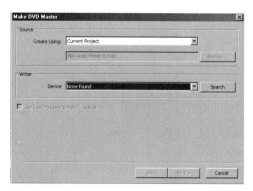

Figure 6.91 The make DVD Master dialog. Making a DVD master requires that a DLT drive be attached.

Choosing a DVD Format

You have several disc formats to choose from. In **Table 6.1**, you'll find a very brief summary of the main DVD formats. For further detail, check the list of resources in Chapter 1.

When evaluating the different formats for your project, the main things to keep in mind are

◆ **Project size.** Project size is one of the determining factors in choosing a disc format. A bit budget calculation will tell you whether your project will fit on one single-sided disc or will require more capacity. See the Appendix for more information on bit budgeting.

◆ **Desktop creation.** If your project requires dual-sided discs or copy protection, you will not be able to use a desktop burner to create your DVDs.

◆ **Mass production.** If you plan to have a very wide distribution of discs, it will be more practical to use the DVD Image option or write a DVD file to a digital linear tape (DLT) drive and employ a replication facility to create many copies. DLT is the generally accepted format for replication, but you should check with the facility you choose for any specifics.

◆ **Rewriteability.** The main differences in disc formats center around their write-once or write-many-times capabilities. Generally speaking, rewriteable discs are great for test runs and for making revised versions of your project. For general distribution or DVD-Video content, rewriteability is not necessary and can decrease playback compatibility.

◆ **DVD burner support.** The burner you use must support the format you want to burn. Older burners may not support the newer DVD+RW formats, for instance.

◆ **Compatibility.** Though compatibility issues will probably lessen over time as new DVD players become more prevalent, DVD-R has the best record for compatibility with a wide range of different DVD players.

The following is a list of common DVD types and capacities. Note that capacities are shown according to the DVD standard, not the computer standard. See Chapter 2 for more information. Different disc formats (DVD-R, RW, etc.) support different disc types and capacities:

◆ **DVD 5.** Single-sided, single-layer disc, 4.7 GB capacity

◆ **DVD 9.** Single-sided, dual-layer disc, 8.5 GB capacity

◆ **DVD 10.** Dual-sided, single-layer disc, 9.4 GB capacity

◆ **DVD 18.** Dual-sided, dual-layer disc, 17 GB capacity

Table 6.1

Comparing Disc Formats

FORMAT	TECHNOLOGY	REWRITEABILITY	USES
DVD-R	Organic dye	Write once	DVD authoring and distribution, data storage
DVD-RW	Phase Change	Rewriteable	DVD authoring and testing, data storage, real-time video recording
DVD+R	Organic dye	Write once	DVD authoring and distribution, data storage
DVD+RW	Phase Change	Rewriteable	DVD authoring and testing, real-time video recording
DVD-RAM	Phase Change	Rewriteable	Data storage, real-time video recording (least suitable for DVD distribution)

Multiple Sides. Multiple Layers. Multiple Choice.

While most users will only need the basics of single-sided, single-layer desktop disc creation, Encore DVD can accommodate both dual-side and dual-layer formats, but it can get a bit complicated and the final DVDs must be created by a disc replicator.

Single-sided/dual-layer means two recordable layers are sandwiched; the laser is refocused to switch between layers. Its capacity may be required by large projects. The disc doesn't have to be flipped to access the second layer, handy if you have a long continuous program. But there still needs to be a "layer break," where the laser switches between layers. To make the switch smooth, as it writes to DLT tape, Encore DVD attempts to set the layer break at a point between menus or timelines close to the end of the disc layer. If it can't find a good point, it will prompt you to select a chapter point for the layer break. Creating a single-sided/dual-layer DVD requires two DLT tapes, one for each side.

The dual-sided/single-layer format also is useful for large projects, but since the disc must be flipped to access the second side, it lends itself to large projects with a different type of content. With the dual-sided format, one side can have a wide-screen version of the content, the other can have a standard version, or one side can have the main content, while the other has the "making of" documentary content. This type of disc requires two DLT tapes and two separate projects, one per side of the disc.

If you like to live large, Encore DVD can even handle the dual-sided/dual-layer format. To create a disc in this format requires two separate projects (one for each side) and four DLT tapes (one for each layer).

Part II:
Beyond the Basics

INTEGRATING
PHOTOSHOP

In earlier chapters, I emphasized the capabilities of Encore DVD and the tools available in the application to create menus, buttons, and other elements for your project. Encore DVD is not an isolated program, however. It's designed to work directly with the rest of the Adobe suite of video and imaging products: Premiere Pro, After Effects, and especially Photoshop. This chapter focuses on the process of moving between Encore DVD and Photoshop, with some features that are specific to Photoshop CS.

If you like, you can do most or even all of your creative work on menus and buttons in Photoshop and then import it directly into Encore DVD. If you have both applications installed on the same computer, you can use Encore DVD's Edit in Photoshop feature to jump back into Photoshop to make changes, and you can move back and forth seamlessly between the two applications.

About Photoshop Integration

The best thing about the close connection between Photoshop and Encore DVD is the way in which Encore maintains the Photoshop layers when you import a PSD (Photoshop) file as a menu. If you follow the correct layer-naming convention in your Photoshop files, Encore DVD will automatically recognize button sets, subpictures, and video thumbnails. (The layer-naming convention is shown in **Table 7.1**.)

Prefixes are added manually to layers and layer sets in Photoshop. You can, of course, create other elements in Photoshop, such as textures, text, and logos. They can be placed inside or outside a button-layer set, and do not need a layer-name prefix.

As you might remember from Chapter 4, many of the creative tasks involving buttons and subpictures can be done within Encore DVD. Photoshop, however, being the world-class graphics application that it is, gives you more tools to design menus with, such as control over all three subpicture layers supported in the DVD standard and the ability to use thumbnails and masks to define elements on its layers.

But because the theme of this chapter is integration, I'll just touch on the most basic implementation of Photoshop in designing menus.

Table 7.1

Naming Layers

Menu Item	Photoshop Element	Layer Prefix
Button	Layer set	(+)
Subpicture 1	Single color image layer	=1
Subpicture 2	Single color image layer	=2
Subpicture 3	Single color image layer	=3
Video thumbnail	Placeholder for video in layer set	%

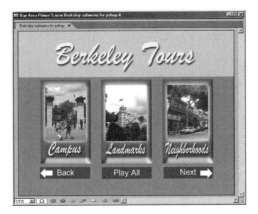

Figure 7.1 A basic menu as a starting point.

Figure 7.2 You can get into Photoshop quickly with this Toolbox shortcut.

Figure 7.3 The menu, now ready for changes in Photoshop.

Using the Edit in Photoshop Feature

Just to keep things consistent, I'm going to start in Encore DVD with one of the menus you've seen in earlier chapters (**Figure 7.1**). I'll make use of some Photoshop tools to embellish it, and show how to traverse back and forth between the applications.

To edit a menu in Photoshop:

1. *Do one of the following:*

▲ Select a menu in one of the Project window tabs and choose Edit > Edit in Photoshop.

▲ Right-click on a menu in the Menu Editor or a Project tab and choose Edit in Photoshop.

▲ Select a menu in the Menu Editor or a Project tab and click the Edit in Photoshop shortcut on the Toolbox (**Figure 7.2**).

If it had been closed, Photoshop automatically launches and displays the same menu that is selected in Encore DVD (**Figure 7.3**).

The file being modified is actually a temp file; *temp.psd* is displayed in the header. This "shared file" scheme allows for easy interaction between the two applications.

continues on next page

2. Make your adjustments in Photoshop. Encore DVD and Photoshop have similar toolsets and interfaces, of course (**Figure 7.4**).

   Note also that any guides created in Encore DVD are available and adjustable in Photoshop (**Figure 7.5**).

3. Continue making changes to the menu (**Figure 7.6**). When finished, choose File > Save in Photoshop.

   In Encore, the menu is automatically updated to reflect the changes as soon as they are saved in Photoshop.

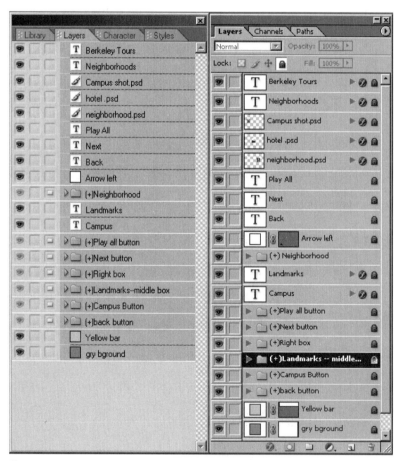

Figure 7.4 As you can see, the way Photoshop and Encore DVD handle layers is virtually identical.

Figure 7.5 Guides set in Encore DVD can be used in Photoshop. (I put this over black so you can see the guides a bit better.)

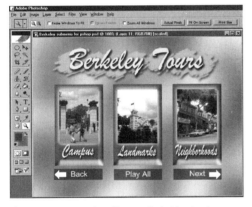

Figure 7.6 Some paint effects, a little blurring here and there, and voilà! Maybe not better than the original, but definitely different.

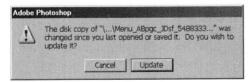

Figure 7.7 You'll get this warning if you make a change in Encore DVD that will also force an update in the temp copy in Photoshop.

✔ Tips

■ Photoshop saves the updated menu file to the Encore DVD Project folder. It does not overwrite the original file.

■ You can also make changes to a menu in Encore DVD and have them reflected in Photoshop. If you happen to reverse the direction of your normal workflow and make a change in Encore DVD while Encore DVD and Photoshop are sharing a temp file, you'll get a warning message in Photoshop (**Figure 7.7**). You can decide to update the temp file with the new changes, cancel the process, or, if you're not sure, perform a Save As in Encore DVD to avoid overwriting the temp file.

■ As you move between Photoshop and Encore DVD, remember that only those layers with their hide/show toggle in the show position (with the eye icon visible in the Layers palette) will "travel" between the applications. Hidden layers will remain hidden in both applications.

■ If at any time you want to save an Encore DVD menu as a Photoshop file, you can select the menu and choose Menu > Save Menu as File. This will preserve all the layers and allow you to keep a copy of your menu design outside of Encore DVD, in case you want to access it directly from Photoshop or another application.

Creating Buttons in Photoshop

You've seen how simple objects can be converted to buttons in Encore DVD, and how subpictures and color sets can be created to manage a highlighting scheme for your whole project (see Chapter 4). In Photoshop, you can design more complex buttons and subpictures, but the basic procedure to start building buttons is quite simple.

To create button layer sets in Photoshop:

1. Launch Photoshop.

2. If you are just starting a new menu in Photoshop, choose Layer > New > Layer Set (**Figure 7.8**).

   Photoshop displays the new layer set in the Layers palette (**Figure 7.9**).

   Or

   If you have existing layers, drag them into layer-set folders.

3. Type the prefix (+) at the beginning of the name of each layer-set folder. Include the parentheses (**Figure 7.10**).

   Inside each layer set, you'll group the elements you want to use for a button in Encore DVD. You may want to have separate layer sets for text elements, logos, and so on, so that these elements can be modified independently of the button sets.

✔ Tips

■ Encore DVD automatically recognizes any layer set with the (+) prefix as a button-layer set. If you don't create a subpicture in Photoshop, you can choose Object > Create Subpicture in Encore DVD to attach one to your button. You also can use Object > Convert to Object to *take away* button attributes.

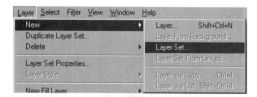

Figure 7.8 Creating a new layer set.

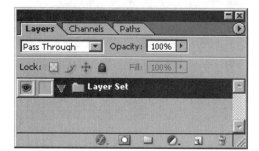

Figure 7.9 Photoshop places the layer set in its Layers palette.

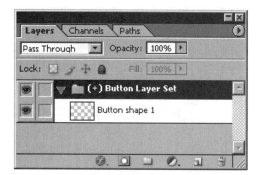

Figure 7.10 This is a button-layer set, now that it has the (+) prefix, and it looks like a graphic element for a button has been added to the set as well.

■ You can create buttons and other menu components as separate items in Photoshop, import them into Encore DVD, and create a menu using Encore DVD's tools. You don't have to design and assemble an entire menu in Photoshop.

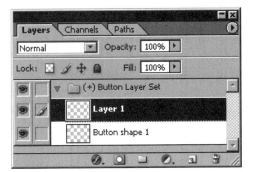

Figure 7.11 For subpictures, a new layer goes inside a layer set...

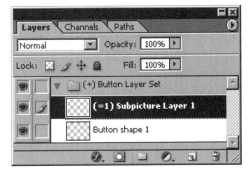

Figure 7.12 ...and is given the prefix that allows Encore DVD to recognize it as a subpicture layer.

Figure 7.13 By drawing this simple shape, I'm defining the shape for a subpicture highlight for a particular button.

Creating Subpictures in Photoshop

Photoshop enables you to work with all three color subpicture layers available in the DVD spec and has more flexibility than Encore DVD in fine-tuning each layer. However, subpictures are somewhat limited. They are simplified color overlays, so note that any gradients, feathering, or antialiasing in a subpicture layer will be lost. That nice Photoshop airbrush effect you want to use for a button highlight will flatten out to a jagged blob when you use it as a subpicture layer. So stick to solid colors and simple, sharp-edged elements, and use a light touch on the opacity settings. Other techniques to use in working with multiple subpicture layers will be covered later in the chapter.

To create a subpicture layer in Photoshop:

1. Choose Layer > New > Layer in Photoshop.

2. Place the new layer inside a button layer set.

   Photoshop may do this automatically if you have the button layer set selected (**Figure 7.11**).

3. Assign one of the three subpicture layer prefixes (=1, =2, or =3) to the new layer and give the layer a custom name, if desired (**Figure 7.12**).

   With the prefix, Encore DVD will be able to recognize any shape in the layer as a subpicture overlay and assign color-set values accordingly.

4. Use the graphics tools in Photoshop to create a shape on the subpicture layer (**Figure 7.13**). Make any necessary adjustments to get the look you want.

continues on next page

CREATING SUBPICTURES IN PHOTOSHOP

5. If desired, create more subpicture layers and name them, following the steps above.

6. When you've finished choose File > Save and import the PSD file into Encore DVD.

✔ Tip

■ The prefixes (=1), (=2), and (=3) each represent one of the three colors available for a subpicture. The three colors (and their opacity) can be created and previewed in Photoshop, but their final values are controlled by the settings in Encore DVD's Menu Color Set. The color values for a subpicture layer with the (=1) prefix are controlled by the Color 1 settings in the menu's color set. Layers with (=2) are controlled by the Color 2 settings, and you can probably guess about (=3).

Figure 7.14 This shape will retain the color and opacity values assigned in Photoshop. The menu's color set needs adjusting.

Figure 7.15 Select the Automatic color set in the Menu Color Set dialog...

Figure 7.16 ...and create a new color set.

Working with the Automatic Color Set

When importing a menu, Encore DVD examines the color and opacity values in the subpicture layers and generates an Automatic color set based on these values. This color set also automatically updates to reflect any changes you make when you edit the menu in Photoshop and re-import it into Encore DVD. Because it is so important to the integration between Encore DVD and Photoshop, it can't be modified directly. It must be saved as a new color set, then the copy can be modified.

To change the color of Photoshop subpicture layers in Encore DVD:

1. With the Encore DVD Project window active, choose File > Import as Menu, or double-click any empty area in the Project tab.

2. Navigate to the PSD file you want to import and select it.

3. Click Open.
   The Menu Editor displays the imported menu (**Figure 7.14**). In the Properties palette, the color set will be defaulted to Automatic.

4. Choose Edit > Color Sets > Menu.
   The Menu Color Set dialog appears.

5. To modify the Automatic color set, select it from the pop-up menu (**Figure 7.15**).

6. Click the New color set button (**Figure 7.16**).
   The New Color Set dialog appears.

continues on next page

7. Name the color set and click OK.

8. Adjust the color and opacity values for the three button highlight states (**Figure 7.17**).

9. Click OK.

The results can be viewed in the Menu Editor. The Encore DVD button highlight is defined by the subpicture shape created in Photoshop (**Figure 7.18**).

✔ Tip

■ To watch the changes to the color set as you make them, click the Preview check box on the Menu Color Set dialog. Use the highlight buttons just below the Preview check box to toggle between the different button highlight states. As you work on the color set, you can continue to use the Edit in Photoshop function to move back and forth between the applications.

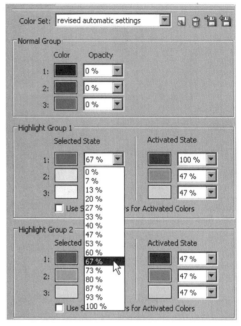

Figure 7.17 Now you can make adjustments to the color set. Opacity will be the first order of business here.

Figure 7.18. Now the button is highlighted with a semi-transparent overlay. The picture is a bit washed out though, so in the next section, I'll cut the overlay away from the picture with a mask.

Using Masks with Subpictures

The previous example covered only the basics of designing and preparing layers (especially subpicture layers) in Photoshop and then importing and customizing them in Encore DVD.

An exhaustive survey of all the ways to use Photoshop in combination with Encore DVD would be exhausting, indeed, so I'll just point out one basic Photoshop feature: the use of *masks* to control the shape and content of subpicture layers. Masking allows you to increase the color saturation and opacity of the subpicture layer without "washing out" the colors of the button layer.

To use Photoshop masks on subpicture layers:

1. Follow the steps outlined earlier to create a subpicture layer in Photoshop with a simple-shaped object applied (**Figure 7.19**).

continues on next page

Figure 7.19 Back in Photoshop, the basic shape for the subpicture is drawn again.

2. Select a Marquee tool or other drawing tool from the Photoshop Tool palette.

3. Draw a shape inside the existing shape (**Figure 7.20**).

4. Choose Layer > Add Layer Mask > Hide Selection.

A "hole" is cut in the subpicture shape, which allows the underlying picture to be seen (**Figure 7.21**).

5. Save the Photoshop file.

6. Import it as a menu into Encore DVD.

In the Menu Editor, the Selected state button will show that the subpicture overlay is now confined by the mask—in this case, the picture on the Campus button is revealed through the "hole" created in the mask (**Figure 7.22**).

✔ Tips

■ The masked overlay's color and opacity can be adjusted via the Menu Color Set controls. It can be repositioned and resized by selecting it with the Direct Select tool.

■ When modifying the masked subpicture overlay, remember to use the Direct Select tool. Otherwise, any modification performed on the masked overlay is also performed on the underlying image.

Figure 7.20 A new shape, sized to the button's picture, is drawn on top of the existing subpicture shape.

Figure 7.21 A hole is cut in the subpicture by the mask and reveals the underlying layer.

Figure 7.22 It might be a bit hard to see here, but in Encore DVD, the picture "pops through" the hole in the subpicture overlay.

Creating a Pop-On Effect

Another technique you can use to add interest to a menu is to take advantage of the opacity controls in a color set. Rather than simply using color overlays to indicate a button state, you can design graphic accents that can get the job done with a bit more style. They "pop on" when a button is activated.

To use opacity values to "pop on" highlight elements:

1. Follow the steps under "Creating Subpictures in Photoshop" to create and name one or more subpicture layers in a Photoshop file.

   In this case, the element on the layer is a shape from Photoshop's Custom Shape library (**Figure 7.23**).

continues on next page

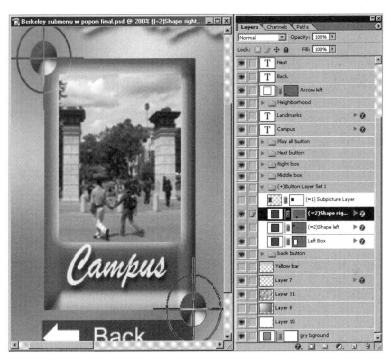

Figure 7.23 The button now has a couple of shapes, assigned to subpicture layer 2, added to it.

2. Import as a menu into Encore DVD.

3. In Encore DVD follow the steps described earlier to modify the Automatic color set.

4. In the Menu Color Set, set the opacity for the pop-on element to zero for the Normal state. Set the opacity high enough to be visible for either the Selected or Activated states, or both (**Figures 7.24–26**).

Figure 7.24 The Normal state: all subpicture layers in the menu's color set are adjusted to zero.

Figure 7.25 The Selected state. Subpicture layer 1's opacity setting is high enough to make the button overlay visible. Subpicture layer 2 still has zero opacity.

Figure 7.26 In the Activated state, subpicture layer 2's opacity setting is raised, and the shape elements pop on.

Figure 7.27 Identifying the layer as a thumbnail.

Figure 7.28 Drawing a shape for the thumbnail...

Creating Thumbnails in Photoshop

In Photoshop, you can also create *thumbnails*, which are button shapes that display small placeholder images that link to the "real" full-size image or moving video. They can be created as an integral part of a menu that is then imported into Encore DVD, or they can be created as separate elements and saved to a folder or stored in the Library tab for future use. The thumbnails can be still or can be "animated"—they can have video playing in them. For more information on animating button thumbnails, see Chapter 9.

Thumbnails are identified as such by the (%) prefix that you assign to them as layers in Photoshop. Include the parentheses with the prefix.

To create simple thumbnail shapes in Photoshop:

1. Follow the steps under "Creating Buttons in Photoshop" to create one or more layers in a button-layer set in Photoshop.

2. Label the layer as a thumbnail with the (%) prefix (**Figure 7.27**).

3. Choose a selection tool from the Tools palette.

Because the default shape for a video or still image is rectangular, the Rectangular Marquee will generally be your tool of choice.

4. With the selection tool, draw a shape on the thumbnail layer (**Figure 7.28**).

Exact proportions won't matter. If the selection is not rectangular, Encore DVD will calculate the smallest rectangle in which the image can fit.

continues on next page

243

5. Define the shape by filling it with a color (**Figure 7.29**).

6. Save the Photoshop file.

7. In Encore DVD, import the Photoshop file as a menu.

   The menu appears in the Menu Editor with the thumbnail shape filled in with gray as a placeholder for an image (**Figure 7.30**).

8. With the Properties palette open, select the thumbnail in the Menu Editor.

   The button properties appear.

9. Using any of the linking methods described in Chapter 5, create a link between the thumbnail and a timeline or menu in one of the Project window tabs (**Figure 7.31**).

   The first frame of the selected image or timeline appears in the thumbnail (**Figure 7.32**).

Figure 7.29 ...and temporarily defining it with a color fill.

Figure 7.30 When imported into Encore DVD, the color fill is now a gray placeholder.

✔ Tips

■ If you are linking to a timeline, you can select a specific chapter point to link to. That point's frame will be displayed in the thumbnail. You can also use the Set Poster Frame feature to specify a particular frame for display. More details on poster frames later in the chapter.

■ Encore DVD has a few default thumbnail buttons already built and stored in the Library palette. You can use them "as is" or use the Edit in Photoshop procedure to modify them in Photoshop.

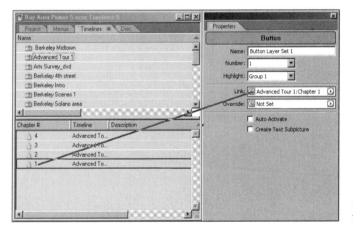

Figure 7.31 Linking the thumbnail to a timeline or menu.

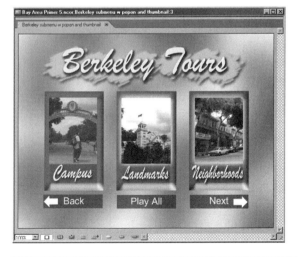

Figure 7.32 The first frame of the selected image or video appears in the thumbnail.

Using Masks with Thumbnails

To have more control over the shape of a thumbnail, you can use the masking capabilities of Photoshop, similar to the process with subpictures outlined earlier.

To create thumbnail shapes with masks in Photoshop:

1. Follow the preceding directions for creating a thumbnail on a layer in a button-layer set in Photoshop.

2. Choose an appropriate selection tool from the Tools palette.

3. Draw a shape over the button (**Figure 7.33**).

4. Fill it with color to define the shape. You can also add layer effects to the shape (**Figure 7.34**).

Figure 7.33 Drawing a shape for a mask in Photoshop.

About Thumbnail Shapes

You can draw any shape in Photoshop for the thumbnail. When the image file or video is linked, Encore DVD will default to the correct rectangular TV aspect ratio. It will reference the thumbnail shape and calculate the smallest rectangle in which the image could fit. You can then resize the image in the menu.

As you resize thumbnails in the menu, you'll get different results with different selection tools. The Selection tool will always maintain the correct TV-aspect rectangle for the image and thumbnail. And any resizing using the Selection tool will be applied to all the objects on the same layer as the thumbnail. The Direct Select tool, on the other hand, allows you to isolate the thumbnail and scale the rectangle freely.

The size of the thumbnail determines the size of the video displayed in the menu. If you want to make a thumbnail larger without degrading the image by blowing it up, it's better to delete the link to the image file first. Resize the thumbnail and then relink the image.

Most important, these methods only apply to static images in the thumbnail. Moving images will ignore any "non-standard" thumbnail shape, and display in buttons in their normal TV aspect ratio, unless a mask is used on the thumbnail. See the next section.

Figure 7.34 The mask shape is defined.

Figure 7.35 The shape, plus any layer effects, back in Encore DVD.

Figure 7.36 After linking, the thumbnail displays a picture frame, which conforms to the shape and style of the mask.

5. Select the shape and choose Layer > Mask > Reveal Selection.

6. Save the file in Photoshop.

7. Import it as a menu into Encore DVD.

The menu is displayed in the Menu Editor. The thumbnail now conforms to the shape of the Photoshop mask, as well as taking on other attributes of the mask's style, such as embossing and shadows (**Figure 7.35**).

8. As in the previous directions, create a link between the thumbnail and a timeline or menu in one of the Project window tabs.

The first frame of the selected image or timeline appears in the thumbnail (**Figure 7.36**).

✔ Tip

- By using the Direct Select tool, the thumbnail can be resized independently.

Setting a Poster Frame

If a button is linked to a timeline, you can choose a particular chapter point to link to, and choose a different point—called a *poster frame*—to display in the button's thumbnail. For instance, you might want to start your playback from the beginning of a timeline, but it fades in from black. You don't want to have a plain black frame displayed as your button's representative thumbnail, so you can select the timeline's Chapter Point 1 as the button link, but then move to a more representative frame in the timeline and set that as the poster frame.

To set a poster frame:

1. Follow the previous steps above to create a video thumbnail button in a menu.

2. Double-click on a timeline in the Project window to display it in the Timeline window.

3. With the Properties menu for the button open, use the pickwhip to create a link to the desired chapter point in the Timeline window (**Figure 7.37**).

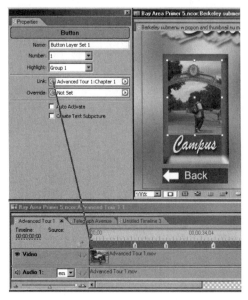

Figure 7.37 Creating a link to Chapter 1 at the beginning of a timeline.

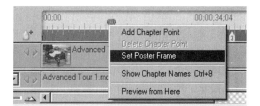

Figure 7.38 Moving to a better frame to display in the Timeline window and selecting it as the poser frame.

4. With the chapter point selected, position the Current Time Indicator (CTI) to the desired frame in the Timeline window

5. Right-click on the CTI and choose Set Poster Frame from the contextual menu (**Figure 7.38**).

A poster frame icon is created at the selected point, with the same number or name as the selected chapter point.

The frame displayed in the button thumbnail is updated to the selected poster frame (**Figure 7.39**).

Figure 7.39 When selected, the timeline will still play back from the beginning, but now the thumbnail displays the new poster frame.

Creating Custom Styles in Photoshop

As you saw in Chapter 4, Encore DVD's Styles palette lets you add layer effects, such as drop shadows, glows, gradients, etc. to objects in a menu. You can create custom styles in Photoshop and add them to Encore DVD's Styles palette. A *style* is defined as a single-layer Photoshop file with effects applied to it via Photoshop's Layer Styles menu. There are three types of layers you can create in Photoshop—image, text, and shape—and this type determines the category that Encore DVD will assign it in the Styles palette. You can create custom styles that will either *replace* or *add to* any existing effects on a layer in Encore DVD.

Creating a custom style (to replace existing styles):

1. In Photoshop, choose File > New.

   The New File dialog appears (**Figure 7.40**).

2. Make sure that the Color Mode is set to RGB and Background Contents is set to Transparent (**Figure 7.41**). Adjust any other parameters and assign a name if you wish, then click OK.

   Parameters such as width and height in the New File dialog will not have an effect on creating styles for use in Encore DVD. For consistency, follow the general guides for creating graphics files outlined in Chapter 2.

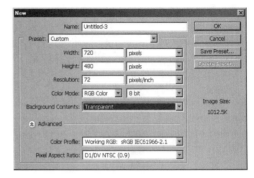

Figure 7.40 Start with a new file in Photoshop...

Figure 7.41 ...and check the background and color mode settings.

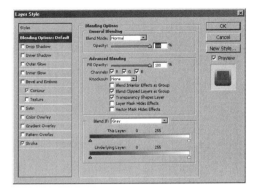

Figure 7.42 You'll use the main Layer Style dialog...

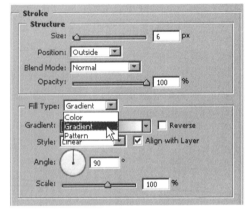

Figure 7.43 ...and its tools to create specific layer effects...

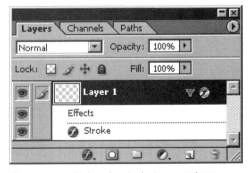

Figure 7.44 ...which end up in the Layers palette.

3. Choose Layer > Layer Style > Blending Options.

The Layer Style dialog appears (**Figure 7.42**).

4. Use the controls in the dialog to select and modify one or more layer styles (**Figure 7.43**).

5. The styles created for the layer appear in the Layers palette (**Figure 7.44**).

6. Choose File > Save to save the layer and style.

continues on next page

CREATING CUSTOM STYLES IN PHOTOSHOP

7. In Encore DVD, click the Add Item button in the Styles palette (**Figure 7.45**).

8. Navigate to the Photoshop file you want to include in the Styles palette (**Figure 7.46**) and click Open.

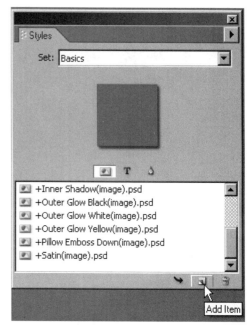

Figure 7.45 You can add your custom styles to the Styles palette...

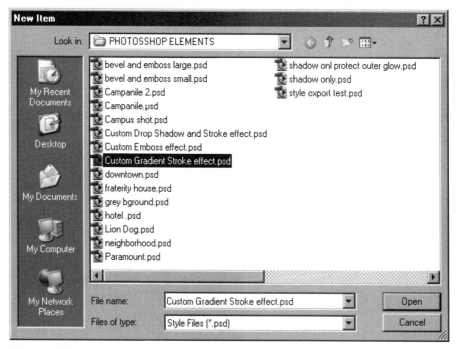

Figure 7.46 ...by navigating to them and selecting them.

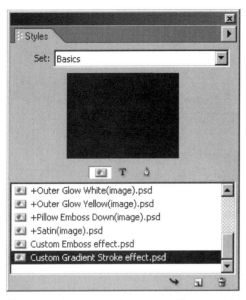

Figure 7.47 The custom styles are sorted by type and stored in the Styles palette.

Figure 7.48 Here's an example of using a custom style. This is "before"...

Figure 7.49 ...and this is "after." The previous style has been replaced by the custom gradient stroke effect.

9. The Photoshop file is imported into the Styles palette and categorized according to its layer type (image, text, or shape) (**Figure 7.47**).

10. Locate an object in the Menu Editor (**Figure 7.48**).

11. Drag and drop the style from the Styles palette onto the menu object.

The style is applied. Any preexisting styles applied to the object are replaced with the new style (**Figure 7.49**).

Creating a custom style (to add to an existing style):

1. Follow Steps 1–3 from the previous task.

2. Select and modify the layer styles as in Step 4 earlier. In addition, select any styles you wish to preserve when applying the style to a menu object in Encore DVD.

   The selected styles appear in the Layers palette.

3. Turn off the eye icon in the Layers palette to hide the effects that you want to preserve in the style (**Figure 7.50**).

4. Follow Steps 6–10 above to import the new style into the Encore DVD Styles palette.

5. Locate an object in the Menu Editor (**Figure 7.51**).

6. Drag and drop the style from the Styles palette onto the menu object.

   The new style is added to the object. Any preexisting styles that were included in your custom style but hidden in the Photoshop Layers palette when you created it are preserved (**Figure 7.52**).

✔ Tips

- Most often, you'll be using the method in the previous section to create a style that replaces any preexisting styles. This will give you more control and consistency when applying styles in your menu.

- In the Encore DVD Styles palette, the prebuilt styles that add to, rather than replace, existing styles have names that begin with a plus sign (+).

- You can apply the Clear All Styles template from the General set in the Styles palette to remove all styles from a menu object.

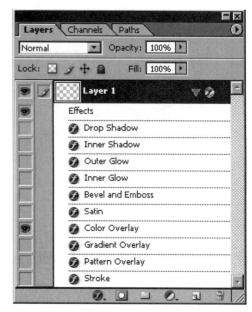

Figure 7.50 Turn the eye icon off for those effects you want to preserve.

Figure 7.51 Again, here's a "before" example...

Figure 7.52 ...and here's after applying the style. Note that the color for the title has changed, but the original drop shadow has been preserved.

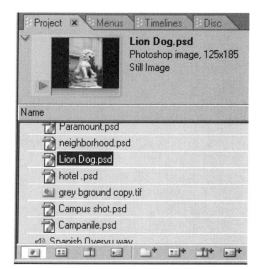

Figure 7.53 A Photoshop file is selected for some changes. In this case, the shot will be flipped horizontally in Photoshop.

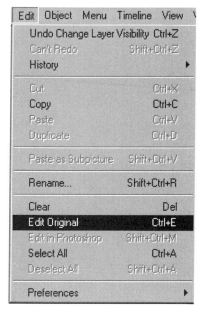

Figure 7.54 Edit Original references the original file and launches Photoshop.

Modifying Assets with Photoshop

Up to now, you've seen how Encore DVD and Photoshop integrate in terms of *menus*. You can also use Photoshop to modify Photoshop files that were imported as *assets* in your project. In this case, the Edit Original command comes into play.

To modify Photoshop assets with the Edit Original feature:

1. Open the Project window if it is not already open and select a Photoshop file from the Project tab (**Figure 7.53**).

2. Choose Edit > Edit Original.

   Photoshop launches and displays the asset (**Figure 7.54**).

3. Modify the asset within Photoshop and save the result.

   The original file is changed. It is automatically re-imported as an asset into Encore DVD, overwriting the previous asset in the Project tab.

✔ Tips

- If the asset is used in a menu, the menu will continue to display the "old" asset until manually updated. You will need to replace the asset in the menu to incorporate the changes made in Photoshop (**Figure 7.55**).

- Changes to assets made with Edit Original cannot be undone. The modifications are made on the original source file that Encore DVD is referencing.

- Edit Original can only be used on one asset at a time.

Figure 7.55 This is the end result. The asset has changed in the Project tab, but any menu like this one will have to be updated individually, to reference the modified asset.

Working with Nested Layer Sets

Photoshop CS has a new feature: Nested Layer Sets. This can be a big help in fighting Layer palette clutter in both Encore DVD and Photoshop CS. In Photoshop CS, you can group your elements into layer sets—even within other layer sets—and move elements around so they are easier to see and access. You might use this feature to group together all of the text elements in a menu, or all of the highlights, or all of the main navigation buttons, and put them into their own specific folders. For a before and after example, see **Figures 7.56** and **7.57**.

Nested Layer Sets can also be useful when it comes time to repurpose your project. If all the text elements, for instance, are in their own folders, replacing and updating the text in your menus is much easier. As long as you are scrupulous about the layer-naming conventions (see the beginning of this chapter for a refresher), Encore DVD can find the neatly-organized nested layer sets in Photoshop CS and correctly construct the menu.

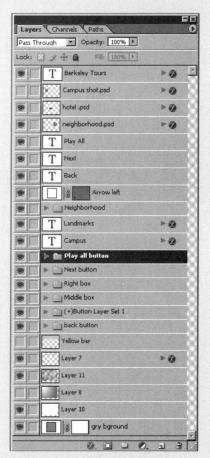

Figure 7.56 An example of Layer palette clutter and confusion...

Figure 7.57 ...and the same layers organized into nested layer sets.

INTEGRATING PREMIERE PRO AND AFTER EFFECTS

As you saw in the last chapter, the integration between Photoshop and Encore DVD can both make your projects look better and save you time in the process. This chapter will highlight the integration between Encore DVD, Adobe Premiere Pro, and Adobe After Effects. The ability to travel seamlessly back and forth between editing, adding effects, and DVD-authoring processes is great for experimentation and creativity.

There are so many ways in which these complementary applications can work together that I've purposely kept this chapter's scope rather narrow. Once you get the hang of the fundamentals, you should be able to move among these apps comfortably. In this chapter, you'll see how the Edit Original function ties Encore DVD, Premiere Pro, and After Effects together. I'll also give an overview of getting menus in and out of After Effects, and show you some techniques to animate a menu in After Effects.

Working with Adobe Premiere

As you no doubt know, Adobe Premiere and Premiere Pro are great tools for editing together content for timelines and motion menus. Either version can be used with Encore DVD, but, as you might expect, Premiere Pro has a few extra features, such as the capability to output video files in AVI, QuickTime, or MPEG-2. With the MPEG-2 capability, many DVD creators will choose to do all their transcoding to MPEG-2 as the last step in the editing process, rather than as part of the DVD authoring process. Premiere Pro also has the ability to embed markers in its timelines, which can be used as chapter points in Encore DVD. For more information on these and other Premiere Pro features, go to www.adobe.com.

It's important to understand that you can use any desktop editing application to cut together your content—Encore DVD is very flexible. However, one big advantage in using Premiere or Premiere Pro with Encore DVD is the Edit Original feature. Similar to what you saw with Photoshop in Chapter 7, Edit Original allows you to quickly reopen a timeline in Premiere, make changes, and then import the updated timeline back into Encore DVD. Since Edit Original works the same in both versions, I'll just refer to Premiere for the rest of this section.

To use Edit Original with Adobe Premiere:

1. Use Premiere to edit together a timeline.

2. Choose File > Export Timeline > Movie.

3. Check the Export Movie Settings dialog and make sure Project is selected in the Embedding Options (**Figure 8.1**).

   Without project link information embedded in the timeline, you will not be able to use the Edit Original feature.

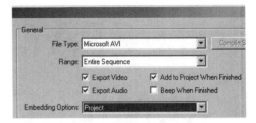

Figure 8.1 In order to use Edit Original, make sure to embed the project link in Premiere's export settings.

Figure 8.2 Here's what the Premiere-originated file looks like on the desktop...

Figure 8.3 ...and here's what it looks like in Encore DVD.

4. Export the timeline.

5. In Encore DVD, navigate to the exported video file and import it as an asset or timeline (**Figure 8.2**).

6. Use the tools in Encore DVD to work with the imported material (**Figure 8.3**).

7. To re-edit the asset, select it in the Project tab and choose Edit > Edit Original. Premiere launches and opens the original timeline (**Figure 8.4**).

8. Make your changes to the timeline in Premiere.

continues on next page

Figure 8.4 If you need to go back to Premiere to make changes (like flopping the direction of a shot), Edit Original puts you right where you left off.

9. As before, choose File > Export Timeline > Movie in Premiere.

When you perform the export, make sure you overwrite the original exported file (**Figure 8.5**).

The confirmation dialog appears.

10. Click Yes.

Encore DVD automatically updates to reflect the changes to the timeline (**Figure 8.6**).

✔ Tips

■ MPEG-2 files exported from Premiere Pro include the project link by default.

■ While not mentioned specifically, the process for exchanging audio between the applications is the same as above, whether the audio is included with the video information or is separate.

Figure 8.5 When you've finished with the changes, overwrite the old file (and make sure your settings— listed in the summary—are correct).

Figure 8.6 Finally, the updated Premiere material is ready to go in Encore DVD.

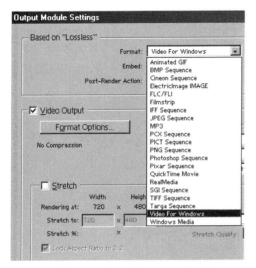

Figure 8.7 There are plenty of output options in After Effects' Output Module.

Working with After Effects

There are so many ways to integrate After Effects into your Encore DVD workflow that they would fill a much longer book than this one. Here are a few to consider:

◆ You can create video content in After Effects and import it into Encore DVD as an asset or timeline.

◆ You can start a menu in Encore DVD and export it to After Effects for animation and embellishment.

◆ You can create multilayered, animated content in After Effects and import it into Encore DVD for use in a menu.

Because these subjects can get very large and detailed, I'll just cover a couple of the most useful integration scenarios and you can experiment on your own.

To start at the most basic level, you can create content in After Effects, export it, and then import it into Encore DVD. Just as with Premiere and Photoshop, After Effects has a number of export options. They are listed in the Output Module Settings dialog (**Figure 8.7**). Generally of course, you'll be using MPEG-2, AVI (Video for Windows), or QuickTime as the video format of choice. Similar to the procedure with Premiere, once the content is exported from After Effects and imported for use in Encore DVD, you can use the Edit Original feature to reopen After Effects and perform any modifications you might need.

To use Edit Original with After Effects:

1. Create a composition in After Effects (**Figure 8.8**).

2. In After Effects, choose Composition > Make Movie.

   The Render Queue window appears.

3. Click the Output Module setting (**Figure 8.9**).

   The Output Module Settings window opens.

4. Select Project Link in the Embed pop-up menu (**Figure 8.10**).

   Without project link information embedded in the composition, you will not be able to use the Edit Original feature.

5. Click OK to render the composition to a video file format.

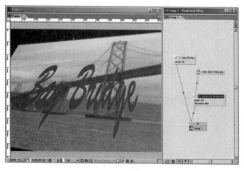

Figure 8.8 The Edit Original process starts in After Effects, with a composition...

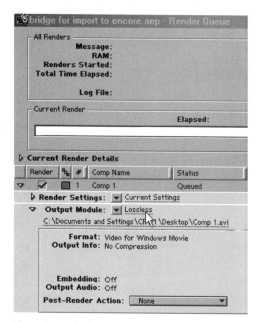

Figure 8.9 ...which goes through the Render Queue...

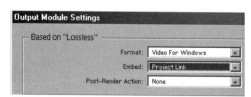

Figure 8.10 ...and the Output Module, where the project link is set.

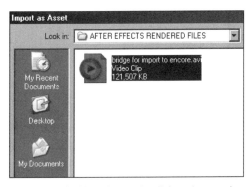

Figure 8.11 The file and its project link are imported into Encore DVD.

Figure 8.12 Once in Encore DVD, you can work with the After Effects–originated material...

6. In Encore DVD, navigate to the file created by After Effects and import it as an asset or a timeline (**Figure 8.11**).

7. Use the tools in Encore DVD to work with the imported material (**Figure 8.12**).

continues on next page

WORKING WITH AFTER EFFECTS

8. With the asset selected in the Project tab, choose Edit > Edit Original (**Figure 8.13**).

After Effects launches, and opens the original composition.

9. Make changes to the composition (**Figure 8.14**).

10. Follow Steps 2–5 above to output the new version and write over the previous version.

Encore DVD automatically updates to reflect the changes made to the After Effects composition (**Figure 8.15**).

✔ Tip

■ Writing over the previous version is necessary to allow the automatic update in Encore DVD. You can save alternate copies of your work, of course, but this will add a step or two as you go back and forth between the two applications.

Figure 8.13 ...and decide to take a step back into After Effects...

Figure 8.14 ...where you can make all sorts of changes...

Figure 8.15 ...and have those changes quickly reflected in your Encore DVD project.

WORKING WITH AFTER EFFECTS

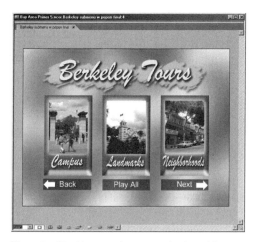

Figure 8.16 In this case, the process begins with a multilayered menu in Encore DVD.

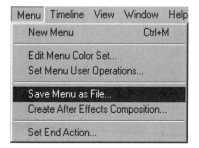

Figure 8.17 Saving the menu as a file keeps all the layers intact, and allows After Effects access to them.

After Effects and Encore DVD Menus

After Effects can be used to create single-layer video backgrounds for motion menus, or video content for timelines. It can also be used in combination with Encore DVD and Photoshop to create menus, and its greatest strength is its ability to work with the different layers in a menu and add animation to them. Any element in a menu can be animated in After Effects and used to create a motion menu. (More on the how-to's of motion menus in Chapter 9.)

If you want to animate buttons along with other elements in your menu in your menu—fly them around the screen, for instance—a typical way to proceed is this: Design a static title in Encore DVD, complete with button highlights, and then import it into After Effects. This template will be the "end position" of your motion menu. Use the features in After Effects to add motion to the layers of menu elements, but have the elements "come to rest" in the end position. When the animated menu is imported into Encore DVD, you can integrate it with the button highlights of the original menu.

Integrating Encore DVD and After Effects for a motion menu

1. Create a menu template in Encore DVD (**Figure 8.16**).

2. Choose Menu > Save Menu as File (**Figure 8.17**).

   The menu is saved as a .PSD file, with all layers intact.

3. Open After Effects if it is not already open.

continues on next page

4. Choose File > Import > File (**Figure 8.18**). The Import File dialog appears.

5. Select Composition from the Import As list (**Figure 8.19**).

The menu is imported into After Effects as a composition, with all the original layers intact.

6. Use the tools in After Effects to animate the layers (**Figure 8.20**).

As noted, the usual design, especially when motion is applied to buttons, is to have the motion resolve to the menu's final, static, end position.

7. Export the final After Effects composition as a video file.

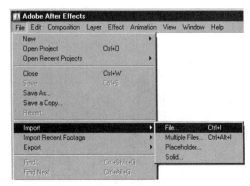

Figure 8.18 Step one in importing a menu into After Effects.

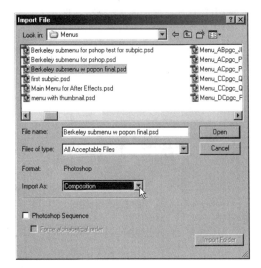

Figure 8.19 Step two in importing a menu—again, keeping the layer structure intact.

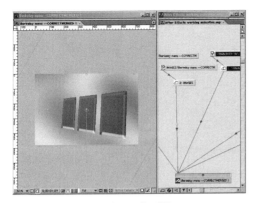

Figure 8.20 You can animate the different menu elements and experiment freely in After Effects.

8. Import the After Effects file into Encore DVD.

9. Open the original menu in Encore DVD.

10. Using the pickwhip or pop-up methods, link the original menu to the imported After Effects asset (**Figure 8.21**). The asset replaces the menu's existing video background. More on this procedure in Chapter 9.

11. Use the hide/show capabilities of the Layers palette to hide all but the menu's highlight layers (**Figure 8.22**).

continues on next page

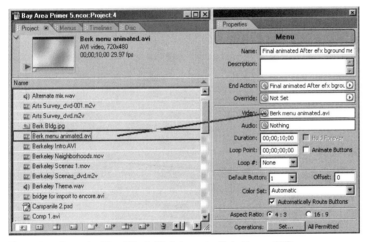

Figure 8.21 Once the After Effects file is imported into Encore DVD, you can link it to a menu with the Properties palette.

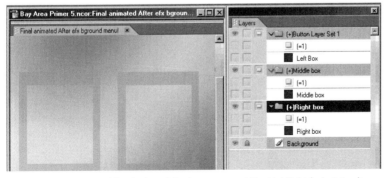

Figure 8.22 Hide everything in the original menu except the highlight (subpicture) information. (I've actually deleted all the extraneous layers in this menu copy.)

AFTER EFFECTS AND ENCORE DVD MENUS

12. Right-click on the Menu Editor and choose Preview from Here in the contextual menu.

The video animation created in After Effects will play as a moving menu background in the Preview window. Once the elements come to their static positions, they will line up with the button highlights (**Figures 8.23–8.26**).

13. To prevent the viewer from selecting and highlighting a button until the buttons are in their proper (static) places, set the Loop Point in the Properties palette to a point after the animation is finished (**Figure 8.27**).

With the Loop Point option set, each time after the first playback of the animated menu, it will loop back to the loop point, and not play the entire animation.

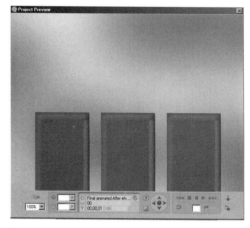

Figure 8.23 Here's a very simple After Effects animation. The blank buttons move in from offscreen...

Figure 8.24 ...the button images appear...

Figure 8.25 ...the titles fade in...

Figure 8.26 ...and the button highlight lines up nicely.

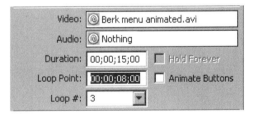

Figure 8.27 The Loop Point can be set to a point after the buttons have come to rest, so the viewer can use them.

✔ Tips

- Because the main purpose here is to show how Encore DVD and After Effects work together, I began my menu design in Encore DVD. You could just as easily start your menu in Photoshop and import it into After Effects for animation. Or do some work in After Effects, then import it into Photoshop, then back into After Effects...(you get the idea).

- This method of creating moving menus has an advantage in that, because all the animation is embedded in the imported After Effects file, the only items being added to the menu in Encore DVD are the button highlights. Because these subpictures are small, static overlays on the moving menu, the menu does not require any extra steps before previewing in motion in Encore DVD. The disadvantage is that any changes in the motion of the menu require re-editing in After Effects. For more information on creating motion menus in Encore DVD, see Chapter 9.

USING
MOTION MENUS

9

In this chapter, you'll learn how to incorporate moving video in your menus. You can put video on your backgrounds, on your buttons, or on both at once. You can also incorporate an audio track to add narration, music, or other sound elements to your menus. The elements you use can be short video bits, brief sound bites, or more complex edited or animated scenes. In the previous chapters, you saw how you can use Photoshop, After Effects, and Premiere Pro to create interesting content, and how to get that content into Encore DVD. This chapter will focus on what you can do inside Encore DVD to take that material and use it to create motion menus.

Building on the techniques discussed in Chapter 7, you'll learn how to use video to animate thumbnail images in buttons. Creating motion menus also requires *rendering*—the compositing of multiple files into a single file—and you'll learn how to manage that process, as well. Finally, you'll see what strategies you can use to control the playback both of video and audio elements in a motion menu.

About Motion Menus

Understanding just what Encore DVD is doing when you create a motion menu will help you better manage the process.

The basic building blocks of menus remain the same, e.g., buttons, layers, links, and so on. In a motion menu, you add a new twist by linking moving video, and possibly sound elements, to buttons and menus.

You also add one more step: rendering. Rendering is the process of combining the various audio and video elements that you select as menu components into a single MPEG-2 file. Without this step, you can't preview your video in motion, nor can you write your project to disc.

Rendered files are stored in a Menus subfolder inside your Project folder (see Chapter 2). Also in that folder are the other components Encore DVD will reference when creating motion menus (**Figure 9.1**).

The main components are

- **The PSD file.** This is the menu file, either created in Photoshop or stored in the Encore DVD Library palette.

- **The MPEG file.** This is the rendered file itself—created from one or more video and/or audio sources.

- **The MCSES file.** This is a "pointer" file that Encore DVD creates along with each rendered file. Whenever the rendered file is updated, this file updates, too.

Figure 9.1 A look inside the Menus folder for this project.

Before You Begin

Here are some things you should know about motion menus and the rendering process:

- Each time you make a change to a menu, it will have to be re-rendered.

- Each time a menu is re-rendered, it *overwrites* the previous version of the menu. If you choose to "undo" a rendering in Encore DVD's Edit menu, you will be able to get back to the earlier state of your menu, but you will have to render it again in order to preview it.

- And most important, because motion menus are based on these rendered MPEG-2 files rather than simply pointers to various elements, you'll have to make sure you have enough space on your drives to accommodate all the rendered files in your Project folder.

ABOUT MOTION MENUS

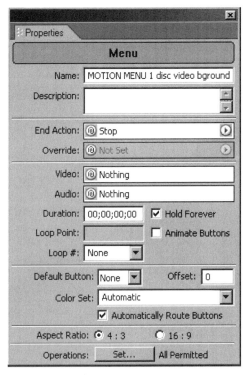

Figure 9.2 The Menu Properties palette controls the links between assets and motion menus.

Adding Video to a Menu

You can use moving video as the background for a menu by creating a link between the menu and a video asset in your project. You do not have to do any rendering, by the way, until you add buttons on top of the background. When you link a menu to a video asset, you cannot choose a particular chapter point as your start point. There are some looping and duration options, however, that can help you optimize your background video's start and end points.

To add video to a menu:

1. Create a new menu, or double-click on an existing menu in the Project window.

   The Menu Editor is displayed.

2. Open the Properties palette (Window > Properties) if it is not already open.

   The Menu Properties are displayed (**Figure 9.2**).

3. Click and drag the pickwhip from the Video pop-up of the Properties palette and point to the video asset you want to add in the Project tab (**Figure 9.3**).

continues on next page

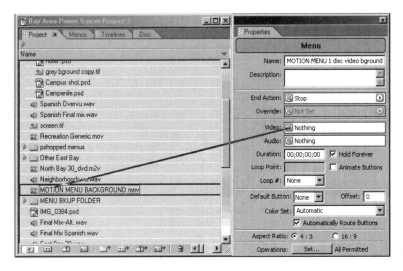

Figure 9.3 Using the pickwhip to link a video asset to a menu.

The selected destination appears in the Video pop-up, and the first frame of the video asset is displayed in the background of the Menu Editor (**Figure 9.4**).

The duration of the asset is displayed in the Duration box (**Figure 9.5**).

4. If you do not want the menu to play the entire video asset, you can type a new duration in the box.

Generally, an alternate duration is shorter than the asset's "native" duration. If it is longer, the last frame of the asset will hold on the screen to fill any remaining time.

5. Right-click the menu in the Project window and choose Preview from Here in the contextual menu.

The Preview window opens and the menu preview begins (**Figure 9.6**).

ADDING VIDEO TO A MENU

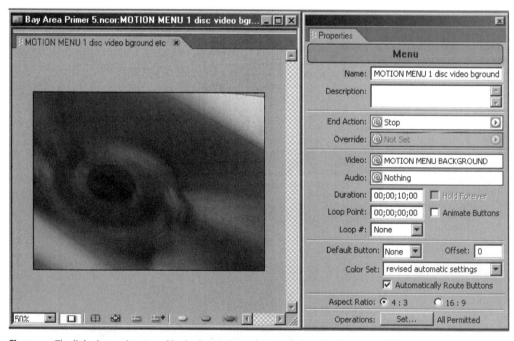

Figure 9.4 The linked asset is entered in the Properties palette and shown in the Menu Editor.

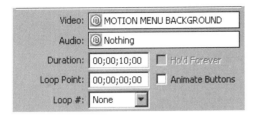

Figure 9.5 The asset duration appears in the Duration box.

✔ Tips

■ Clicking and dragging with the pickwhip is the only method you have of linking menus to video and audio assets. The pop-up menu and Specify Other selections are unavailable.

■ To clear a link to a video or audio asset in the Properties palette, right-click on the pop-up and choose Delete from the contextual menu. The pop-up will display Nothing after the link is cleared.

■ Although I'm starting this chapter by talking about background video in a menu and working forward to buttons with animated video, it's actually faster and easier to start by building your buttons against a plain static background. Once you're satisfied with them, you can add the moving video background as described earlier. Trying to design buttons with moving video *and* a moving background will mean a lot of time spent rendering and re-rendering.

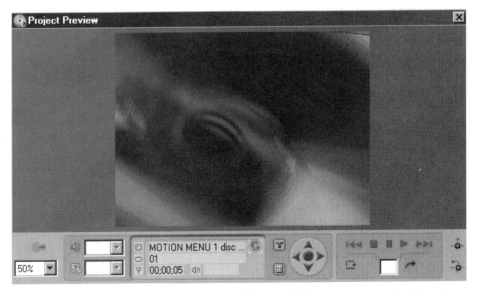

Figure 9.6 Choose Preview from Here and watch the video play. This is a pretty unassuming, abstract video background.

Adding Audio to a Menu

You can add audio to a menu as well as video. The audio you select can be music, narration, sound effects—whatever works to enhance the viewer's "menu experience" (a convenient term I just made up).

The process of linking a menu to an audio asset is similar to that of linking a menu to a video asset. Audio can be added to a menu with moving video or a menu with static visual elements. The destination selected in the Audio pop-up can be the same as the one selected in the Video pop-up, or it can be any other audio asset in the project.

To add audio to a menu:

1. Follow Steps 1 and 2 in the preceding section.

2. Click and drag the pickwhip from the Audio pop-up of the Properties palette and point to the audio asset of your choice in the Project tab (**Figure 9.7**).

   The selected destination appears in the Audio pop-up of the Properties palette (**Figure 9.8**).

3. Follow Steps 4 and 5 in the preceding section to adjust the duration and test the playback of the menu.

✔ Tip

■ If your motion menu has both video *and* audio sources, pay attention to the length of each. When audio is linked to the menu, the audio source's duration is applied to the menu, and appears in the menu's Duration box in the Properties palette. See the sidebar, "Loop Points and Animated Buttons," later in this chapter for more information on looping and durations.

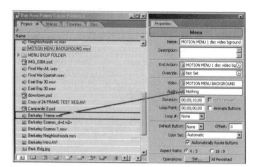

Figure 9.7 Linking an audio asset to a menu.

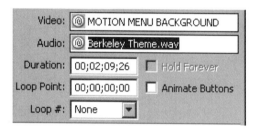

Figure 9.8 The audio asset is listed in the Properties palette.

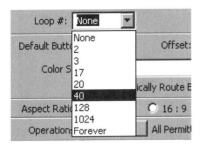

Figure 9.9 Choosing the correct number of loops. Go ahead and select Forever and see what happens.

Looping Video and Audio Assets

You have several options when determining how many times the audio and video portions of your menu will play while waiting for viewer interaction. This is called *looping*. You'll need to consider the durations of both the audio and video assets of your menu. You want to make sure that you don't cut the audio or video too short, leaving "dead air" after the audio or video has finished playing.

(If you have trouble getting the timing of your audio and video elements to work, you may want to edit and modify them in an editing program and then import the finished asset into Encore DVD.)

To loop a video or audio asset linked to a menu:

1. Open a menu, if it is not already open.

2. With the Properties palette open, *do one or more of the following:*

   ▲ Click the Loop # pop-up menu (**Figure 9.9**).

   Several loop (repetition) options are displayed, from None to Forever, with several increments in between. Select the one you want or type an alternate number in the Loop # box.

   Unless interrupted by viewer interaction, Encore DVD will play the menu asset for its entire length and then repeat it for the selected number of loops. It will then execute the end action or override displayed in the Properties palette.

continues on next page

▲ Type a new entry in the Duration box, if necessary. The asset will stop play at the end of the newly specified duration and then loop to the beginning to play again.

▲ If you want to begin your loop at a particular place in the video or audio asset, type the timecode value of that point in the Loop Point box (**Figure 9.10**).

On its first play, the menu will still play the asset from the beginning. However, on all subsequent loops, it will begin play from the loop point, play the asset for the selected duration, and then return to the loop point.

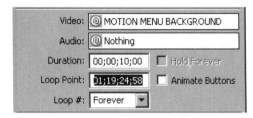

Figure 9.10 You can choose a different point to begin your loop.

✔ Tips

■ The loop point also determines when the buttons are active in a menu. When a loop point is set in a menu, it acts as the *on* switch for button selection. The buttons are turned off until the loop point is reached. Buttons then remain active during loop play.

■ The background video loops are not seamless. There is a half second or so of black between loops, due to the inherent playback characteristics of a DVD. You may want to use Premiere or another editing solution to program a fade to (and from) black in your video asset to mask the slight delay when looping video.

■ Your video or audio assets might "stutter" a bit in playback during preview. I've found that this is an artifact of previewing. The stutter disappears when the material is rendered or burned to disc.

■ To clear loop or duration displays in the Properties palette, select all the numbers entered in a display, right-click, and choose Delete from the contextual menu.

Looping and Durations

Now that you've added motion to your menus, you'll need to coordinate the timing of all the moving parts. A motion menu can have an audio track, a moving background, and multiple animated buttons, and they all need to work together.

Audio and Video Duration Considerations

By default, it's all about the audio. If the audio in a menu is *shorter* than the video, the video portion of the menu will stop when the audio stops. If the audio is *longer* than the video, the video portion will hold on its last frame until the audio stops. In either case, if you have programmed an end action or override for the menu, it will be executed when the audio stops.

This default can be overridden by typing a new menu duration in the Duration box. The end action or override will take place when the specified new duration of the menu is finished. If the specified duration is *shorter* than the menu's audio source, both video and audio will be interrupted by the end action or override. If the specified duration is *longer* than the audio source, the audio will stop when it's done, but the video will continue (and even hold on the final frame, as above, if necessary) until the new duration is complete.

Animated Button Timing

The rules are slightly different for animated buttons. Their run times are constrained by the duration of the menus in which they appear. So if the time displayed in a menu's Duration box is shorter than the "native" duration of a thumbnail video displayed in a button, the button video is interrupted. However, if the native duration of the button video is *shorter* than the specified menu duration, the button's video will repeat until the menu loops or ends.

Loop Points and Animated Buttons

Establishing a loop point can very useful when using animated buttons, which often are linked to long-duration timelines. Consider this situation: Your project is a feature-length movie, and you want to have thumbnail videos of each scene playing in animated buttons on your Scene Select menu. However, to save both disc space and rendering time, you want your button loops to be relatively short, and each scene may be many minutes long. When you set a loop point, the video will play in the button thumbnail only for the length of time specified in the Loop Point box, rather than for the entire scene.

Here are some rules that apply to using the Loop Point option with animated buttons:

♦ Setting a loop point to shorten the playback of an animated button, as above, is only necessary if the background of the menu is static. If the background has a moving audio or video element to it, *that* element's duration establishes the duration of the entire menu and any buttons in it.

♦ The loop point applies to the whole menu, so all the animated buttons have the same duration.

Using Buttons in Motion Menus

A button can be a static graphic element over a moving video background, or it can display a frozen thumbnail image of the video to which it is linked, or the button can be "animated," meaning it can have video playing in its thumbnail shape. The basic structure of thumbnails, creating them in Photoshop, and linking them to destinations is covered in Chapter 7. Thumbnail button templates are also available in Encore DVD's Library tab.

Unlike menu backgrounds, buttons cannot be linked to raw assets; they can only be linked to timelines (specific chapter points, if desired) or menus (specific buttons, if desired).

Displaying moving video, rather than static frames, in a button thumbnail is controlled by the Animate Buttons option in the Properties palette.

To animate a video thumbnail button:

1. Follow the steps outlined for thumbnail button creation in Chapter 7.

   You'll have one or more buttons in a menu that are linked to timelines and are displaying a frame from a timeline (**Figure 9.11**).

2. To animate the buttons in the menu, click the Animate Buttons check box in the menu's Properties palette (**Figure 9.12**).

   With Animate Buttons selected, the linked timeline video will play in the buttons' thumbnails after the menu is rendered. See the next section for more information on the rendering process.

Figure 9.11 An example of video thumbnails combined with a moving video background.

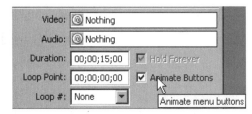

Figure 9.12 Select Animate Buttons to get video playing on a menu's buttons.

✔ Tips

- All the buttons in a menu must be either animated thumbnails or static—no mixing the two.

- You'll need to use the Render Motion Menus function when a button (static or animated) is added to a moving video background. You'll also need to use it whenever animated buttons are used, whether the background is moving or static. More on the rendering procedures next.

- To reduce rendering time, you should start by building your animated buttons against a blank or plain background. If you do have animated buttons and a moving background in your menu design, the render time will be very high.

Figure 9.13 Bringing up the Preview window.

Figure 9.14 You can render just the current motion menu with this selection in the Preview window.

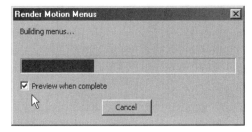

Figure 9.15 This indicates the progress of rendering motion menus.

Rendering a Motion Menu

Whether you want motion in the menu's background or in the button thumbnail, once you combine the elements of button, background, and moving video, you will have to render the menu in order to preview it. You can either render an individual menu in the Preview window, or have Encore DVD render all the motion menus (that require rendering) in the project.

To render a motion menu:

1. Follow Steps 1 and 2 in the previous task to create a menu and buttons.

2. Right-click on the menu in the Menu Editor and choose Preview from Here from the contextual menu (**Figure 9.13**). The Preview window appears.

3. Click the Render current motion menu button in the Preview window control panel (**Figure 9.14**).

   The Rendering Menu progress dialog appears. Click Cancel to abort rendering.

To render all motion menus:

◆ With the Preview window closed, choose File > Render Motion Menus.

   The Render Motion Menus progress dialog appears (**Figure 9.15**). All unrendered menus in the Project will be rendered.

continues on next page

RENDERING A MOTION MENU

If you click the Preview when complete check box when the rendering process is finished, the Preview monitor will display the animated buttons (if any) and background video, according to your First Play and the selections you've made in the Duration, Loop Point, and Loop # areas of a menu's Properties palette (**Figure 9.16**). You can use the navigation controls in the Preview monitor to view and test your links.

✔ Tips

- The time it takes to render a motion menu depends on the number of elements needing to be rendered, their file sizes, and the speed of your computer and hard drives. My system is a 1 GHz Pentium III processor with a standard 20 GB internal hard drive and a 200 GB FireWire drive. On my system, rendering 10 seconds of video (approximately 8 MB) in a button over a blank background took about 1 minute and 45 seconds. Adding a 10 second, 8 MB background video and rendering the two items took approximately 2 minutes and 10 seconds. This is only an estimate, but you can extrapolate from there to estimate your rendering time.

- Other factors that will affect the speed of rendering and the final size of the rendered files have to do with Encore DVD's bit budget calculations. When you're figuring out a bit budget, consider that each motion menu will require approximately 8 megabits of the video data stream. You'll find more information on that in the Appendix.

Figure 9.16 The final result: moving video in the foreground, moving video in the background.

Managing Rendered Files

When you create and render motion menus, the rendered files are written to your hard drive. As noted in Chapter 6, "orphans" (menus you created but didn't use in your final project) can be detected by using the Check Project function. See Chapter 6 for more details.

You can decide to incorporate these orphans into the project, if they are useful, or delete them. However, at the moment, there is no automatic way in Encore DVD to delete both a (very small) motion menu and its associated (probably multi-megabyte) rendered file. When you compare the size of the rendered files to the enormous capacities of today's typical hard disks, however, this is not a huge issue. You could manually view, compare, and delete the unneeded rendered files, but this is tedious at best, and the chances of deleting a rendered file you really want to keep are fairly high.

So you might as well archive even the unused menus and render along with your project rather than trying to get rid of them.

SUBTITLES AND SOUND TRACKS | 10

DVD technology allows for a wide range of alternate viewing and listening choices on the same disc, and you can take advantage of this flexibility when you design your Encore DVD project.

If you'll be distributing your DVD to different countries or to different language groups in the same country, or if you plan to make your programs accessible to the hearing-impaired, you need to know how to use subtitles.

In this chapter, you'll learn how to create and modify subtitles using Encore DVD's text tools. I'll also show you how to import subtitles from text files or specific subtitle formats, if you'd rather do it that way, and how to position and size subtitle clips on a timeline.

You may also want to take advantage of the eight audio tracks available to you, on which you can include alternate languages, alternate sound mixes, and even alternate content, such as an actor's commentary on a scene. You can choose any of the audio formats outlined in Chapter 2 for your alternate tracks and use the techniques described in Chapter 3 to move them around. Later in the chapter, I'll demonstrate how to lay out your subtitle and audio tracks to work with DVD player controls, and how to enable the viewer to choose among track options.

About Subtitles

Here are some quick facts about the way subtitles work in Encore DVD:

◆ The DVD you create can have up to 32 subtitle tracks, but can play only one at a time.

◆ The viewer can select a subtitle track from a menu or set the selection on a DVD player.

◆ You can either import subtitle files that already have been created with timing information already in place, or you can use the Text tools in Encore DVD to type subtitles directly into the Monitor window.

◆ Unlike audio or video tracks, subtitle tracks can have multiple subtitle clips on them.

◆ Subtitles can be trimmed and repositioned on a timeline.

◆ Subtitles are subpictures, with the same characteristics and limitations as the subpictures (button highlights) discussed in Chapter 4.

◆ Subtitles have their own timeline color set, similar to but separate from the menu color set.

Anatomy of a Subtitle

A subtitle is essentially a subpicture—a very small file used as an overlay on top of a video track or still image (**Figure 10.1**). Subtitles are stored in the Sources folder inside your Project folder.

Each subtitle has three parts: fill, stroke, and antialias (**Figure 10.2**).

Each of these parts can be assigned a color value and, in the Properties palette, you are also given some control over the outline width—the *stroke*—of the subtitles you use.

Figure 10.1 A basic subtitle. In this chapter, the subtitles are large and garish to illustrate my point. Your project's subtitles will be nicer looking.

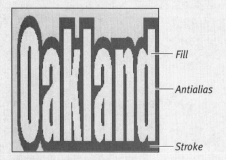

Figure 10.2 The three parts of a subtitle. The antialias segment is hard to see—it's the thin black line between the fill and the stroke.

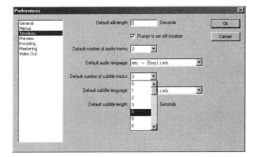

Figure 10.3 Select the number of subtitle tracks you think you'll need on your timelines.

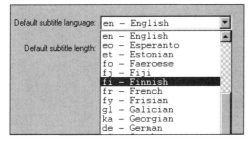

Figure 10.4 The default language you select here will be displayed at the top of the list in subtitle tracks' language pop-ups.

Figure 10.5 If you make subtitles in Encore DVD, this setting establishes the default duration (in seconds) for which each subtitle will show up on the timeline.

Setting Subtitle Preferences

Like transcoding presets, the TV standard, and other basic functions of Encore DVD, subtitles have default settings in the Preferences menu. You can change them to suit your needs, and as with all the preference settings, any change you make will apply to all subsequent projects (until, of course, you change them again).

To set the project subtitle preferences:

1. Choose Edit > Preferences > Timelines.
   The Timeline Preferences dialog appears.

2. *Do one or more of the following:*

   ▲ Click the pop-up menu housing the default number of subtitle tracks (0–32) and select the number you want (**Figure 10.3**).

   ▲ Click Subtitles in the box on the left and select from the Default subtitle language pop-up menu (**Figure 10.4**).

   ▲ Click Subtitles in the box on the left and type a number in the Default subtitle length box (**Figure 10.5**).

3. Click OK.

SETTING SUBTITLE PREFERENCES

Choosing Subtitle Color Sets

Subtitle color sets are very similar to menu color sets. Each timeline can reference one color set, and each color set can assign three groups of colors to the subtitles, with separate controls for the fill and border colors of text. You can use the color groups, for instance, to differentiate between the lines of dialogue spoken by a narrator and those spoken by the characters in the program.

The different color groups can be applied both when text is imported and also via the Properties palette while you're working on the project.

To determine a subtitle color set:

1. Choose Timeline > Edit Timeline Color Set.

   The Timeline Color Set dialog box appears (**Figure 10.6**) and the default color set is displayed.

   The default color set can be modified, but in order to maintain a consistent base setting, it's a good idea to follow the steps that follow to create new color sets and give them specific names.

2. Click the New Color Set button to create a custom color set.

   The New Color Set dialog appears (**Figure 10.7**).

New color set   Import from color set

Delete color set   Export color set to file

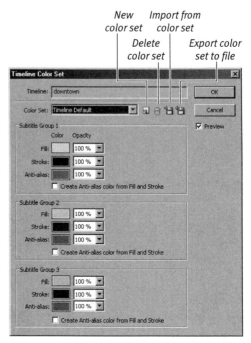

Figure 10.6 The starting point in dealing with timeline color sets. The controls are essentially the same as those for menu color sets.

Figure 10.7 Name and save that new color set here.

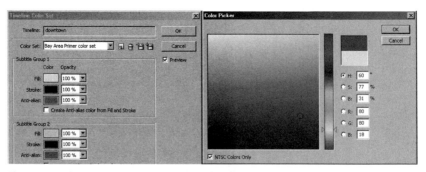

Figure 10.8 Selecting a swatch brings up the Color Picker.

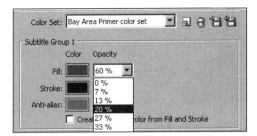

Figure 10.9 You can set opacity in the dialog box, as well.

3. Type a name for the new color set and click OK.

   The Timeline Color Set dialog reappears.

4. Click the color swatch for the fill, stroke, or antialias settings in any of the three available color groups.

   The Color Picker appears (**Figure 10.8**).

5. Use the Color Picker controls to adjust the color for the selected subtitle attribute.

   You'll be able to see your changes in the Monitor window if you have the Preview box checked.

6. Click OK.

   The new color replaces the original color in the Color Set dialog.

7. Click the Opacity pop-up menu to the right of any selected color swatch to choose an opacity value (**Figure 10.9**).

8. Repeat Steps 4–7 to adjust any other color value in the Color Set dialog.

9. Click OK.

✔ Tips

- Of course, even with all the control you'll have over the color and "look" of the subtitles, remember that their main function is to convey information without distracting from the program itself. Generally, you'll want to keep them simple and understated. Psychedelic color treatments are fun to play with while adjusting the color sets, but you probably won't want them in your final DVD.

- Timeline color sets behave much like menu color sets: You can export, import, delete, and share color set files between projects, and you use the same controls to accomplish those things. See Chapter 4 for more information on managing color sets.

- You can use any number of color sets in a project, but each timeline can reference only one color set. If you modify a color set, Encore DVD will update all timelines that use that color set and will apply the last color set you used to any new timelines.

CHOOSING SUBTITLE COLOR SETS

Adding Subtitle Tracks

Before you add subtitles to a timeline, you
have to have a place—a subtitle track—to
put them. The number of subtitle tracks and
the language in which they are written can
be set as defaults in the timeline preferences,
but you can later add, subtract, and make
changes to those tracks as needed in each
timeline.

To add a subtitle track:

◆ Right-click on a timeline in the Timeline
window and choose Add Subtitle Track
from the contextual menu (**Figure 10.10**).

A subtitle track is added to the timeline.

✔ Tip

■ Subtitle tracks behave essentially like
audio tracks in terms of adding, deleting,
copying, numbering, and so on (see
Chapter 3). The main difference in managing subtitle tracks is that subtitles are
discrete clips on the track, and can be
manipulated individually.

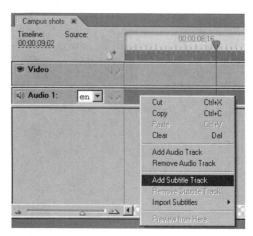

Figure 10.10 Adding a new subtitle track.

Creating and Importing Subtitles

There are four ways to get subtitles onto a subtitle track in a timeline:

◆ You can simply park on a frame in the timeline, select a Text tool from the Toolbox, and begin typing in the Monitor window. A subtitle clip is created on the active subtitle track (with a default duration determined by your Project Preference settings). You can freely size and position the text at any time.

◆ You can park on a frame in the timeline and click the Add Subtitle button in the Monitor window. The Add Subtitle button creates a subtitle clip as above, but provides a template for you to type the text in. You get less flexibility, but more speed and consistency with this method (which is generally more important).

◆ You can create your subtitles using specialized captioning formats, such as Captions Inc. or FAB, and then importing the finished files to a subtitle track. Text attributes are fixed by the external program's format and can't be modified.

◆ You can create subtitles in a text application and format the text file with information to determine the placement of the subtitles in the timeline. You can modify this text after it is imported.

I'll go through the importing steps later. First, take a look at the first two methods of adding subtitles directly into the Monitor window.

To add subtitles by typing in the Monitor window:

1. With a timeline selected in the Timeline window, choose Window > Monitor (if the Monitor window is not already open).

2. Open the Character palette (if it is not already open) and select the text attributes (**Figure 10.11**).

3. Select the subtitle track where you want to put the subtitle and toggle its display to On (**Figure 10.12**).

4. Turn on the Safe Area guides in the Monitor window (**Figure 10.13**).

5. Position the CTI (Current Time Indicator) at the frame you want to use for the subtitle's in-point.

6. Select one of the Text tools in the Toolbox (**Figure 10.14**).

7. Move the pointer over the Monitor window. The pointer changes to an I-beam inside a dotted box.

8. Click and drag the I-beam to define a bounding box for your text (**Figure 10.15**).

   Or

   Position the bottom edge of the I-beam at the point where you want to define the bottom edge of your text and click to set the position.

9. Type the text (**Figure 10.16**).

10. When the text is entered, reposition the CTI on the timeline to the next subtitle's in-point and repeat Steps 6–9.

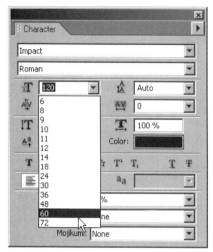

Figure 10.11 Selecting the text attributes for a typed-in subtitle.

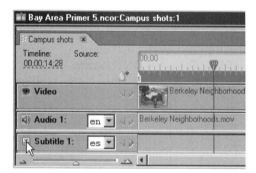

Figure 10.12 Toggling on the display for your selected subtitle track.

Figure 10.13 The Safe Area guides are turned on.

CREATING AND IMPORTING SUBTITLES

Figure 10.14 Selecting a Text tool.

Figure 10.15 A bounding box in the Monitor window, ready for text to go inside it. (Safe Area guides are off so you can better see the box in this example).

Figure 10.16 Typing the subtitle text.

✔ Tips

- A default subtitle clip is created as soon as you draw a bounding box or click to set the type in the Monitor window. The duration is determined by the settings in your Project Preferences.

- It's generally best to type in text immediately after setting a cursor or bounding box in the Monitor window, *then* modify the text attributes through the Character palette or by repositioning the bounding box. Interrupting the process of typing text into the Monitor window usually means deleting the current subtitle and creating it all over again.

- You can modify the text of subtitles in terms of font, positioning, sizing, and so on. See the section on modifying subtitles later in the chapter for more information. Be careful when making changes to maintain consistency, so your subtitles don't distract the viewer

- The color values and antialiasing, or edge, style for a subtitle are determined by your timeline color preferences, not by the text attributes in the Character tab. The Character tab can control font and sizing, but not color and edges. Adjust these two things in the Properties palette.

- You can also copy and paste subtitles (and their attributes) from one timeline to another.

To create subtitles with the Add Subtitle button:

1. Follow Steps 1–5 from the previous task.

2. Click the Add Subtitle button in the Monitor window (**Figure 10.17**).

   A bounding box for text appears in the lower third of the monitor, and the Horizontal Text tool is automatically enabled in the Toolbox.

3. Begin typing text (**Figure 10.18**).

4. After the text is entered, position the CTI to the next point in the timeline and repeat Steps 1–3.

✔ Tips

- The Add Subtitle button is designed to give you speed and consistency by providing the same "starting point" in terms of screen position. For best results, type in text first and then use the Character tab to adjust font size, kerning, and so on. All subsequent subtitles created with Add Subtitle will maintain those attributes.

- You can also use the Previous/Next Subtitle buttons in the Monitor window to quickly navigate between subtitles, no matter what method you use to create or import them.

- Another way to create a consistent "look" in your subtitles is this: Create a subtitle using either of the above methods and modify it to fit your needs. Copy and paste this "slug" on a subtitle track wherever a subtitle is needed. Then you can simply retype the text in each copy of the "slug" on the subtitle track.

Figure 10.17 Using the Add Subtitle feature can speed up the subtitling process substantially.

Figure 10.18 The bounding box is set automatically, and you can type text and then move on to add the next subtitle.

Moving Subtitles on a Track

Once subtitles are on a track, you can move them around in several different ways.

To move subtitle clips on a subtitle track:

Do one of the following:

◆ Click a subtitle clip in the timeline (**Figure 10.19**) and drag it to a new position (**Figure 10.20**).

◆ Ctrl-click to select multiple subtitle clips on a subtitle track and drag them to a new position.

Their position relative to each other is maintained.

continues on next page

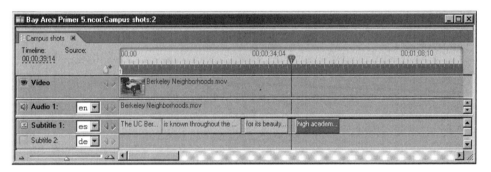

Figure 10.19 You can select a subtitle clip...

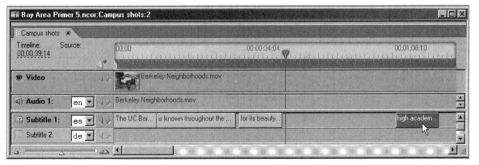

Figure 10.20 ...and drag it to a new position.

◆ Ctrl-click to select multiple subtitle clips on multiple tracks and drag them to a new position (**Figures 10.21** and **10.22**). Their position relative to each other is maintained.

✔ Tips

■ Subtitle clips show as light blue on the timeline. When selected, they change to purple.

■ A subtitle clip pasted onto an existing subtitle clip on the timeline will replace that clip. The position of the surrounding clips is not altered.

■ Subtitle clips can be moved or trimmed freely to fill any empty space on the subtitle track. One subtitle clip cannot "push" another clip out of position or affect its length by partially overwriting it.

■ When a subtitle clip is dragged on top of another on a track (as opposed to being copied/pasted on top of another clip), their positions in the timeline are swapped. Surrounding subtitle clips are unaffected.

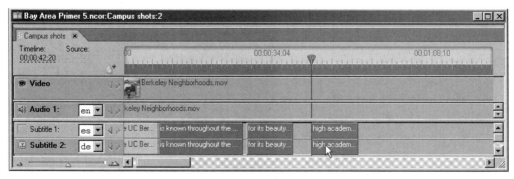

Figure 10.21 If you need to change the timing of more than one set of clips on different tracks, grab them all...

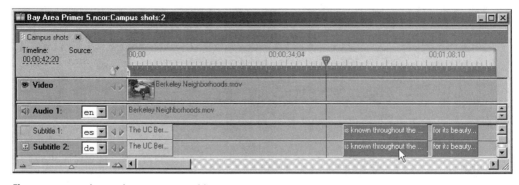

Figure 10.22 ...and move them to a new position.

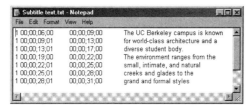

Figure 10.23 An example of a text file to be imported for subtitles.

Importing Subtitles

Importing text or image files to create subtitles has many advantages over typing each one manually. The main advantage is that the subtitles are imported as a group, with timing information included, so that the need for customizing each subtitle clip is minimized. Two of the formats available to you—FAB and Captions Inc.—are actually rendered images instead of text, so the only attribute change you can make is to the subpicture color for these files. (For further information, go to www.fab-online.com or www.captionsinc.com.)

For standard desktop DVD production, you will probably be using text files to compose your subtitles, because text files can be updated and modified relatively easily. In order to import text files successfully, you'll need to prepare them properly:

◆ The text file will need to have timing information and text information in it, in a particular tab-delimited format (**Figure 10.23**).

◆ The basic structure of the file is: in-point, out-point, and text information for each subtitle, with these fields separated by tabs.

◆ Encore DVD is rather flexible regarding the number of digits necessary to define the positions on the timeline where the subtitles will be placed. To avoid confusion, however, use the eight-digit format that is standard in the timeline, showing *hours, minutes, seconds, and frames,* in that order, separated only by semicolons (00;00;00;00).

To import text scripts:

1. Select a subtitle track in the Timeline window.

2. Right-click in the timeline's track area and choose Import Subtitles > Text Script from the contextual menu.

3. Navigate to the text file from which you want to import subtitles (**Figure 10.24**). Select it and click Open.

4. The Import Subtitles (Text Script) dialog opens.

5. Use the controls in the dialog to set up the attributes of the imported subtitles.

   See the following sidebar for more information on what the controls do.

6. Click OK.

   The Import Progress window appears (**Figure 10.25**).

   Click Cancel to abort the import process.

   The subtitles are placed on the selected track and positioned according to the text file's position information and the Import Subtitles dialog settings. Each subtitle clip is named according to its text.

✔ Tip

■ Subtitles can be imported to a track that already has subtitles on it. If there is no overlap between the position information in the imported subtitles and the position of the existing subtitles, there will be no change to the existing subtitles. If there is any overlap, the existing subtitle will be deleted.

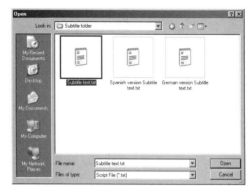

Figure 10.24 Selecting a text file with subtitle information in it that you want to import.

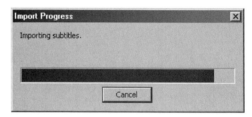

Figure 10.25 The Import Progress window.

Import Dialog Controls

You can tweak text using the controls in the Import Subtitles dialog (**Figure 10.26**).

- **Text attribute options.** These controls are generally the same as in the Character palette (font type, kerning, and so on).

- **Stroke weight options.** Controls the width of the text outline.

- **Text position settings.** These four buttons align the text against the top, bottom, or sides of the text box. Next to each button, you can specify the distance (in pixels) that the text will be offset from the edges of the text box.

- **Vertical/horizontal text controls.** You can have vertical or horizontal subtitles.

- **Vertical position (from top).** Sets the position of text relative to the top of the bounding box. A setting of 100% represents the bottom of the box.

- **Asian Text options.** There are several options here for formatting imported Asian text—determining line breaks and comma and period positions, for instance.

- **Subtitle settings.** You can select track and language settings here. They will override any existing settings for the selected subtitle track in the timeline.

- **Color set options.** Like subpictures, subtitles have color sets, associated with timelines. See "Choosing Subtitle Color Sets," earlier in the chapter.

- **Color group options.** Each color set has three customizable color groups. You can use this menu to select one of the color groups to apply to the text.

- **Timecode options.** Choose Absolute if the timecode values in the text file and your timeline match. Choose Relative if you wish to import the text files starting at a particular point in the timeline. Type that point in the box.

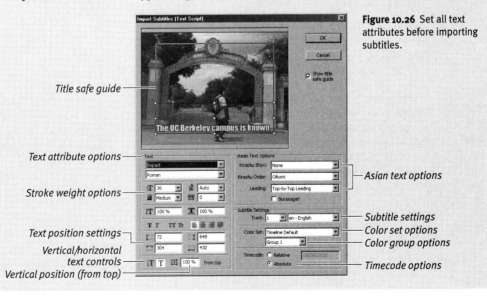

Figure 10.26 Set all text attributes before importing subtitles.

Trimming Subtitles

No matter how you got your subtitles onto the track, they probably will need some timing adjustments. You can use the Trim tool (see Chapter 3) to extend or shorten subtitle clips, and there is also a Monitor window feature that allows you to quickly shorten subtitle tracks, even while playing the timeline.

To trim a subtitle clip on a subtitle track:

1. In the Timeline window, position your pointer near the left or right edge of a subtitle clip.

   The Trim tool appears (**Figure 10.27**).

2. Click and drag the left or right edge of the subtitle clip to increase or decrease its length (**Figure 10.28**).

   Subtitle clips can only be trimmed to fill empty space on a subtitle track. The surrounding subtitle clips remain unaffected by a trim operation.

Figure 10.27 The Trim tool returns.

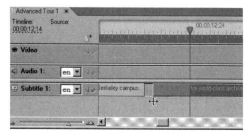

Figure 10.28 Just as with other tracks, you can extend or shorten subtitles at either end.

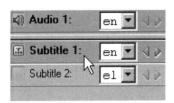

Figure 10.29 Selecting a track.

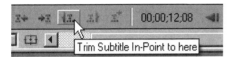

Figure 10.30 Clicking a Trim Subtitle button on the Monitor window.

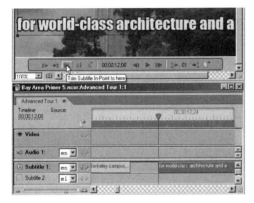

Figure 10.31 The subtitle track is trimmed to the position of the CTI.

To trim a subtitle clip in the Monitor window:

1. In the Timeline window, select a subtitle track by clicking in its Name area.

   The name of the selected track appears in bold (**Figure 10.29**).

2. Open the Monitor window (choose Window > Monitor) if it is not already open.

3. Position the CTI at a point in a subtitle clip.

4. Click one of the Trim Subtitle buttons on the Monitor window (**Figure 10.30**).

   The subtitle track is trimmed to the position of the CTI (**Figure 10.31**).

✔ Tip

- The Monitor trim buttons can be used during playback to shorten subtitle tracks. You'll need quick reflexes to use this method.

TRIMMING SUBTITLES

Modifying Subtitles

To edit text file subtitles, whether entered directly or imported, you can use the standard procedures as described in Chapter 4 to resize, reposition, and change attributes of the text. However, there are some limitations:

◆ The Arrange/Align/Distribute functions of the Object menu are grayed out.

◆ Color can be modified only via the Color Set preferences, not in the Character tab.

◆ Modifications to size and position made with the selection handles on the text bounding box will apply only to the currently selected subtitle clip.

For efficiency and consistency, you can modify subtitles using the Properties palette. These modifications can be applied to one subtitle, or to groups of selected subtitles.

To modify subtitles with the Properties palette:

1. With the Properties palette open, select a subtitle clip in the Timeline window (**Figure 10.32**).

2. *Do one or more of the following* in the Properties palette:

   ▲ Click on the Color Group pop-up menu and select a new color group for the selected subtitle (**Figure 10.33**).

   ▲ Click on the Stroke pop-up menu and select a new stroke style for the selected subtitle (**Figure 10.34**).

   ▲ In the Alignment box, type a new value for the vertical alignment of the text within the bounding box (**Figure 10.35**).

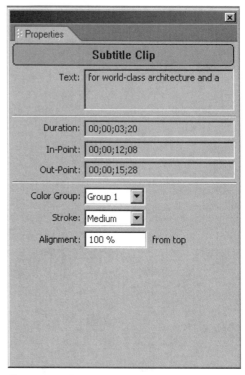

Figure 10.32 All set to modify the properties of a subtitle clip.

Figure 10.33 It might be a bit hard to see, but a new color group has been applied to the subtitle.

Figure 10.34 A new stroke value has been added.

Figure 10.35 Lastly, you can realign the onscreen text within the bounding box.

✔ Tips

■ Values can be modified for multiple subtitle clips as well. Ctrl-click to select several subtitle clips and adjust values in the Properties palette. The new values will be applied to all selected subtitle clips.

■ You can also Ctrl-click to select several subtitle clips and make some adjustments with the Character palette (such as font, size, kerning, and so on). However, the trick is to view one subtitle clip, Ctrl-click the others you want to adjust, and make changes in the Character palette without touching the bounding box or text of any of the clips. Doing so will deselect all subtitle clips other than the one you're directly modifying.

■ If you want to select all of the subtitle clips on a subtitle track, you can double-click or Ctrl-click the track header and choose Select All from the contextual menu.

MODIFYING SUBTITLES

Previewing Subtitles

Once you've got your subtitles imported, placed on timelines, sized, trimmed, and colored to taste, you'll want to see how they work with the rest of your project. You can do simple previewing of individual timelines in the Monitor window. You can also use the Preview window for more of a real-world test, to see how the subtitles work with navigational controls and how well they fit in with the rest of the elements in your project.

To view subtitles in the Monitor window:

◆ In the Timeline window, display the subtitles for a particular track by clicking the Toggle Subtitle Display button in the track's Name area to the On (show) position (**Figure 10.36**).

The subtitles are now visible in the Monitor window (**Figure 10.37**).

✔ Tips

■ When the timeline is played via the keyboard (by pressing the spacebar), a subtitle track can be toggled between show and hide modes while playing.

■ The show/hide state of multiple subtitle tracks also can be toggled during playback in the Monitor window.

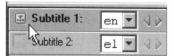

Figure 10.36 This subtitle track is now set to display.

Figure 10.37 This is what you'd see in the Monitor window.

Figure 10.38 The little symbol for *no* indicates that the subtitle track is not visible in the Preview window.

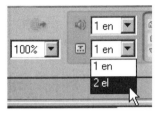

Figure 10.39 You can also switch between different languages with the small control on the bottom of the window.

To view subtitles in the Preview window:

1. With the Preview window active, click the Toggle Subtitle Display button to the On position to see subtitles displayed.

   The default setting for subtitle display is Off (**Figure 10.38**).

2. Use the subtitle track selector's pop-up menu to switch between subtitle tracks (**Figure 10.39**).

✔ Tip

■ As with the Monitor window, subtitles can be shown or hidden in the Preview window, and different subtitle tracks can be selected while the timeline is playing.

Setting the Default DVD Navigation

Now that you have your subtitle and audio tracks lined up consistently throughout your project (see the sidebar), the next step is to set up a scheme that will allow the viewer to choose among the available tracks. You have both default settings and custom links to work with, as you create the navigational structure.

You don't have to adjust your project's default Disc settings, but by doing so you can exercise some control over the initial state of the DVD player as it cues up your First Play selection. In Disc properties, you can

♦ Set a default to allow the current DVD player's subtitle track and audio track selection to remain unchanged while your project is being viewed.

♦ Set a default to determine which subtitle track (if any) and which audio track will be initially selected for your project.

To set the default subtitle or audio track:

1. With the Disc tab active, open the Properties palette.

   The disc properties are displayed (**Figure 10.40**).

2. *Do one of the following:*

   ▲ To leave the DVD player's current sub-title or audio track setting unchanged, select No Change from the appropriate pop-up menu. This is the default set-ting for Encore DVD (**Figure 10.41**).

Figure 10.40 The Disc tab and its properties.

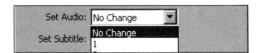

Figure 10.41 Checking the default audio track setting for the project...

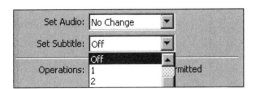

Figure 10.42...and the default subtitle settings, as well.

▲ To change the default so that subtitle tracks are turned off for the entire project (until the viewer makes a selection), select Off from the Set Subtitle pop-up menu (**Figure 10.42**).

Off is not an option for the audio track selection. If there is no selection made here, the DVD player will default to Audio 1.

▲ To select a default subtitle track for the entire project, select a number from 1 to 32 from the Set Subtitle pop-up menu.

▲ To select a default audio track for the entire project, select a number from 1 to 8 in the Set Audio pop-up menu.

Arranging Subtitle and Audio Tracks Consistently

You have several options for arranging your subtitle tracks and audio tracks, but the most important factor is *consistency*. The DVD player can only play one audio track and one subtitle track at a time. Once a track is selected by default or viewer choice, it will remain selected for all the timelines in a project. During playback, if there is no audio on a selected track, the DVD player will switch to Audio 1 for the rest of the project. The player will do the same for subtitle tracks, defaulting to Subtitle 1 if it hits a "gap" in the information on a selected track.

For example, if you have an Icelandic translation you want to put on audio track 4, make sure it's on audio track 4 *for all the timelines in your project.* The same applies to those French subtitles you imported—if they're assigned to subtitle track 2 in one timeline, make sure they're on the same track throughout the project. Otherwise, there could be unintended (and possibly hilarious) results.

Consistency also applies to sound mixes. Some viewers may have the home theater set up to take advantage of a surround-sound mix, while many will be limited to the stereo capabilities of their TV speakers (and a few may still be watching reruns of *Dobie Gillis* and listening in mono). You can decide how many alternate mixes you'll need to accommodate your target audience, and once you do, you'll need to consistently assign tracks to the different mixes (each track on a DVD contains a complete mix, so even if you have multichannel surround sound in your project, it will only take up one audio track).

SETTING THE DEFAULT DVD NAVIGATION

Adding Subtitle and Audio Links

The default settings for your project will remain in effect unless overridden by the user or by a link that specifies a particular subtitle or audio track. You can create a set of links in your project—end actions, overrides, and/or button links—which include subtitle and/or audio track information. Link-based selections override disc- or project-based defaults.

For instance, you could design a menu that lists the subtitle choices available. A viewer could press a button and choose to watch a version of your *Coming Attractions* video with Japanese subtitles. When the button executes its link to the *Coming Attractions* timeline, it will also have to "turn on" the correct subtitle track. The same would apply for an alternate audio selection—the link would have to incorporate the audio track selection as well.

And it doesn't end there. If *Coming Attractions* is actually a *series* of timelines, you will want to have the subtitle and/or audio track selection specified in each timeline's end action (or override), so they can link to one another with the correct subtitles or audio selections playing along seamlessly. You also have to figure out the navigation for where the viewer will be taken next: To a Japanese version of a Scene Select menu? To the English version of the main menu? Or...? No one said figuring out the pathways of DVD navigation would be easy.

To add subtitle or audio track selections to a button link:

1. With the Properties palette open, click a menu in the Menus tab to select it, and then select a button from the bottom pane of the Menus tab (**Figure 10.43**).

   Or

   Double-click a menu in the Menus tab to open it in the Menu Editor and select a button in the Menu Editor (**Figure 10.44**).

   With either method, the button properties are displayed in the Properties palette.

continues on next page

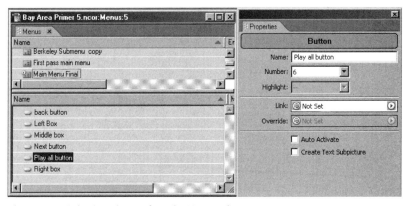

Figure 10.43 Selecting a button from the Menus tab.

Figure 10.44 Selecting a button from the Menu Editor.

ADDING SUBTITLE AND AUDIO LINKS

309

2. Click the Link pop-up menu and choose Specify Other.

The Specify Link dialog appears.

3. Click on one of the items listed to select it as a target (**Figure 10.45**).

4. Click the Subtitle pop-up menu and select the subtitle track you want (**Figure 10.46**).

Or

To add an audio track, select it from the Audio pop-up menu.

5. Click OK.

When the button is activated, it will execute the link and "turn on" the selected subtitle and/or audio track as well.

✔ Tips

■ The same process can be used for end actions, overrides, and First Plays.

■ These choices determine subtitle and audio track selection for the entire DVD. Whichever track is currently selected, either by default or by the viewer, remains selected for the entire DVD, unless it is overridden by a subsequent link or by the viewer adjusting the DVD player controls.

■ If the DVD player has a subtitle or audio track currently specified and begins playing a timeline with no information on that track, it will default to subtitle or audio track 1.

Figure 10.45 Selecting a chapter point as a target.

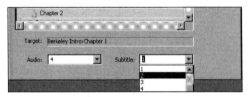

Figure 10.46 From the pop-up menu, a subtitle track (or other options) can be associated with a link.

MORE ON BIT BUDGETING

Bit budgeting is the process of estimating how much space a project will take up on the final DVD. A certain number of bits are available for storage and playback, and your bit budget determines how you will "spend" those bits. Encore DVD has several ways of tracking how the bits are being spent. It automatically performs bit budget calculations as part of its disc management tools, and displays a running total of its estimates in the Disc tab. (See Chapters 2 and 6 for more information.)

However, in addition to relying on Encore DVD's calculations, you'll have to estimate your storage needs at the beginning of a project. This way, you'll be able to plan for the disc type and capacity you'll need, and decide on the optimal data rate you'll want to use to maximize picture and sound quality with the space available on the disc.

Converting to Megabits

Since the data rate of your final DVD is expressed in megabits per second (Mbps), it's a good idea to break down the data requirements for each element all the way to the megabit level, and to do the same with the capacity of the disc. (Note that I'm using the DVD standard for measuring capacity, where a gigabyte is equal to 1 billion bytes.)

A 4.7-GB disc can store 4,700,000,000 bytes. Since there are 8 bits in a byte, the disc can store 37,600,000,000 bits (4,700,000 x 8). This huge number can be made more manageable by converting it to megabits, which, conveniently, is the measurement you're going to end up with when you do the final DVD data rate calculation. There are a million bits in a megabit, so dividing the number we arrived at earlier by 1 million (a simple task, even for someone like me, burdened with a liberal arts education but armed with a powerful laptop) gives the result that the disc capacity for a 4.7-giga*byte* DVD is 37,600 mega*bits*.

Calculating Your Content

The first step in creating a bit budget is to figure out (manually or via a spreadsheet) how much space will be taken up by the project's *non*video content—audio tracks, subtitle tracks, motion menus, and any DVD-ROM or "extra" content. (Subpictures and still menus take up so little space that you don't have to account for them in a bit budget.)

Once the nonvideo content has been calculated, the rest of the capacity of the DVD (less 5% or so reserved for headroom) is available for the stuff that takes up the most space: the video content. The final and perhaps most important calculation is what level of MPEG-2 compression will be needed to get all your video content onto the remaining disc space and have it play back within the 9.8 Mbps maximum DVD video data rate. (And remember, you'll probably want to keep your data rate well within that maximum, to ensure trouble-free playback on a variety of DVD players.)

Now, on to calculating the data requirements for the nonvideo elements in the project (in megabits). Since calculating the audio data requirements can be a bit more involved than the other elements, I'll start there.

Audio

The space requirements for your audio tracks will depend on which audio format you choose in the Project Transcode Preset window (see Chapter 6). You have three choices for transcoding:

◆ **Dolby Digital.** This is by far the most common choice. The bit rate (and therefore the amount of space required to store the audio on disc) is scalable, from 128 kilobits per second (Kbps) to 448 Kbps. The 448 Kbps setting is typically used for tracks with surround sound. The default data rate setting for a common stereo track is 192 Kbps, which balances high quality with efficient storage. The data rate conversion looks like this: 192 Kbps = 0.192 Mbps.

◆ **MPEG Audio.** This option also allows you to choose from a range of bit rates, from 64 to 384 Kbps. It is a less-common format, and for NTSC DVDs, you cannot use MPEG audio only; your DVD must have either Dolby Digital or PCM audio tracks as well.

◆ **PCM Audio.** The bit rate is not selectable for this format, and its data rate is quite high: 1.536 Mbps, approximately eight times what the typical Dolby Digital stereo setting requires. You'll get great sound but a large "footprint" on the final disc.

To calculate how much disc capacity will be taken up by the audio tracks in your project, you can use this formula:

(Amount of audio in minutes x 60 seconds/ minute x bit rate) x number of audio tracks

This calculation can be a bit confusing. See the sidebar "An Example Bit Budget" to get an idea of how it works in the real world.

Subtitles, Motion Menus, and DVD-ROM Content

Estimating the necessary disc space for these elements is less involved, as you don't have to deal with variable bit rates. And while subtitles and motion menus are small compared to a disc's overall video content, they can have a significant impact on your bit budget's video data rate calculations:

◆ **Subtitle tracks.** The rule of thumb from Adobe is to use 0.010 Mbps for the data

rate. Multiply this by the number of subtitle tracks in your project and the length of each track.

◆ **Motion menus.** These are typically transcoded at 8 Mbps, multiplied by the total number of motion menus and the length of each one. (If the native video format for a motion menu is MPEG-2, it will not be transcoded. If you know its native MPEG-2 data rate, you can use that to calculate its space requirements. However, unless you have a very large number of motion menus, using 8 Mbps for the bit budget calculation should be fine.)

◆ **DVD-ROM content.** If you are including any extra files, documents, or applications on the DVD, you just need to add up the file sizes of each and add the total to the overall bit budget.

Video

Once you've calculated all the previous elements, the remaining available disc space can be used for your comparatively large MPEG-2 video files. Native AVI video assets will definitely be compressed as they are transcoded into MPEG-2, but if you have a lot of material to fit in the space available, even native MPEG-2 files (or QuickTime files that were transcoded to MPEG-2 on import) may need to "get small" in order to fit on the disc. Double-transcoding MPEG-2 files should definitely be avoided if at all possible. If you're really tight on space, it would be better to reimport QuickTime files and transcode them with a lower data rate. And it might be necessary for you to consider going all the way back to the pre-MPEG-2 state of other video elements (such as all the way back to the original source tapes) and recompressing them into MPEG-2 at a lower data rate as well.

An Example Bit Budget

Let's say you're working on a DVD project that will have the following elements:

◆ 80 minutes of video content (timelines)

◆ 4 tracks of Dolby Digital audio (transcoded at 0.192 Mbps), each track 80 minutes long

◆ 4 subtitle tracks, each running 80 minutes

◆ 4 motion menus, each 20 seconds long

◆ 100 MB of DVD-ROM content

The storage calculations would go like this:

Audio: 4 x (80 minutes x 60 seconds/minute) x 0.192 Mbps = 3686.4 megabits (Mb)

Subtitles: 4 x (80 minutes x 60 seconds/minute) x 0.010 Mbps = 192 Mb

Motion menus: 4 x (20 seconds x 8 Mbps) = 640 Mb

DVD-ROM content: 100 MB = 800 Mb (1 megabyte = 8 megabits)

When added up, the total storage required for this project's nonvideo content is, rounded off, 5318 Mb.

The capacity of the selected disc type (after setting aside 5% for overhead) is 35,720 Mb. After you subtract the space required for the nonvideo elements, the disc space available for the video content is 30,402 Mb.

To find out what the data rate of the video content will be, the next step is to divide the available disc capacity by the amount of video, in seconds:

Video: 30,402 Mb / (80 minutes x 60 seconds/minute) = 6.33 Mbps

The final calculation is to ensure that the combined data rate of the audio tracks, subtitle tracks, and video content is below the maximum video data rate for a DVD. In this case:

4 audio tracks at 0.192 Mbps = 0.768 Mbps

4 subtitle tracks at 0.010 Mbps = 0.040 Mbps

Video data rate = 6.33 Mbps

Total data rate = 7.14 Mbps

Your project is well within the maximum video data rate of 9.8 Mbps. All the required elements will fit onto a 4.7-GB single-layer, single-sided disc, which can be burned conveniently on your desktop.

More Options

In general, your planning and the bit budgeting function within Encore DVD will complement each other. For many projects, the main benefit of working out a bit budget is that it will give you the confidence that your content will fit within the limits of a particular DVD's capacity, with no rude surprises as you get ready to make the final disc. Once that's established, you can let Encore DVD take care of the transcoding tasks with its Automatic transcode presets.

Of course, you can also continue to massage the numbers, if you like. For instance, you may want to take a more conservative approach in terms of the maximum data rate than your initial bit budget indicates. You can use one of the existing project transcode presets, or create a custom one, to bring the video data rate down to the rate you want. You can also decide whether to transcode with a CBR (Constant Bit Rate) or VBR (Variable Bit Rate) setting. The general rule is that if the calculated video data rate is above 6 Mbps, the video content can be transcoded using a CBR setting. VBR transcoding can achieve improved visual results when the video data rate for a project goes below 6 Mbps, as it "spends" its limited number of bits on video frames with complex content, and "saves" bits on frames with less complexity. Because of the extra calculations in the VBR selection, however, it is a slower process.

If you experiment with the transcode settings for your assets in the Project tab, keep an eye on the Disc Information section at the top of the Disc tab (you can drag the tab out of the Project window into its own separate window to do this). The Disc Information section will update its estimates of how much space is available each time you apply a different transcode setting, without actually having to transcode the asset. You can also use the columns in the Project and Timelines tabs to keep track of the size of your various assets and the bit rate of their current transcode settings.

You also have the option to evaluate the transcoded picture quality of each video element while you are previewing the project. If while you are previewing you see a video clip that just doesn't look right, you can assign or create a different transcode setting for that clip's timeline, in an effort to improve its playback. This is another good reason to have that 5% (or more, in a larger project) disc space held in reserve. You can then decide to spend more of your bit budget to improve the picture quality of selected assets and use up some of the reserve without having to redo all your calculations for all the elements in the project. If the quality of the compressed video is still unacceptable after you experiment with different settings, you may have to increase the video data rate (lower the compression) by eliminating content, writing to a higher-capacity DVD format, or going back to your original source video and recompressing it into MPEG-2 and then reimporting it into Encore DVD.

INDEX

INDEX

M

INDEX

Digital Video For All

Whether you're shooting your first home movie or finishing your latest feature film, we've got just the book you need to master digital video editing and DVD creation using the newest, hottest software. iMovie, Premiere Pro, Final Cut Pro, DVD Studio Pro—we cover them all and more. So toss the manual! We've got the only digital video instruction you need.

Getting Started

After Effects 6.5 for Windows and Macintosh: Visual QuickPro Guide
By Antony Bolante
0-321-19957-X • $29.99 • 632 pages

Adobe After Effects 6.0 Classroom in a Book
By Adobe Creative Team
0-321-19379-2 • $45.00 • 392 pages

Adobe Premiere Pro Classroom in a Book
By Adobe Creative Team
0-321-19378-4 • $45.00 • 520 pages

DVD Studio Pro 3 for Mac OS X: Visual QuickPro Guide
By Martin Sitter
0-321-26789-3 • $29.99 • 656 pages

Apple Pro Training Series: DVD Studio Pro 3
By Adrian Ramseier and Martin Sitter
0-321-25610-7 • $44.99 • 656 pages

Apple Pro Training Series: Final Cut Pro HD
By Diana Weynand
0-321-25613-1 • $44.99 • 872 pages

iMovie 4 and iDVD 4 for Mac OS X: Visual QuickStart Guide
By Jeff Carlson
0-321-24663-2 • $19.99 • 288 pages

QuickTime 6 for Macintosh and Windows: Visual QuickStart Guide
By Judith Stern and Robert Lettieri
0-321-12728-5 • $21.99 • 520 pages

Beyond the Basics

Premiere Pro for Windows: Visual QuickPro Guide
By Antony Bolante
0-321-21346-7 • $24.99 • 584 pages

Apple Pro Training Series: Advanced Editing and Finishing Techniques in Final Cut Pro 4
By DigitalFilm Tree
0-321-19726-7 • $49.99 • 960 pages

In-Depth Reference

Real World Digital Video, Second Edition
By Pete Shaner and Gerald Everett Jones
0-321-23833-8• $49.99 • 480 pages

Technique & Inspiration

Editing Techniques with Final Cut Pro, 2nd Edition
By Michael Wohl
0-321-16887-9 • $39.99 • 584 pages

For these titles and lots more, go to www.peachpit.com!

Peachpit
Essential books for the creative community

Visit Peachpit on the Web at www.peachpit.com

- Read the latest articles and download timesaving tipsheets from best-selling authors such as Scott Kelby, Robin Williams, Lynda Weinman, Ted Landau, and more!

- Join the Peachpit Club and save 25% off all your online purchases at peachpit.com every time you shop—plus enjoy free UPS ground shipping within the United States.

- Search through our entire collection of new and upcoming titles by author, ISBN, title, or topic. There's no easier way to find just the book you need.

- Sign up for newsletters offering special Peachpit savings and new book announcements so you're always the first to know about our newest books and killer deals.

- Did you know that Peachpit also publishes books by Apple, New Riders, Adobe Press, Macromedia Press, palmOne Press, and TechTV press? Swing by the Peachpit family section of the site and learn about all our partners and series.

- Got a great idea for a book? Check out our About section to find out how to submit a proposal. You could write our next best-seller!

You'll find all this and more at www.peachpit.com. Stop by and take a look today!